RELAND

INDUSTRY AND ECONOMIC DEVELOPMENT
THE CHALLENGE FOR THE LATECOMER

" Industry and Economic Development
The Challenge for the Latecomer "

Eoin O'Malley

Published in Ireland by
Gill and Macmillan Ltd
Goldenbridge
Dublin 8
with associated companies in
Auckland, Delhi, Gaborone, Hamburg, Harare,
Hong Kong, Johannesburg, Kuala Lumpur, Lagos, London,
Manzini, Melbourne, Mexico City, Nairobi,
New York, Singapore, Tokyo
© Eoin O'Malley, 1989
Print origination by Typeform Ltd, Dublin
Printed by Billing & Sons Ltd, Worcester

British Library Cataloguing in Publication Data
O'Malley, Eoin
    Industry and economic development : the
    challenge for the latecomer.
    1. Ireland. Economic conditions
    1700-1987
    I. title
    330.9415'07

    ISBN 0-7171-1682-4

Contents

Acknowledgments

Many people have been of help to me in writing this book. My greatest debts are to Professor Reginald H. Green and the late Professor Dudley Seers of the Institute of Development Studies at the University of Sussex, and to Professor Kieran Kennedy of The Economic and Social Research Institute, who made detailed comments and suggestions on a good deal of the research on which this book is based.

A number of other people also helped me by providing the nucleus of ideas, by offering comments or by discussions of relevance to parts of the book. They include Manfred Bienefeld, Martin Godfrey, Robin Murray and Professor Hans Singer of the Institute of Development Studies at the University of Sussex; a number of my fellow students when I was at the IDS some years ago, especially Neil Rosser; Raymond Crotty and Professor Dermot McAleese of Trinity College, Dublin.

Others have helped me to develop ideas in the course of carrying out joint work on subjects related to this book, particularly Ronan O'Brien and Dermot O'Doherty, while we were engaged in work for the National Board for Science and Technology; John Blackwell and Gerard Danaher, while preparing a report for the National Economic and Social Council; and Rosheen Callender, Alan Matthews and Paul Sweeney, while preparing publications by a group of socialist economists.

I am also indebted to the Industrial Development Authority for providing some of the necessary data; to The Economic and Social Research Institute for financial support; to the library staff of the IDS and ESRI; and to Mary Cleary, Pat Hughes, Regina Moore and Mary O'Sullivan for their efficient typing of several drafts.

List of Abbreviations

AIFTA	Anglo-Irish Free Trade Area
B&ICO	British and Irish Communist Organisation
CIO	Committee on Industrial Organisation
CIP	Census of Industrial Production
CSO	Central Statistics Office (Ireland)
ECLA	Economic Commission for Latin America
EEC	European Economic Community
EFTA	European Free Trade Area
EPTR	Exports Profits Tax Relief
IDA	Industrial Development Authority (Ireland)
IRA	Irish Republican Army
LDC	Less-Developed Country
MITI	Ministry of International Trade and Industry (Japan)
NESC	National Economic and Social Council (Ireland)
NBST	National Board for Science and Technology (Ireland)
NIC	Newly Industrialising Country
OECD	Organisation for Economic Co-operation and Development
OEEC	Organisation for European Economic Co-operation
R & D	Research and Development
SFADCO	Shannon Free Airport Development Company
SFWP	Sinn Fein The Workers Party
SITC	Standard International Trade Classification
TNC	Transnational Corporation

List of Tables and Figures

1

Introduction

For a long time after the beginning of Great Britain's Industrial Revolution over two hundred years ago, Britain remained the world's principal industrial economy. Her early and long-sustained lead in industrialisation made Britain the 'workshop of the world' and gave her a position of global economic and political influence unequalled by any state of her relative size before or since. There was a lag of several generations before other countries could catch up, until Britain's industrial output was eventually exceeded by the United States in the 1860s and by Germany early in the twentieth century. Having lost its former dominance, however, British industry has for long been in relative decline.

Economic historians have discussed at length the advantages and disadvantages of being an early leader in industrialisation, as compared with the situation of later developers. It has been suggested that Britain's early lead gave her unique competitive advantages over other countries for a time, so that the industrialisation of latecomers may have been delayed due to the difficulties they faced in competing with established British producers. It has also been argued that Britain's early and long-sustained lead as an industrial power ultimately burdened her with inflexible and archaic business structures, technologies and attitudes, so that she had no adequate response when new dynamic competitors finally emerged.

The issue concerning the advantages and disadvantages of early and late development surfaces again in development economics, which deals with less-developed countries in more recent times. Since early in the present century, few late-industrialisers have emerged to join the ranks of advanced industrial countries. Arguably, the established competitive strength of the developed countries has constrained the industrialisation of the modern generation of latecomers in the less-developed world, since they would find it difficult to match the established competitive capabilities of more advanced economies.

This book aims to make a contribution to understanding the general implications of making a relatively late start to industrialisation, mainly by reviewing the experience of industry in Ireland. At the same time, it offers an interpretation of the experience of Irish industry and aims to clarify the problems for Ireland's own industrial development which remain to be resolved. It also outlines the type of strategy which would be needed to do so.

Although Ireland has frequently been overlooked both in discussion of the nineteenth-century latecomers and the twentieth-century less-developed countries, it is in some respects a case of special significance for both issues. For Ireland was the first colony of Great Britain and during the period of Britain's industrial leadership was fully incorporated into the United Kingdom. So if relatively late-industrialisers in the nineteenth century suffered ill effects due to competition from earlier established British industries, one would expect to see clearly the result of these effects in the economic performance of Ireland at that time. Of course, the small relative size of the Irish economy today might appear to take from its significance as a case study of general interest. But then it should be remembered that until the 1840s Ireland had a population and labour force about two-fifths as large as Britain's, with quite a high proportion employed in industry by the standards of the time. In most parts of Ireland, however, industry declined rapidly during the nineteenth century, so that people leaving the land and seeking employment generally had to emigrate, which resulted in a continuous fall in population and a relatively declining economy. The causes of this industrial decline and the role played by Ireland's position as a latecomer relative to Britain are examined in chapter 3 of this book.

By the time when the Irish Free State was established in the 1920s, there was little manufacturing industry left in the country. Thus the Irish situation in the twentieth century was comparable to that of countries which are more conventionally recognised as less-developed or underdeveloped, in so far as Ireland had to start its industrialisation almost from the beginning. The special significance of the Irish experience of industrialisation in this century lies in the fact that the country has tried both of the principal strategies recommended by contending schools of thought in development economics. From the early 1930s until the 1950s, an 'inward-looking' strategy of protectionist import-substitution was implemented, with results which are discussed in chapter 4.

Perhaps of wider general interest, because it is more unusual among late-developers, is the fact that Ireland, since the 1950s, has switched to an 'outward-looking' free market strategy. This type of strategy is now widely recommended for developing countries by many economists and by influential bodies such as the World Bank and the International Monetary Fund. It involves integrating fully with the international economy by dropping protectionist measures, promoting exports and welcoming foreign investment to contribute to export growth. It also involves relying mainly on free market forces and private enterprise to make investment decisions, rather than on detailed state intervention to direct the process of industrialisation. Although this strategy is now widely recommended by what has become the conventional wisdom on industrial development, few late-industrialising countries have actually implemented it so fully or for so long a period as Ireland. Since much of the interest in Ireland's experience therefore lies in the fact that it is one of only a small number of genuine test cases for this strategy, this book focusses largely on her experience with outward-looking free market policies, in chapters 5, 6 and 7.

In order to clarify the general theme of the book, it may be useful at this stage to outline briefly the main lessons which are drawn from the Irish case, before going into greater detail. The theoretical discussion, which is contained in chapter 2, argues that late-industrialising countries cannot generally rely on free trade and free market forces. This is because latecomers face inherent disadvantages in trying to break into international competition with the strong established industries of earlier developers. The promotion of industrialisation in late-developing countries, therefore, generally requires substantial state involvement in the economy if there is to be any hope of real success. The decline of Irish industry in the nineteenth century, under classic *laissez-faire* free market policies and free trade with Great Britain, is seen as supporting this general argument. The reversal of decline and the growth of Irish industry under a policy of protection against imports after the early 1930s is seen as further support for this view. But it is also recognised that protection alone ultimately proved inadequate to overcome the problem of late development since industrial growth slowed almost to a halt in the 1950s. Protection on its own, therefore, is not seen as a satisfactory strategy.

After the 1950s, under outward-looking free market policies, Ireland experienced a sustained increase in the rate of industrial growth as well as a particularly rapid expansion of manufactured exports and diversification of production into a wider range of activities. But it will be shown that these developments have been due very largely to foreign direct investment which has occurred on a scale that could not be expected in most late-industrialising countries. Ireland's indigenous or native-owned industries, on the other hand, remain mostly confined to a limited range of generally less advanced products. The indigenous industries have been in relative decline for two decades, since they have shown rather little increased ability to export and their shares of the home market have been eroded since the introduction of free trade. Thus foreign direct investment on an exceptionally large scale has been primarily responsible for the apparent transformation of Irish industry since the 1950s. This suggests that in the absence of this exceptional factor the *general* disadvantages of late industrialisation would be well exemplified in Ireland as would the shortcomings of the strategy adopted — if the general applicability of that strategy is considered rather than its possible suitability for certain exceptional cases at certain times. Furthermore, as unemployment has reached new heights, and industrial performance has weakened in several respects since the early 1980s, some serious doubts concerning longer-term prospects for development based largely on foreign investment have been raised in Ireland.

While the apparent transformation of *industrial* production in Ireland since the 1950s has been largely due to foreign investment, this factor was also important, but not the only exceptional factor contributing to raising average incomes with the consequent appearance of substantial progress in overall economic development. One important factor which contributed to average income growth was emigration, except in the period 1971-79, on a scale which would not be possible for most latecomers. The emigration of large numbers of people of working age would have contributed to restraining open unemployment and reducing underemployment in agriculture, and thus had the effect of raising average incomes for those remaining in Ireland.

Another exceptional factor which boosted Irish average incomes was the sharp rise in prices for agricultural exports, gained as a result of joining the EEC in 1973. Few late-industrialising countries could hope to gain access to such a large and highly subsidised market for their principal exports of primary products. In addition, a rapid expansion of foreign borrowing by the public sector was another factor contributing to supporting demand, employment and incomes. But because the continuous expansion of foreign borrowing can scarcely be regarded as sustainable, it too must be regarded as a special factor which added to the appearance of success for Ireland's development strategy for some time. This rather temporary appearance looked more promising than the underlying reality.

For the reasons mentioned above, then, Ireland's apparently successful industrial development from the 1950s to the 1980s could be seen as largely due to special or exceptional factors, in the absence of which the difficulties of late industrialisation would be more immediately apparent. This book suggests that Ireland's experience with a relatively pure form of outward-looking free market strategy points, therefore, to defects in the *general* applicability of this type of policy.

There are, however, a number of other countries which are (or have been only recently) latecomers, and which are often thought to have achieved great progress in industrialisation with the same type of conventionally recommended strategy adopted by Ireland. Several of these countries are discussed briefly in chapter 8, where it is suggested that they are either very small cases which are exceptional for reasons similar to Ireland (e.g. Singapore), or else that they have adopted policies which actually depart significantly from the conventional approach used in Ireland (e.g. Japan and South Korea). The policies of the latter group have generally been 'outward looking' only in the limited sense of emphasising the attainment of an ability to export, but they have not in practice greatly favoured free trade or freedom for foreign investment as a means of promoting late industrialisation. Neither have they exercised as much faith in free market forces as Ireland has, but rather they used systematic selective intervention by the state to develop internationally competitive indigenous industries in a range of advanced sectors which show little sign of emerging among Irish indigenous industries.

Because these countries have had greater success than Ireland in overcoming the constraints on the development of the indigenous industry of latecomers, it is suggested that their *departures* from the conventional strategy are probably crucial in accounting for their results. Thus it is concluded that the common practice of lumping together strategies such as Ireland's, South Korea's and Japan's under a general label such as 'outward-looking' or 'export-oriented' policies is unhelpful. Greater attention needs to be devoted to the selective and interventionist element in the strategy of these other countries which seems capable of producing results which are qualitatively different to those observed in Ireland. Chapter 9 draws partly on the experience of these other countries in suggesting an appropriate industrial development strategy for Ireland.

Finally, it might be thought that Ireland is not really a suitable case study for drawing lessons of relevance to less-developed countries, due to its relatively high living standards and developed infrastructure. In fact, however, Ireland is a particularly useful example to look at for the particular purpose of pin-pointing the constraints on the late-industrialisers. The general theme of this book is that a common set of difficulties face all aspiring latecomers, even though they may have different capacities to overcome the difficulties. These constraints still have to be faced even by a latecomer which does not show the more obvious symptoms of 'underdevelopment' or which does not suffer markedly from the conditions conventionally regarded as the causes of underdevelopment or economic backwardness. Ireland is a particularly useful case to examine in order to see, in a fairly pure and isolated form, the operation of these constraints on latecomers. This is because most of the conditions which are put forward as the conventional explanations of underdevelopment either do not exist or are not very severe in Ireland — i.e. conditions such as 'traditional' attitudes and a lack of enterprise, capital shortage, poor education, political instability or a poor infrastructure. Yet although such conditions are not very marked, one can still identify serious deficiencies in the country's industrial development, especially in its indigenous industry. This makes it plausible to suggest that — and to demonstrate how — the effects of being a latecomer play the major role in constraining the country's industrial development. If this is so, it points to the conclusion that the removal of certain conditions which inhibit industrialisation, such as those just mentioned, is generally not *sufficient* for successful industrialisation without strong government policies specifically aimed at overcoming the disadvantages of making a relatively late start.

The next chapter discusses the general problem of late industrialisation. First it outlines what is described as the 'conventional' view, which takes little specific account of the problems confronting latecomers and leads to a recommendation of outward-looking policies without selective state intervention. This is followed by an outline of an alternative view stressing certain constraints on latecomers and leading to different policy conclusions. Most of the rest of the book examines the experience of industry in Ireland, as well as in some other countries, suggesting that the facts are consistent with this alternative view.

2

The Problem of
Late Industrialisation

2.i. THE CONVENTIONAL VIEW

There is a fairly well-recognised conventional or orthodox view
on industrial development, which is held by many economists
and also underlies the approach of influential bodies such as the
World Bank and the International Monetary Fund.[1] This view,
which has been important in shaping official policy in Ireland, is
based on a number of key assumptions about the way modern
economies work. Since the assumptions and principles of
conventional neo-classical economics are well known, there is
no need to go into great detail here, but the general implication
of the assumptions adopted is that the free operation of markets
leads to efficient and rational use of productive resources of
capital and labour. This comes about because the process of
competition between many producers forces each to be
efficient in order to survive, and it also forces them to
concentrate on what they can do best. Since it is generally
assumed that each industry consists of a large number of
companies, each of which is relatively small, no company has
special advantages which would allow it to dominate
competitors, and newcomers are not inhibited from competing
on equal terms with the established firms.

The conventional view also assumes that market economies
can generally function well enough to allow productive
resources to be virtually fully employed. Unemployment,
therefore, when it occurs, arises from some 'distortion' or
interference in the market, such as misguided government
intervention or excessive wage levels brought about by strong
trade unions. Given this faith in the benefits of the operation of
free markets, the problem of securing maximum industrial
growth generally reduces to two principal issues. First, savings,

or the supply of capital for investment, must be increased as far as possible. And second, capital must be invested and production carried on in the most efficient way possible — which is believed to be generally achieved by allowing markets to operate quite freely.

When it comes to applying this general view to the particular question of industrial development in less-developed countries, this approach assumes that underdevelopment must be due to some barriers to development *within* the underdeveloped country, because there is no fundamental defect in the international market economy. So it attempts to identify these barriers to development and to find ways to overcome them. When this is done, it is expected, the operation of market forces will produce the same results which they are said to have produced in the advanced countries. Probably the major barrier to development suggested by the conventional analysis is a shortage of capital. If the rate of investment is limited by the rate of savings, this is a problem because small incomes in poor countries generate small savings. The effect of inadequate education has also been widely regarded as an important barrier to development, as has rapid population growth because it reduces the growth of average incomes (and hence the savings available for investment).

The conventional view also recognises that sociological or political factors can be important barriers to development. But attention is focussed very much on the society of the underdeveloped country itself, rather than the effects of external influence from dominant advanced countries in affecting the formation or continuance of certain types of society. Thus, the conventional approach focusses on the 'traditional' nature of society and institutions within less-developed countries as barriers to development, which must be overcome by 'modernisation' which takes the advanced countries as models.

On the question of achieving full employment in less-developed countries, the faith of the conventional view in the ability of markets to function smoothly leads to the conclusion that full employment is essentially a matter of creating a good business climate and getting the right balance between the price of capital and the price of labour. Thus unemployment could indicate that government policy is detrimental to business. Or it could indicate that labour costs are too high for all to be employed (due to a 'distortion' such as strong trade unions), or perhaps that capital costs are too low due, say, to government capital subsidies leading to a substitution of capital for labour.

The Conventional Policy Recommendations

The conventional view leads naturally to recommendation of policies which are outward looking in several respects. If capital shortage is a constraint, foreign investment and aid can help. If poor education and traditional attitudes are problems, foreign cultural influences and technical aid can help. If natural resources are lacking, they (along with capital-intensive goods) must be imported, and paid for by export-oriented development. The general basis of the approach in neo-classical economic theory leads also to a favouring of free market forces, including free international trade. For free trade opens the economy to competitive pressures from abroad, promoting both efficiency in production and rational allocation of investment in accordance with comparative advantage, which for an underdeveloped economy would mean initial concentration on labour-intensive, technically undemanding industries. In a low-income country, especially, production for a small protected home market would be considered not to allow sufficient advantage to be taken of economies of scale, unlike production for export. Besides leading to economic inefficiency and misallocation of productive resources, protection (and other forms of intervention) is said to provide too much scope for corruption and bureaucratic interference in favour of dominant interests, which is said to be part of the less-developed country's basic problem arising from the attitudes of a 'traditional' society.

In its purest form, therefore, the economic strategy favoured is outward looking in three important respects: (a) encouragement of, or at least non-discrimination against exports; (b) acceptance or encouragement of foreign investment; and (c) favouring of free trade. The term 'outward-looking policies', from here on in this book, refers to all three aspects, although the term has been used rather more loosely elsewhere. Besides being outward looking, the strategy recommended by the conventional view also favours reliance mainly on market forces within the less-developed country. It aims to establish favourable general conditions for private enterprise, with any business incentives or tax concessions being generalised to all firms and automatically available, and the state refraining from very specific or discretionary intervention in the market designed to achieve precise pre-determined aims.

While these are the basic principles of the conventionally recommended strategy, some small modifications may be conceded in practice. Thus Balassa (1980) suggests that temporary difficulties in starting up new industries may call for temporary protection against imports — but only on a very moderate scale 'to avoid the establishment and maintenance of inefficient industries'. On foreign investment, he also says that while export-oriented investment will contribute to growth, foreign investment in industries producing for the local market could entail a net foreign exchange loss, due to profit outflows without offsetting export earnings, and it may therefore be discouraged. But apart from these considerations, Balassa recommends minimal intervention in the market economy, reliance on the price mechanism, and stability and automaticity in any incentive systems. There is conclusive evidence, he says, that this strategy has had the best results, mentioning Japan, South Korea, Taiwan and Singapore as examples of its success. In chapter 8 of this book these countries will be considered briefly, and it will be suggested that they are not in fact convincing examples of the success of the conventional strategy. Little, Scitovsky and Scott (1970) also recognise that certain difficulties in starting up new industries may call for some modest intervention, but they counsel against the use of protection since it would mean foregoing some gains from the specialisation attainable through international trade. Rather, they suggest, promotional subsidies should be used, particularly labour subsidies if unemployment is a problem.

2.ii. CONSTRAINTS ON LATE-INDUSTRIALISERS

At variance with the conventional neo-classical view outlined above, there is a fairly wide range of literature which stresses the special difficulties faced by late-industrialisers. Despite the diversity in emphasis and style of argument in this literature, there are a number of points on which there is broad agreement and which, taken together, amount to a reasonably coherent statement of the problem of late development.

Barriers to Entry for Newcomers

At the heart of the argument that late-industrialisers face special difficulties is the view that there are 'barriers to entry' for newcomers in many industries, i.e. structural features of an industry which give the established producers strong competitive advantages over aspiring new entrants. Since the established producers are mainly based in advanced industrial countries, the common occurrence of barriers to entry would be a general constraint on the development of new indigenous or native industries in late-industrialising countries.[2]

The idea that entry barriers for newcomers are widespread (and have been for a long time past) occurs both in discussion of the nineteenth-century latecomers and the twentieth-century less-developed countries. In fact, going back to Hamilton in the USA in the eighteenth century and List in Germany in the nineteenth century, the existence of entry barriers has been a basis for rejection of the liberal argument for free trade for latecomers, and for support of protection for 'infant' industries. Economic historians such as Habakkuk (1962), Gerschenkron (1962) and Landes (1965) have analysed the effects of a relatively late start to industrialisation in countries such as the United States and Germany in the nineteenth century.[3] They have argued that the earliest starters, such as Britain, tended eventually to experience *disadvantages* compared with these later developers, due to inflexibility in adapting existing industrial structures, which slowed down innovation and replacement of plant. However, while this *could* give certain competitive advantages to latecomers eventually, it has also been noted that the increasing scale of plants, and the advantages of large agglomerations in major industrial centres, made it increasingly difficult for latecomers to take the *first* step of breaking into competition with the established industries. As time went on, it became necessary for latecomers to start with plants of an increasingly large scale and, because of the necessity to develop and take advantage of linkages between plants, to start with whole industries on an increasingly large scale. Gerschenkron argues that this created special needs for active policies and strong institutions, which had to be seen and met by the state in late-industrialising countries before any possible advantages of lateness could be realised. Landes goes on to draw the conclusion for latecomers today: 'The burden has tended to grow with the increasing size of industrial plant, so that today many of the so-called underdeveloped countries are trapped in a vicious circle of poverty and incapacity. The much vaunted freedom of the latecomer to choose the latest and best equipment on the basis of the most advanced techniques has become a myth.'

Among development economists in the 1950s, Myrdal paid particular attention to the problem of entry barriers, emphasising the barriers to newcomers in underdeveloped countries created by the advantages of agglomeration or 'external economies' in established industrial centres. Thus Myrdal (1956) argued that local industries in late-developing countries cannot generally compete profitably with the 'progressive countries whose manufacturing industries have the lead and are already fortified in surroundings of external economies'. Barriers to entry for firms in underdeveloped countries are also widely mentioned in the work of the Dependency school. In particular, the technological lead of established producers in the advanced countries is commonly put forward as a constraint on the development of competitive, technologically advanced industries in underdeveloped countries, rendering them crucially dependent on imports of most capital goods. In the Latin American Dependency literature, for example, this factor is mentioned by Dos Santos (1973) and Cardoso and Faletto (1979). Sunkel (1973) mentions a related point, saying that the technological advantages of transnational companies (TNCs) based in the advanced countries enable them alone to satisfy much of the type of consumer demand generated by their marketing activities and by the broader socio-political influences of international capitalism on poor countries. And Furtado (1971) also argues that the large scale and capital-intensity necessary for efficient production in many industries imposes barriers to entry on latecomers. This is both because large-scale production creates substantial demands on capital, and because of the need to gain a large market for efficient production, while domestic markets (even if protected) are usually small and international markets are dominated by established producers. Similar points are also mentioned in Dependency-type literature dealing with countries outside Latin America, as for instance in Thomas (1974) and Seers (1980).

In the mainstream of the Marxist literature, too, barriers to entry for newcomers arising from the competitive strength of established producers have come to be regarded as important constraints on latecomers, although this was not originally the case in Marxist thinking. Karl Marx himself did recognise that the larger scale and advanced techniques used in the most developed countries could enable them to capture foreign markets, 'in competition with commodities produced in other countries with lesser facilities for production . . . in the same way that a manufacturer exploits a new invention before it has become general' (Marx, 1977, vol. III, ch. 14).[4] But he still undoubtedly expected the penetration of capitalism into the more backward countries to result in their ultimate development. It seems, however, that Marx expected that some protection, at least, against competition from the advanced countries, would be necessary to foster relatively late development.[5]

Marx's analysis was based on the highly competitive capitalist system of the mid-nineteenth century, when most industries were composed of a large number of relatively small firms; but as larger, more dominant companies emerged, different conclusions concerning prospects for late development began to be drawn by Marxist economists.

By now, a general emphasis on the dominance of large firms and recognition of the consequent barriers to newcomers is widespread among them. This point features, for example, in Barratt Brown's (1974, p. 63) summary of a Marxist critique of conventional neo-classical thinking. Various aspects of this point are discussed, too, in Sutcliffe's (1971, ch. 9) review of literature on the consequences of lateness. The same point is also quite central to Bienefeld and Innes' (1976) analysis of the continuing weakness of indigenous manufacturing even in such a relatively high-income late-developer as South Africa. Bienefeld and Innes attribute the dominance of existing producers in advanced countries to 'enormous resources of capital, technology, marketing, management and political influence', which have been built up over a long time.

It is evident, then, that in several different strands of thought on industrial development, barriers to entry of one sort or another are considered to be important obstacles to newcomers. In most of the historical or development literature, however, the nature of entry barriers is not analysed in great detail, so it is helpful to turn to work on industrial economics and business studies for further clarification. The nature of barriers to entry is examined closely in these fields of study (e.g. see Bain, 1956 and Porter, 1980, ch. 1), and it is generally concluded that such barriers are quite common. Thus Porter (1980, p. 6), for example, refers to the 'economist's perfectly competitive industry, where entry is free' as the 'extreme case', rather than treating it as typical.[6]

Probably the most widely recognised source of entry barriers in this literature is *economies of scale* (or increasing returns to scale), which arise when a company's average costs decline as the scale of production increases. This creates barriers to entry because large existing firms have already achieved low costs due to scale, so that newcomers would have to enter on a similarly large scale in order to be competitive. But newcomers may have little hope of quickly capturing a sufficiently large market share and therefore they risk going through a period of chronic losses. Alternatively, if they try to enter on a small scale, they must accept persistently higher average costs than large established competitors, which is also an unattractive option. Economies of scale, in the broadest sense of advantages of large size, are very common, arising not only in the manufacturing process,[7] but also in purchasing, research and development, marketing, operating after-sales service networks and distribution.

An impression of the general importance of economies of scale can be gained by looking at the structure of existing successful industries in advanced countries. Where one finds that an industry has become highly concentrated in a relatively small number of large firms, one can take it that there are probably significant competitive advantages in a large scale of operation, since the process of competition has squeezed out smaller firms and favoured larger ones. In the USA, for example, the *Census of Manufactures* distinguishes 449 manufacturing industries, and in 223 of these the largest eight firms accounted for over half of shipments in 1977. These 223 highly concentrated industries together accounted for just over half of US manufacturing output (value-added). To put these figures in perspective, one must remember that the USA is an exceptionally large economy. If the top eight firms produce over half of output in a US industry, on average each one produces more than 6% and up to 12.5% of US output, which would usually be a very large scale of production compared with the market size in most countries. For example, a company producing 10% of output in a US industry would typically be capable of supplying roughly the equivalent of the whole Canadian market, more than twice the Mexican market, twelve times the Egyptian market or seventeen times the Irish market.[8]

The importance of economies of scale, however, varies considerably between different types of industry. Table 2.1 gives a broad indication of the types of industry which are most and least affected, by ranking the 20 major Industry Groups in the USA according to the proportion of their output (value-added) which is accounted for by the highly concentrated industries within them. (For this purpose, highly concentrated industries are those in which the top eight firms account for at least half of shipments.) Industry Groups placed towards the top of table 2.1 would tend to be most characterised by entry barriers due to economies of scale, unlike those nearer the bottom of the table. As would be expected, the industries in the top half of the table tend to be those which indigenous private firms in LDCs have had little success in developing to competitive standards, unless perhaps they are aided by protection. Of course, it is usually still possible for small firms and newcomers to find *limited* niches even in the most highly concentrated industries, for example by focussing on specialised segments of the market or on selling in particular geographical areas. But there would tend to be only limited opportunities of this type in the highly concentrated industries while the major activities in them are dominated by large established companies.

A second widely recognised source of barriers to entry is *product differentiation advantages*, which means that established firms have advantages of brand identification and customer loyalties stemming from past advertising, a long record of customer service or high quality, or simply from being one of the first into the industry. Differentiation creates entry barriers by forcing new entrants to spend heavily to overcome established customer preferences, at a considerable risk of failure. Porter (1980, ch. 1) suggests that this is a major barrier to entry in industries such as drugs, cosmetics and baby care products. In some industries, such as tobacco products and brewing, product differentiation can be coupled with economies of scale in marketing or production to create high entry barriers.

Capital requirements are a third important source of barriers to entry. In part, this arises from the large scale of capital equipment necessary for competitive production in many modern industries — a factor which caused little difficulty for the earliest industrialisers. Thus Hobsbawm (1969, p. 39) remarks that the production techniques used in Britain's pioneering industrial revolution 'required little initial investment, and their expansion could be financed out of accumulated profits. Industrial development was within the capacities of a multiplicity of small entrepreneurs and skilled traditional artisans. No twentieth-century country setting about

Table 2.1: Relative Importance of Highly Concentrated Industries, * by Industry Group, USA, 1977*

Major Industry Group	Number of Industries In Group	Number of Highly Concentrated Industries	Concentrated Industries' Share of Group's Value-Added (%)
Tobacco Products	4	4	100.0
Transportation Equipment	18	14	96.0
Petroleum & Coal Products	5	3	93.8
Primary Metals	26	16	70.9
Electric & Electronic Equipment	37	27	66.0
Machinery, except Electrical	44	23	58.5
Chemicals & Allied Products	28	19	57.9
Textile Mill Products	30	17	53.2
Instruments & Related Products	13	5	49.9
Stone, Clay & Glass Products	27	16	49.3
Food & Kindred Products	47	29	38.7
Rubber & Plastic Products	6	4	28.5
Fabricated Metal Products	36	13	25.5
Paper & Allied Products	17	7	23.2
Miscellaneous Manufacturing	20	8	20.6
Apparel & Related Products	33	6	18.7
Furniture & Fixtures	13	4	16.6
Lumber & Wood Products	17	2	11.0
Printing & Publishing	17	4	6.0
Leather & Leather Products	11	2	4.7
TOTAL	449	223	50.6

Source: Derived from US *Census of Manufactures, 1977, Concentration Ratios in Manufacturing.*

* *Note:* Highly Concentrated Industries are defined here to be those in which the top eight companies account for at least half of shipments.

industrialisation has, or can have, anything like these advantages.' However, as Porter (1980) points out, capital requirements can also create particularly difficult entry barriers in cases where large amounts of finance are required for working capital purposes, e.g. for investment in advertising, research and development or customer credit; such investments may not be recoverable in the event of failure, whereas plant and machinery at least have some resale value. Capital requirements present entry barriers even when capital is not generally in short supply, because financial institutions may be justifiably reluctant to take the risk of lending to new and unproven manufacturing ventures faced with strong established competitors.

There is a long list of further possible barriers to entry which apply in different industries. In engineering industries, for example, *customers' switching costs* can deter buyers from switching to a new supplier, due to costs such as retraining employees to handle different machines, the need to change ancillary equipment, or the cost of testing and approving the new product. *Access to distribution channels* can present entry barriers for consumer goods especially, since existing producers are well established with distributors whereas new firms must persuade them to accept new products through price concessions, favourable credit terms etc., which reduce the prospects of making profits. *Proprietary technology*, in the form of product designs or process know-how developed by established firms and protected by patents or secrecy, can create entry barriers in technologically advanced industries. This is because newcomers would have to take the risk of investing heavily in their own research and development, with uncertain prospects of earning any returns, if they are to match the existing technology of established competitors. And in many industries there are entry barriers caused by *learning or experience curves* — which mean that average production costs decline and quality improves as engineers, technicians and skilled manual workers acquire practical on-the-job experience in complex and intricate tasks. This effect would impose higher costs and initial losses on newcomers as compared with experienced firms, thus deterring new entrants.

Finally the advantages of agglomeration or *external economies*, which are enjoyed by firms in large established industrial centres, represent a further barrier to entry for newcomers in late-industrialising countries. External economies consist mainly of the advantages of proximity to related firms, specialist services and suppliers, a pool of skilled labour and a large local market. That they are very important is evident from the fact that, although cheaper labour was generally available outside the main industrial centres, industrialisation was highly centralised in the advanced countries and this continued to be the case until about the early 1960s. Many of the small manufacturing firms which remain in the advanced countries, despite the growth of very large firms, are in fact closely linked to larger firms, supplying components for instance.[9] Thus, although barriers to entry may be low for some of these smaller-scale activities, the importance of external economies means that this is only true for new entrants in the locality. The tendency for industry to become more spatially dispersed (both within countries and internationally) over the past two or three decades is made possible by improved communications and transport, the deskilling of many production jobs, and by the development of very large firms which have internalised what were formerly external economies. Much of this dispersal, in fact, results from the relocation or extension of such large firms and, to this extent, is not an indication that the importance of external economies is declining in a sense that reduces the difficulties for new indigenous firms in late-developing countries.

It appears to have generally been the case that external economies have a strong effect on each generation of new, fast-growing industries based on new technologies in the early stages of their development — from textiles in the nineteenth century to electronics in recent decades. In newly developing industries, many new initially small firms do appear, suggesting that some barriers to entry such as economies of scale are not decisive at this stage. But if external economies are particularly important in such activities, this does create a serious entry barrier for new firms situated in late-industrialising countries. For new small high-technology firms often arise out of, and continue to depend on close links with existing advanced industrial structures. Many of them are 'spin-offs' — created by professional or technical staff leaving existing industries in advanced industrial areas with the benefit of knowledge, experience and ideas gained in their former employment. They generally also require continuing close links with such an advanced industrial area, because they may be engaged in supplying components to larger firms and because, more generally, they depend on the pool of specialised skills and knowledge and the easy exchange of information available in concentrated areas of their industry. Hence such geographically concentrated developments as 'Silicon Valley', California.[10]

To conclude this discussion of barriers to entry for newcomers, one indication of their overall importance is the fact that most of the major industrial firms today are not newcomers, but rather have been established for a very long time. Vernon (1970) mentions, for example, that at least 187 of the largest American multinationals, which together account for 80% of US foreign manufacturing investment, can trace their origins back further than the year 1900.

Instability in the International Economy
The argument that late-industrialisers face special difficulties begins with the contention that widespread barriers to entry seriously limit the opportunities for new indigenous firms in late-developing countries. Taken on its own, this point would mean that indigenous industry in the latecomers would tend to be concentrated in sectors with relatively low barriers to entry, if they are exposed to open competition with advanced countries. These industries would probably provide only relatively low incomes, due to the intensity of competition in easily entered activities as compared with the higher incomes which would be sustainable in industries with restricted entry in the advanced countries.

The problem of late development is further compounded, however, by the instability of the international economy, which tends to experience recurring recessions or depressions with consequent unemployment. If this were not so, and if full employment of productive resources worldwide were the normal situation, then late-industrialisers could at least expect to have full employment even if their incomes were relatively low. For, in accordance with the principle of comparative advantage, the stronger advanced countries would concentrate their productive resources exclusively in sectors in which their competitive advantage is *greatest*. Less-developed countries would then find employment for their productive resources in the remaining sectors — including some in which advanced countries might have an *absolute* competitive advantage, but which would be left to the less-developed countries because advanced producers would concentrate all their resources in those sectors where their advantage is comparatively even greater.

The instability of the international economy means, however, that there is no general tendency for productive resources to be fully employed, even if 'supply-side' conditions such as savings rates, business incentives and social and institutional conditions are satisfactory. It means, too, that one of the conditions required for the principle of comparative advantage to operate so as to benefit all parties in international trade does not generally exist. So, the *absolute* competitive advantage enjoyed by the stronger established producers causes less-developed countries to suffer disproportionately from underemployment of productive resources. This would be true particularly of the recessionary periods themselves, both because of increased competitive pressure from exports from the advanced countries, and because recession tends to generate protectionism in advanced countries, often directed particularly against latecomers. But, even in periods of recovery and expansion, the time available for adjustment to full employment worldwide may well be inadequate, while the intense competition resulting from the expectation of recurring shortages of profitable markets would force the strongest producers to seek to hold as much of the market as possible. Besides implying fairly persistent (though fluctuating) underemployment of productive resources in late-developing countries, this would also considerably reduce the opportunities for their indigenous industries to make progress in diversifying the range of their activities. This restriction of opportunities would arise from the desire of the established industries based elsewhere to retain control of as many activities as possible. And such a desire is frequently backed by their ability to do so as long as *some* entry barriers exist in the activity concerned — even if what would be their *comparative* advantage in a situation of persistent full employment is passing away.

The view that there is a continual tendency for international recessions to recur could be argued quite effectively on the grounds that historically this has clearly been the case. This point is underlined by the sluggish international growth and widespread unemployment which have prevailed for much of the time since about 1974 — after this problem might have appeared to have been finally overcome during the preceding period of more than 20 years of almost unbroken expansion.

The theoretical analysis which suggests that instability is an inherent feature of capitalist or market economies, which cannot readily be controlled, is perhaps most characteristic of Marxist economics but is by no means confined to that body of theory. Thus, although Marxist economics is based on a labour theory of value and uses different concepts from those of conventional economics, there is some similarity between several of the tendencies it identifies as leading to recession, stagnation or 'crisis' and concepts which appear in branches of conventional economics. The Marxist approach identifies four tendencies which are said to result from the process of sustained capital accumulation (or economic growth), one or more of which ultimately causes economic crises:—

1. The tendency of the rate of profit to fall as capital is accumulated so that the ratio of capital and material inputs to labour rises.[11]

2. A tendency for wages to rise, squeezing profits and deterring investment, as demand for labour increases due to capital accumulation increasing the stock of capital equipment which needs labour to operate it.

3. Should the (first-mentioned) tendency of the rate of profit to fall be counteracted by some means, then profits would be taking an increasing *share* of income, so that consumer demand (which arises primarily from wages) would tend to decline relative to the growing productive capacity. This would cause a 'realisation' crisis, or a crisis of deficient demand.

4. The tendency of sectors to grow at different rates in an unplanned or anarchic manner, causing disproportionalities to develop, thus precipitating crises in excessively large sectors which can spread more widely through effects on demand. In particular, sectors producing capital or intermediate goods receive excessive stimulation from the acceleration of demand for producers' goods in the upswing of a boom (when recovering from a recession or, perhaps, war damage). This causes them to overinvest in productive capacity which proves to be excessive once investment settles at a more normal rate.

Views differ among Marxists as to which of these tendencies is most important in practice, though all of them are found (with some inconsistencies of emphasis) scattered throughout Marx's own works.[12]

More conventional theories of the trade cycle have developed fairly similar concepts to several of these ideas, which do not depend on acceptance of Marx's labour theory of value. Thus Keynes suggested that persistent demand deficiency would be likely to tend to cause depression (though for different reasons). Many others (including many governments) have also considered that government intervention to boost demand and sustain full employment would — in the absence of a disciplined incomes policy — cause wages to rise excessively. Excessive wage rises would either squeeze profits and deter investment or else they would fuel inflation, which would ultimately call for deflationary measures resulting in recession. The 'accelerator' principle in the trade cycle literature draws attention, too, to the problem of disproportionate growth and wide fluctuations in the capital goods sector. The solutions required to control these difficulties and avoid recession can be identified in principle but would be very difficult to implement for a sustained period. What is required is, first, the ability to identify the problems emerging in good time. Then all major countries, in co-ordination, must regulate demand, control income increases, and influence the amount and direction of investment — in the context of competitive rivalry between firms and nations and frequently conflict between capital and labour as well. The practical difficulties of carrying this out suggest that instability and recurring recessions or depressions are likely to remain features of the international economy.

Foreign Direct Investment in Latecomers
The problems for late-developers outlined above, concerning the effects of barriers to entry for newcomers compounded by international instability, are relevant to the *indigenous* or native industries of latecomers. But these countries also have the further possibility of attracting direct investment by established firms based in advanced countries, which would not be subject to the constraints imposed by entry barriers on new firms. Thus the role and potential of foreign direct investment as a possible solution to the problem of late industrialisation must be considered too. In fact, there are good grounds for suggesting that it cannot provide a general solution to the problem. This is mainly because foreign direct investment in late-developing countries occurs only in certain circumstances, which are such that it could be of substantial economic benefit to relatively few of these countries. This issue is considered only briefly here, since a more detailed discussion

follows in chapter 7 leading into some analysis of the nature of foreign investment in Ireland.

Before the Second World War, there was little foreign direct investment in manufacturing. When it began to grow rapidly after the war, it was largely aimed at production for the local market of the host country. Consequently most of it was going from one developed country to another, while the smaller markets of most underdeveloped countries proved less attractive.[13] This type of investment, however, did become quite important in some less-developed countries with relatively large protected markets and an acceptable infrastructure built up during earlier periods of protected import-substituting industrialisation; the main examples are certain Latin American countries. Consequently, the first critical studies of foreign direct manufacturing investment were mainly those of the Latin American Dependency school.

One of the main criticisms made in the Dependency literature concerns the effect on the balance of payments of foreign investment in production for the local market. It is pointed out that while such investment involves some inflow of capital, much of the capital is also raised locally (e.g. Sunkel, 1973). Subsequently, profit repatriation builds up leading to an outflow of capital (Sunkel, 1973; Frank, 1969). In addition, a large proportion of inputs for these industries tends to be imported, particularly since production of capital goods and other technically advanced and large-scale industries remain in the advanced countries (Dos Santos, 1973; Furtado, 1971). And finally, the inflow of capital initially associated with this investment tends to run down as the scope for further investment in suitable, technically mature industries becomes exhausted. Balance of payments problems tend to arise eventually from the combination of these factors and the rather limited development of production for export (given that the desire to gain access to the protected home market was the principal motivation for such investment, which frequently does not attain the scale or efficiency required for internationally competitive production). Conventional neo-classical analyses, such as Balassa (1980), would also recognise that such results can occur with protected domestically oriented industrialisation.

The chronic balance of payments difficulties, arising both from the process outlined above and from generally slow growth of demand for primary exports, impede further industrial growth. For further growth requires more imports of capital goods and other inputs as well as some consumer goods as incomes grow, but chronic balance of payments problems inhibit this. Furthermore, the fact that balance of payments problems cause governments to seek to restrict profit repatriation by foreign firms tends to make further investment unattractive to foreign capital. Another point made in the Dependency literature concerning foreign investment in manufacturing of this type is that such investment may be in competition with existing or potential domestic producers. At the least, this would have the disadvantage of leading to the export of profits which would otherwise have accrued locally. And it would also pre-empt some desirable longer-term effects such as development of more local managerial and technical skills and the development of more backward linkages within the country.

The growth of foreign direct investment in *export-oriented* manufacturing, which became of some importance in a number of countries during the 1960s, naturally has not been so much associated with the same problems concerning the balance of payments, competition with domestic producers or the inefficiencies of too small a scale. But, although arguably more beneficial, export-oriented foreign investment seems unlikely to represent anything like a general solution to the problems of latecomers. This is mainly because it has occurred on a relatively small scale, having no great impact on the vast majority of underdeveloped countries. Nayyar (1978) found that in the early 1970s only four countries accounted for nearly half of the manufactured exports from LDCs or NICs. These were Hong Kong, Singapore, Taiwan, and South Korea — none of them very large, while in all except Singapore foreign investment was only a supplement to a more substantial expansion of indigenous industry. Among the remaining LDCs which were leading exporters of manufactured goods, he says, transnational corporations (TNCs) played an important role only in Brazil and Mexico (Puerto Rico is not included in his analysis). Furthermore, US-based multinational corporations, which account for about 40% of all foreign direct investment in the world, employed only 1.38 million people in manufacturing in all of the less-developed countries by 1985 (US Department of Commerce, *Survey of Current Business,* June 1987). Clearly this is no more than a drop in the ocean in a group of countries whose population amounts to some 3,900 million.

Few latecomers, therefore, can expect export-oriented foreign investment to make a major impact on their industrial development. It also appears that, although it may be beneficial for some time in certain countries, it is not ultimately a satisfactory substitute for indigenous industrial development. For export-oriented foreign investment has been highly concentrated in certain types of activity — usually technologically undemanding, very often relatively labour-intensive, and usually employing few highly skilled people. Often, too, it involves only some stages of a manufacturing process which meet these conditions while other more technically advanced stages are carried out elsewhere. Since there is a limited range of such activities, and because they are sufficiently 'mobile' or 'footloose' to choose from a large number of less-developed sites, the ability of any particular country to attract many of them depends on keeping labour and other costs relatively low as compared with other sites regarded as suitable alternatives.[14] For some countries with special attractions this may allow wages to rise well above the norm for LDCs, but still constrains them to remain below the level of acceptable alternative sites with the same advantages. For example Ireland, with its access to the EEC market, and Puerto Rico, with access to the USA, have had high wages by LDC standards while successfully attracting much export-oriented foreign investment. But the wage levels attainable with a development process based primarily on foreign industry are probably limited to about the minimum level found in comparable locations elsewhere in the EEC or USA respectively.[15]

For most LDCs with no exceptional advantages, the successful attraction of export-oriented foreign investment probably depends on keeping wages and other costs very low, in competition with many other low-cost countries with a combined labour force far in excess of that required by mobile foreign investors. A further important point is that political stability of a type favourable to private capital, and a docile or repressed labour force, are also generally prerequisites for substantial foreign investment (Nayyar, 1978). This can lead to or reinforce tendencies to political repression.

The Nature of the State
Some of the literature on the problems of late-developers also stresses certain constraints on the role of the state. It is argued

that the apparatus of the state is not completely above or outside the economic situation, capable of selecting and implementing economic policies at will, on the basis of good (or bad) advice. Rather, the state is influenced by classes or groups which have definite interests and attitudes arising from their position in society. Thus, the range of policies which may be chosen and implemented by the state is limited (in ways which differ depending on the country), though not precisely determined. In a late-developing country, the question of which social classes or groups have important positions in society and strong influences on the state is, in turn, at least partially influenced or 'conditioned' by the latecomer's history of economic and political domination by more advanced countries.

This point is identified by Godfrey (1980) as one of the principal characteristics of the Dependency school — 'the endogenisation of the State,' as he puts it, 'as the crucial battleground between the different social groups'. The degree of economic determinism suggested in this matter varies between different writers, but a particular aspect of it which all regard as being important is the question of the influence of *external* relations with the dominant advanced countries on the internal economic and social structure of the latecomer, and hence on the state. Frank (1969) suggests that there are quite rigid hierarchical relations between 'metropolis' and 'satellite', whereas Dos Santos (1973) for instance, puts rather more emphasis on the internal structure of a dependent country itself, which is conditioned by the international relations of dependence in ways which vary depending on the country. The relation between external and internal forces is described by Cardoso and Faletto (1979) as 'a complex whole whose structural links are not based on mere external forms of exploitation and coercion, but are rooted in coincidence of interests between local dominant classes and international ones and, on the other side, are challenged by local dominated groups and classes'. Thus, the external influence, in this formulation, operates through local allies with similar interests and would continue to do so in the absence of substantial political change, which may be resisted by dominant local groups with the help of external support. The historical studies of such Dependency writers attempt to show these relationships at work, and the way in which social formation and policy-making is influenced by them. To the extent that the social structure and policies which result may not be conducive to successful industrial development, this factor may be an obstacle of primary importance.

2.iii.   SUMMARY OF THE ISSUES

The issues raised in this chapter can now be drawn together to contrast the analysis of the conventional view with that of the alternative approach outlined in section 2.ii.

The conventional analysis suggests that less-developed countries should adopt outward-looking policies, rely mainly on market forces rather than government intervention (except for fairly generalised or automatic incentives), and aim to overcome backward or 'traditional' characteristics which inhibit development. In this way they will achieve the best results in industrialisation — with output and employment expanding at a rate determined primarily by the availability of capital for investment. The process would begin with labour-intensive, technologically undemanding industries and would be characterised by growth of exports in particular, which would enable other sorts of industrial products to be imported. In the course of time, as capital is accumulated and skills are developed, the country would become increasingly involved in more capital-intensive, technologically demanding industries, thus evolving into an advanced industrial country with higher incomes (e.g. see Balassa, 1980).

The alternative approach outlined in section 2.ii stresses the special difficulties faced by latecomers which make such an outcome unlikely, as the general case. *Under such policies*, it is suggested, the development of *indigenous* industries would be largely confined to a limited range of activities, beyond which further progress would be difficult and slow or perhaps would not be achieved at all. This limited range of activities would include some which are effectively sheltered from foreign competition and others which are open to international competition but have exceptionally low barriers to entry. Activities sheltered from foreign competition would include some protected by transport costs (e.g. building materials), some protected by the advantages of proximity to the local market if local knowledge, contacts and flexibility of response are important (e.g. printing and packaging), and also some which may develop exports but are 'sheltered' by the advantage of proximity to local primary resources for low value-added processing (e.g. basic food processing). Unsheltered activities with low barriers to entry would be those characterised by a relatively small scale of firms, mature standardised products, an absence of major sales promotion activities (usually because of little product differentiation), and relatively small capital requirements. They would also be characterised by a relatively small demand for specialised industrial skills and little need for close contact with related industries. Commonly cited examples of such easily entered industries are branches of clothing, footwear, household goods, and their inputs such as certain textiles, leather and wood, though there are others.

It is necessary, however, to point out at this stage that barriers to entry for newcomers do change over the long term. Industries which once were inaccessible to new entrants can gradually become more open to them, mainly as a result of the maturation and standardisation of technology removing the advanced countries' advantage over low-cost competitors.[16] At the same time new, technologically advanced activities are continually appearing at the other more inaccessible end of the scale. Consequently, the latecomer trying to close the gap with the advanced countries has the added difficulty of pursuing a moving target, but also some opportunity gradually to diversify its range of industries, thus making some absolute progress in industrialisation even while making no progress in closing the gap. The critical analyses on which this alternative view is based, however, clearly mean to suggest that the difficulties for latecomers are somewhat more serious than merely an inability to *catch up* with the advanced countries. Rather, it is suggested that, at the least, the absolute progress which may be made would persistently be insufficient to achieve full employment of productive resources. Thus this alternative view suggests that in a latecomer adopting the conventionally recommended policies, one would observe: (a) confinement of indigenous industry very largely to sheltered activities and others with *relatively* low barriers to entry; (b) a slow rate of diversification, or a slowing down after an initial spurt at the start of industrialisation, *leading to* (c) a marked slowing down in the rate of growth of, or a decline in indigenous industrial employment while unemployment still persists; and (d) competitive pressures from other low-cost NICs becoming involved in the same limited range of easily entered activities. In other words, the latecomer following the conventional strategy would generally find progress in 'upward' diversification of its indigenous industry too slow, and the competition from so many others in so limited a range of accessible industries too strong, to achieve anything close to full employment.

In the alternative view, it would be expected too, that periods of recession or depression would create the greatest difficulties for latecomers — a point scarcely disputed in the conventional analysis, but the difference lies in whether such periods are regarded as exceptional aberrations or inevitable recurring features of the international market economy.

It would also be expected that, in latecomers with outward-looking free market policies, the amount of foreign direct investment in production for the local market would be quite limited. Foreign export-oriented manufacturing would have an important role only in exceptional cases, since its overall scale worldwide is not great. Due to its generally technically undemanding and relatively labour-intensive nature, it would also have limited beneficial secondary effects, and it would tend to become vulnerable to competition from other low-cost NICs if labour costs were to rise continuously over time. Rising labour costs over time would also tend to reduce the attractiveness of the latecomer for new investors.

In addition it should be possible, according to this alternative view, to trace some relationship historically between the policy stance adopted by the state and the interests of dominant groups. The development of internal politics would also be expected to be somewhat influenced by external relations, or rather, the contrasting interests of different social groups in various forms of external relations.

By formulating the view of the prevailing constraints on the industrialisation of latecomers in this way, it can be seen that one way in which a *small number* of small economies could partially evade the constraints, while adopting the conventional strategy, is by successfully attracting an exceptionally large *share* of the limited amount of export-oriented mobile foreign industries. Observation of such cases might appear to justify the conventional view, which does not make a point of distinguishing between indigenous and foreign industry. But a satisfactory assessment of which view is justified by such cases must make this distinction, and must regard the experience of their indigenous industries as the consideration most relevant to drawing *general* conclusions since foreign investment of the type mentioned occurs on so limited a scale worldwide. Another type of experience with the conventional strategy which might, for a time, appear to justify the conventional view would be that of countries which rapidly build up sheltered and easily entered industries from an initially very backward position, thus achieving rapid industrial growth before reaching the point where the suggested constraints on latecomers really begin to apply. A satisfactory assessment of which view is justified by such cases must await further developments.

If this alternative view is broadly correct, it suggests that the type of strategy most likely to achieve the best results would involve active and selective state policies to build up industries capable of overcoming barriers to entry. Protection against imports, without much further systematic and purposeful intervention, has been widely used with only limited or temporary success to achieve this end. In chapters 8 and 9, where reference is made to the policies of relatively successful latecomers such as Japan and South Korea, further suggestions are made concerning the type of action that needs to accompany or substitute for protection — suggestions which are supported by the industrial success of these countries.

Most of this book, however, is a case study of the Republic of Ireland since the 1950s. The strategy adopted by the country has, with some qualifications, been close to that which is conventionally recommended and the results, at first sight, appear to have been quite good, at least in the 1960s and 1970s, so that Ireland is now widely regarded as an advanced industrial country and an example of the success of that strategy. It will be shown, however, that Ireland is one of the handful of exceptions which could achieve such results by attracting a greatly disproportionate share of the limited amount of mobile export-oriented foreign industry. At the same time, its indigenous industry shows clear signs of experiencing the suggested constraints on latecomers — which is the more important consideration in drawing general conclusions.[17] For Ireland itself, which has recently experienced greater difficulty in attracting a sufficient inflow of new foreign industry, this weakness of indigenous firms has become an increasingly obvious and serious problem.

Before going on to consider the period since the 1950s, however, the next two chapters briefly outline the historical experience of industry in Ireland up to that time. This experience itself illustrates the disadvantages of being a relative latecomer in close competition with more advanced industrial economies and the devastating economic and social effects which the free play of market forces can have on such a latecomer.

3

Irish Industry Before
the Twentieth Century

Although this book is quite largely concerned with the experience of industry in Ireland since the 1950s, this chapter and the next outline the earlier historical background. This earlier background seems worthy of attention since, as was mentioned in chapter 1, it illustrates the evolving effects of the problem of late development as it gradually emerged during the nineteenth century, following the start of Great Britain's industrial revolution.

The main points of interest in the historical background outlined here include the fact that industrial development had already proceeded quite far in Ireland by the early nineteenth century, suggesting that local economic and social conditions were not markedly unfavourable for development. But there followed a very substantial industrial decline in most of the island. This indicates that the attainment of relatively favourable local conditions was by no means *sufficient* to generate sustained industrialisation in a country making a relatively late start on a relatively small scale in developing mechanised industry (i.e. relative to Great Britain — the pioneer of the Industrial Revolution). Ireland's position in the nineteenth and early twentieth centuries, as a relative latecomer in a relationship of free trade with Great Britain, was somewhat analogous to that of latecomers adopting the conventional strategy today, so that the devastating results cast doubts on the wisdom of such a strategy. It is possible to observe in Ireland's historical experience relative to Britain how the growing importance of economies of scale, external economies, specialised technological capabilities and other factors created ever stronger concentrated industrial centres in those areas which began the process of mechanised industrialisation on a large scale first. Meanwhile the areas which started relatively late and/or on a smaller scale were gradually eliminated by the competitive process. What one observes, in other words, is the effect of the process of the most advanced industrial areas building up cumulative competitive advantages, eliminating lesser competitors, and simultaneously raising ever higher barriers to entry for newcomers.

3.i. EARLY INDUSTRIAL DEVELOPMENT

At the beginning of the seventeenth century, the Irish economy was distinctly undeveloped compared with other Western European countries. The population was probably only about one million, the land was still heavily wooded and the main exports were fish and hides (Cullen, 1976, ch. 1). Although the English crown controlled a small area (the Pale) in the environs of Dublin, political authority beyond the Pale was highly decentralised in the hands of Gaelic clan chiefs and descendants of earlier Norman invaders. This picture changed greatly in the course of the seventeenth and eighteenth centuries. Growing exports of cattle, wool and butter, which had come to exceed those of fish and hides by 1641, indicated more extensive settlement and more sophisticated agricultural organisation. The defeat of Irish rebellions, followed by extensive confiscations of land which was awarded to soldiers and financiers of the English armies, extended English political power and economic interests to a position of effective dominance for the first time. The change is illustrated by the fact that while Catholics (who were mainly natives) still owned 60% of the land in 1640, this dropped to 14% in the 1690s, and to 5% by 1775 (Johnston, 1974; and Wall, 1968). But despite plans to colonise large parts of Ireland with British settlers, these plans were not effective in most of the island and native Catholics generally stayed on as tenants under new English Protestant landlords. Only in the northern province of Ulster, which was the most thinly populated and the most recently subdued area, did a substantial plantation of British settlers occur in the seventeenth century, with others following independently of the official plantation policy.

The extension of English control over the island extended the market economy, or capitalism, and resulted in increasing exports in the second half of the seventeenth century. These began to include woollen cloth and a rapidly growing trade in salted provisions to the West Indian colonies. Expansion of the woollen industry was also reflected in a sharp decline of imports of some woollen cloths after the 1680s. That decade also saw the beginnings of a long-sustained growth of linen exports, which rose from 23,000 yards in 1683, to 520,000 by 1705 (Cullen, 1976, p. 24; and Gill, 1964, p. 10). By the end of the seventeenth century the population was about 2½ million, Dublin was already bigger than any English town except London, and Cork was a major transatlantic port.

The general trend of economic expansion, although of a changing nature, continued in the eighteenth century, with some temporary interruptions. This expansion was increasingly linked with the needs of the British economy as British demand increased and the West Indian trade declined. Thus the proportion of Irish exports going to Britain increased from 44% in 1720 to 85% in 1800 (O'Tuathaigh, 1972, p. 2). Linen cloth became the largest component of these exports, but export growth was fairly broadly based after the 1730s — involving provisions and grain as well (Cullen, 1976).

By the 1790s, cotton had also become an important industry, which mainly supplied the home market. The woollen industry, too, although excluded from export markets by an English Act of 1699, had expanded due to its dominance of the growing domestic market until the closing decades of the eighteenth century. The general impression of fairly broadly based economic expansion is strengthened by the acceleration in population growth around the middle of the eighteenth century to over 5 million by 1800, and by the large and increasing quantities of consumer goods such as tea, tobacco and sugar which were imported. There also arose in the eighteenth century an important native Catholic middle class (Wall, 1968). Thus by the beginning of the Industrial Revolution in the late eighteenth century, Ireland had experienced considerable development of a capitalist market economy and the linen, woollen and cotton industries were well established.

The Textile Industries

An important feature of the process of merchanised industrialisation which occurred in the Industrial Revolution, beginning in Britain around the 1770s, was the fact that industry became highly centralised. The development of a wide range of industries in any one industrial centre was also apparently quite specifically linked to, and depended heavily on, the success of leading sectors, or its earliest major mechanised industries. In Ireland, which lacked large deposits of coal and iron and therefore also lacked large mining industries, the various textile industries had the best potential for acting as such leading sectors (they were also very important in Great Britain). In order to explain the long-term decline of industry in most of Ireland in the nineteenth century (except in the north east), it is therefore important to outline in a little more detail the history of textiles. A description later in the chapter of the subsequent development of a wider range of industries in the north east, which can be traced back to the local success of linen, will then serve to illustrate both the process which caused nineteenth-century industrialisation to be so centralised and the long-term consequences of the failure of textiles elsewhere in Ireland. This concentration on the history of textiles is not to suggest that this was the only important manufacturing sector in eighteenth-century Ireland, which was not lacking in other industries such as milling, brewing, distilling, shipbuilding, sugar-refining and the manufacture of consumer luxuries.

The growth of linen exports had been quite spectacular in the eighteenth century, from 520,000 yards in 1705 to over 40 million yards annually in the 1790s. Linen manufacture was an ancient craft in Ireland as evidenced by records of yarn exports as early as 1542 (Gill, 1964). But the type of narrow finished cloth made then was not in demand outside the country and when significant cloth exports began in the 1680s, its weaving and finishing were mainly concentrated in the north east, in the province of Ulster. It is generally agreed that the seventeenth-century immigration of British settlers and Huguenots to the north east was an important part of the explanation for this location. For many of them were skilled in the weaving and finishing trades and used to the manufacture of broadcloths for English or continental markets. With a supply of Irish yarn they could produce such cloth to supplement the incomes from their small farms.

It has sometimes been argued, e.g. by Gill (1964) and the British and Irish Communist Organisation (1972), that the linen industry had to remain concentrated in Ulster because rack-renting of tenants in the rest of Ireland did not allow a class of petty commodity producers to emerge and engage in industrial production. Cullen (1976, ch. 3), however, disputes this, saying that the land system in most of the island did not cause such extreme insecurity and that the linen industry expanded over quite a wide area. This view, in fact, is supported by Gill's own statistics. According to his figures (pp. 161 and 271), sales of linen outside Ulster were 8 million yards in 1770, 9 million in 1784, and 14.3 million annually in 1816-21; this represents a fairly consistent proportion of total Irish sales, at 19% in 1770 and 1784, and 16% in 1816-21. Thus the available evidence suggests that linen weaving and finishing were growing outside Ulster at much the same rate as in Ulster itself. Spinning certainly grew faster outside Ulster, especially in some counties in Connaught where the highest proportion of employment in manufacturing was to be found by the early nineteenth century — mainly among women engaged in domestic spinning. Both developments suggest that the social class formation and land tenure system outside Ulster did not prevent the growth of a rural textile industry in the crucial period leading into the Industrial Revolution. Nevertheless, due to its origins in the north east, the weaving and finishing stages of the linen industry remained *relatively* concentrated there and this was to have a decisive effect on later developments.

The mechanised technology of the Industrial Revolution first became evident in Ireland towards the end of the 1770s in the cotton industry, which also led the way in Great Britain. The Irish cotton industry was probably larger than, or certainly comparable in size in the early 1780s to that of Scotland, which was to develop in the Glasgow area a cotton industry second only to that of Lancashire (Cullen and Smout, 1978). Dickson (1978) shows that this industry too was by no means confined to Ulster, but rather was quite widely dispersed with Dublin being a larger regional centre than Belfast or Cork. Again, this suggests that suitable conditions for industrial development were fairly widespread. The Irish cotton industry, however, grew quite slowly, and was probably only about one-quarter of the size of the Scottish industry by the turn of the century. It appears that the Irish showed a stronger tendency to keep to the still less mechanised linen industry, in which they had a strong competitive position. Also, the mainly coarser types of cotton produced in Ireland were not so easily sold outside the home market, which had the additional benefit of protective tariffs in the 1790s.

By the 1790s, according to Dickson (1978), Belfast, the major town in the north east, was becoming the main location of cotton *spinning* (the most highly mechanised stage of its production) with 54% of Irish spinning capacity in 1800. The advantage of Belfast was due, as Dickson argues, to the presence in the adjacent Lagan valley of an established large population of skilled weavers of finer linens who could readily work with cotton yarn. The displacement to this extent of linen weaving by cotton in the north east, while Irish linen output continually grew, is a further indication that linen weaving could spread effectively beyond this area.[1] This tendency of mechanised spinning mills to concentrate in Belfast shows, too, that even at this early stage there were signs of a centralising tendency in mechanised industry in locations influenced by the availability of related skilled labour.

The woollen industry had been excluded from export markets by an English Act in 1699, which is in itself an indication of the contemporary English evaluation of the competitive potential of early Irish industry. But it still continued to grow during much of the eighteenth century due to its dominance of the expanding home market, although remaining smaller than the English woollen industry. Following the transformation of the English industry in the Industrial Revolution, Irish imports of some woollens rose during the 1780s, while the relatively small exports of worsted, made possible by the repeal of the 1699 Act in 1779, declined quickly after 1785. The emergence of some factory-type firms in Ireland eventually halted the decline for a time and imports levelled off between 1799 and 1825 despite rising demand (Cullen, 1976, p. 105). But there emerged no large mechanised centre of the industry comparable in scale to that in Yorkshire.

To conclude, by the end of the eighteenth century, Ireland had a strong linen industry, exporting a good deal and with its weaving and finishing stages relatively concentrated in the north east. The woollen and cotton industries were well established in the home market but exported little and were a good deal smaller than British competitors. Some of the non-textile industries had met increasingly strong British competition around the 1770s, but they had mostly been successful in reorganising on a larger scale, as in Britain, during the 1770s and 1780s and thereby maintained their position (Cullen, 1976, ch. 4).

Political Developments in the Late Eighteenth Century

During the 1770s, the American War of Independence and the state of hostility existing between Great Britain and much of Europe led to a reduction in the British forces stationed in

Ireland. Consequently, to meet the danger of a French invasion, the Irish Protestant upper classes in 1778 organised a militia force, the Irish Volunteers. This force of about 80,000 to 100,000 armed men was for several years beyond the effective control of the British government. When its leaders and its allies within the Irish Parliament chose to demand free trade (i.e. free from the Navigation Acts and other British restrictions on Irish trade with Europe and the colonies) and the repeal of Poyning's Law (which allowed the British Parliament to make laws binding for Ireland), the British government found it prudent to comply. In this way there began the era of 'Grattan's Parliament' in which the Irish Parliament had a greater measure of independence. The traditional nationalist view of Irish economic history, perhaps best exemplified by the works of O'Brien (1918 and 1921), regarded this period as one of unprecedented economic expansion, and therefore an illustration of the benefits of Irish independence. However, as has been indicated above, a considerable volume of more recent historical research suggests that economic expansion had also prevailed before this time (see also Cullen, 1968a and 1968b).

Some of the more radical elements in the Irish Volunteers also sought universal suffrage and the repeal of the Penal Laws against Catholics, but few of the Protestant landed aristocracy or middle class were prepared to back these demands. The landowners were especially conscious of the insecurity of their position in view of the claims of the larger population of native Catholic Irish to be rightful heirs to the land. Unlike the American colonists, for instance, they needed the security of British support and they eventually allied with Britain to oppose the radical Volunteer elements, which were mainly composed of Presbyterian middle-class intellectuals and landless men. In the end the radicals gave in without a battle.

Nevertheless, the radical intellectual tradition, inspired by the American and French Revolutions and based mainly among a minority of northern Presbyterians, lived on in the United Irishmen, founded in 1791. This movement sought the unity of all Irishmen in a common struggle for democracy and independence from Britain. Many Catholics joined it, but inevitably in the south many of them identified Protestants with the English — and both with their landlords — and the movement there began to take on a sectarian character. In the north, Protestants, especially men of property including the relatively secure tenant farmers, increasingly saw their interests as opposed to those of Catholics. By the time of the 1798 Rebellion, Protestant participation was quite limited. But, significantly, some of the Protestant Belfast cotton manufacturers, whose interests (unlike those of the linen manufacturers) lay increasingly in economic separation from Britain, were prominent in the Rebellion.[2]

Following the defeat of the 1798 Rebellion, the British government moved to enact the Union of Britain and Ireland. The threat to security made evident by the Rebellion and the narrow failure of the French to land large armies in Ireland on two occasions, as well as their success in landing one small force, was the main reason for the Union. Also, by that time British industry had advanced to the point where few manufacturers objected to free trade with Ireland, as many had done in reaction to Pitt's commercial propositions in 1785. In Ireland itself militant opposition to a Union was weak after the defeat of 1798, while the Protestant ascendancy parliament was sufficiently shaken to abandon its earlier pretentions to some independence. In this way there was established by the Act of Union in 1800 the United Kingdom of Great Britain and Ireland, which abolished the existing degree of legislative independence held by the Irish parliament and instituted full economic union as well. The Union was the political context for the subsequent long-term decline of industry in most of Ireland and the diverging industrialisation of the north east.

3.ii. NINETEENTH-CENTURY DECLINE

By the early nineteenth century Ireland had a fairly substantial industrial sector by the standards of most countries at that time, except Great Britain, the pioneer of the Industrial Revolution. According to the 1821 Census, one-third of the Irish counties, including six out of 23 outside Ulster, had a greater number of people engaged in manufacturing, trade or handicraft than in agriculture. And in 1841, 700,000 people — one-fifth of the working population — were reported to be occupied in textile manufacturing alone.[3]

During the nineteenth century, however, industrial activity declined in most of Ireland. As industry declined, offering diminishing prospects of employment to the masses being forced out of agriculture, emigration rose to proportions unparalleled in any other country. The labour force of the 26 counties of the present Republic of Ireland dropped from 2.7

million in 1841 to 1.3 million in 1911. This represents a decline from 38% of the size of the British labour force in 1841 to just 7% in 1911 (Crotty, 1986, p. 2). By the 1920s little more than 100,000 workers (8% of the labour force) were employed in industry in the new Irish Free State.

In the Belfast area in the north east, however, growth continued in a manner similar to that of large industrial centres in Britain. After the mid-nineteenth century Belfast became the largest centre of linen manufacture in the world and by the 1900s the Belfast shipyards were building up to about a quarter of the total United Kingdom tonnage (Goldstrom, 1968).

A number of different explanations have been suggested for the decline of most of Irish industry (see O'Malley, 1981, for a short review of this literature). These include some which stress the poor quality of Irish entrepreneurship (especially Lee, 1968 and 1973; and Sinn Fein The Workers' Party, 1978). It has also been suggested that the main factors were the lack of coal and/or iron (Connolly, 1973; and O'Tuathaigh, 1972), or the decline of the local market due to changes in agriculture (Crotty, 1979). Others stress particularly the importance of centralising tendencies and/or growing advantages of large-scale firms, and the damaging effects on Ireland of these tendencies in the United Kingdom of Great Britain and Ireland as a whole — given that Britain was the most advanced industrial economy in the world. Variations of this type of explanation are found in O'Brien (1918, ch. 34) and Cullen (1968b and 1976), and it was also apparently the view of Marx (see Marx and Engels, 1971). The emphasis of this type of explanation seems the most convincing, though agricultural change played an important part too.

In most of the main nineteenth-century industries, survival and successful development required that relatively large-scale, specialised and centralised production should be achieved in the quite early stages of mechanisation, while proximity to large markets was also sometimes important. Unprotected industries generally could not develop smoothly from relatively small beginnings on the eve of, or after, the start of mechanisation elsewhere, into successful large-scale producers. Rather, only the few largest, most favoured regional centres of an industry at the time when mechanisation got under way were able to develop successfully, disposing of lesser competitors as they did so. As was mentioned above, the demise of Irish textiles except linen, for these reasons, was particularly important as can be illustrated by the later experience of Belfast where linen developed successfully.

The contraction of Irish textiles began in the depression of 1825-26 as competition quickened considerably from the larger more advanced British industries which urgently sought new markets, forcing prices down. Many Irish woollen manufacturers closed down permanently and woollen imports more than doubled between 1825 and 1835. By 1838, the Irish woollen industry supplied only about 14% of its home market (Cullen, 1976). Similarly, the late 1820s was a traumatic period for the cotton industry, particularly outside Ulster (Dickson, 1978). In Ulster, handloom cotton weaving and embroidery continued on quite a large scale for several decades. But an increasing proportion of the yarn began to be imported from Glasgow, so that the number of cotton spinning mills in the Belfast area fell from 22 in 1824 to ten in 1840. The contraction and decline of the cotton industry in Ireland, as Dickson concludes, may be regarded as 'only one aspect of the general concentration of the industry on Lancashire and Glasgow, in the second generation of industrialisation'. Cullen (1976) similarly remarks that the decline of the Irish woollen industry was comparable to the decline of smaller British woollen centres such as Norwich and the south west in the face of the growing dominance of Yorkshire.

In the mid-1820s, a successful process for powered spinning of fine linen yarn was developed for the first time and many of the Belfast cotton mills, under severe competitive pressure, changed over to linen. Because the Belfast-based Irish linen industry had no very large British competitors, and itself had large established markets, a large population of skilled weavers living nearby, and existing mills and factory hands available when the new technology first appeared, Belfast was in an excellent position to become an early major centre of mechanised fine linen spinning.[4]

The centralisation of linen spinning in Belfast and the decline of the woollen industry had very severe consequences for the rural poor — i.e. households in which the men were landless labourers or very small tenant farmers. For spinning, mostly by women, had provided an important supplement to their household incomes, especially those in Ulster and Connaught. The decline of domestic spinning also coincided with the early stages of a long-term rise in the price of beef relative to more labour-intensive agricultural products, as a result of growing incomes in Britain changing the pattern of demand. This trend began to limit the demand for agricultural workers, so that it became increasingly difficult for the still growing numbers in the poorer classes to earn a living. (This argument on the effects of agricultural change is put strongly by Crotty, 1966, and is modified by Lee, 1969.) Consequently emigration was growing in the 1820s and 1830s, but it was only during and after the Great Famine of 1845-48 that it rose to levels which resulted in population decline. The severity of the famine was due less to an absolute shortage of food than to unemployment (agricultural and industrial) and lack of access to sufficient land among the poorer classes, many of whom came to have little income and to depend heavily on intensive small-scale cultivation of the unreliable potato crop for subsistence. In the course of the Great Famine, which occurred when the potato crop failed in successive years, about a million people died and another million emigrated, out of a population of about 8½ million.

The industrial crisis in the first half of the century was confined to textiles. Other sectors, including milling, brewing, iron-founding, shipbuilding, rope-making, paper and glass continued to grow. The growing advantages of large-scale production and centralisation were also evident in these sectors since the number of firms declined as the larger companies, generally situated in or near the towns, gained larger market shares (Cullen, 1976, p. 123). But outside textiles, this process had not yet gone so far that an Irish regional market was inadequate for competitive production.

Demographic and Political Change

After the Great Famine, emigration continued at a rate which resulted in population decline in every decade until well into the twentieth century. As emigration proceeded, the numbers of agricultural labourers and small tenant farmers on scarcely viable holdings declined very rapidly. Farms were consolidated into larger units and labour-intensive tillage increasingly gave way to grazing as the latter became more profitable due to changing relative prices (Marx's *Capital*, vol. 1, ch. XXV, and Crotty, 1966). The virtual elimination of the poorest classes was accompanied by important effects on the social structure remaining. As the very small land holdings disappeared, the typical holding grew larger and capable of providing more than the barest subsistence, as competition for land was reduced. At the same time, family labour increasingly took over from hired labour due to the decline in labour-intensive tillage. These changes meant that the conflict of interest between farmer and labourer became relatively less important in much of the country, while a broad class of economically stronger tenant farmers emerged. They were to prove more capable of engaging in a struggle with their landlords, which now came to be a more dominant issue.

During and after the 1880s the tenant farmers were able successfully to challenge the landlords whose power was being eclipsed by the rising industrial bourgeoisie in Britain. As a result of the farmers' campaign in the Land War, a series of Acts was passed to facilitate the transfer of land ownership to the tenants. By 1917 about two-thirds of them owned their holdings.

This rising agricultural bourgeoisie, together with the Catholic commercial and professional middle class, was to dominate the mainstream of the nationalist movement which generally depended on parliamentary action to win Home Rule. Just before the First World War, Home Rule was won, postponed and then apparently lost due to a shifting balance of power in Britain during the war. As a result of this experience, combined with popular resentment against the executions by the British of the leaders of the 1916 Rebellion and against the threat of conscription in 1918, most of the mainstream of the nationalist movement became more militant. They joined with the existing militant Republicans in a united front party, Sinn Fein, which won a general election victory in 1918 and gave political leadership in the subsequent war of independence.

Further Industrial Decline and the Contrast with Britain
A further industrial crisis occurred in the 1870s, sparked off by the onset of the 'Great Depression' in Britain in 1874 leading to stiffer competition. In addition, there was weak demand from the agricultural sector due to bad harvests and falling grain prices caused by cheap North American grain. But more fundamentally, in many industries considerable progress had been made in methods of large-scale production in Britain and elsewhere. In Ireland, the relatively small, declining and dispersed nature of local markets (as a result of a declining agricultural population since the 1840s and the earlier failure of textile-based industrialisation) gave Irish firms little incentive to introduce new methods of large-scale production. But British or European firms, with larger growing markets nearby, had that

incentive and they could then go on to capture export markets such as Ireland. Irish industries which declined from this time included iron-founding, milling, paper, tanning, chandling and rope-making. There was no significant industrial recovery up to the 1920s and the insignificance of industry in the new Irish Free State is indicated by the figure mentioned above of an industrial labour force of just over 100,000.

In Britain the major industrial areas throughout the nineteenth century continued to be the original large centres where textiles were the leading sectors — such as Manchester, Glasgow and West Yorkshire. Apart from Belfast, there was no such centre in Ireland. There were also some important industrial centres in Britain built on areas of rich resources of coal and iron (often but not always coinciding with textile centres), and again none of these could arise in Ireland.[5] But towards the end of the nineteenth century and later, a new type of major industrial area arose in Britain with the mechanisation of consumer metal goods production and the development of new consumer durable products requiring precision engineering, such as sewing machines, bicycles, motor cars and electrical goods. These new industries were virtually confined to a belt stretching from London to Birmingham, taking in towns such as Coventry and Slough. Their location was probably determined originally by the development in the Birmingham and London areas of light precision engineering skills, particularly for the production of firearms. The same skills and technology could then be applied to development and production of other precision engineering goods.[6] In addition, proximity to the major markets in the southern part of England probably helped these industrial centres to grow. In these industries, economies of scale and specialisation became increasingly important as technology developed, so that the earliest major centres gained cumulative advantages and eventually wiped out the smaller-scale competitors operating in northern Britain and in Belfast.

The early failure of this new generation of light precision engineering industries in the Belfast area was thus not exceptional, but was part of the general pattern in the UK (see Hobsbawm, 1969, p. 219). In the rest of Ireland the chances of significant success in these sectors were virtually non-existent due to the unattractive local market, the poor development of engineering skills in the absence of an earlier industrial centre, and the absence of a substantial firearms industry.

To strengthen the argument that industrial decline in most of Ireland was mainly due to the early advantages gained by British industries in large-scale and centralised production and proximity to major markets, it is necessary to mention some other conceivable causes of industrial failure which may be dismissed. Lee (1968) shows that there is considerable evidence that capital shortage was not a problem since it was available in sums quite adequate for industry. Nor is it likely that the price of coal was an important problem. For Coe (1969) points out that contemporary commentators generally agreed that on Ireland's east coast coal was cheaper than in much of Britain, including London. While coal would still have been dearer in Dublin than in Glasgow for instance, R. R. Kane calculated in 1844, from numerous examples, that expenditure on coal in British and Irish spinning mills was only in a range of about 1% to 4% of production costs. The price difference on this small fraction of costs would have been of little overall importance and easily offset by cheaper labour in Ireland.[7] Cheap labour, too, was clearly available in abundance, while poor basic education could scarcely have been a problem since Ireland was a relatively literate society by 1841. The possibility that a lack of entrepreneurship may have been a major cause of the failure of Irish industry can be more conveniently considered later, after examining the industrialisation of the north east.

To conclude this section, it would be fair to say that the Act of Union introduced by Britain in alliance with the Irish elite played a significant part in the decline of Irish industry. This is not simply to agree with the traditional nationalist interpretation which regarded British rule *per se* as the cause of Ireland's economic ills. For British rule had been compatible with economic expansion in an earlier period. But the inability of Ireland to protect its industries and to introduce suitable policies for development became an increasingly serious handicap as the need became greater during the nineteenth century due to growing advantages such as economies of scale and external economies which accrued to the earlier developers once the process of mechanisation began. In fact, all the other nineteenth-century latecomers which industrialised successfully after Britain used protection for a time against their more advanced competitors. It seems clear that with effective protection the Irish textile industries in particular could have survived and expanded for much longer. In an age of simple and newly developing engineering technology, in which engineering industries arose spontaneously to meet local needs (unlike in the twentieth century), the benefits for the development of machinery and related industries could have been considerable. Recognition of the relationship between the development of a leading sector such as textiles and a wider range of industries is important for an understanding both of the centralised nature of industrialisation and of the consequent difficulties for industrialisation in most of Ireland. The next section considers an example of this pattern of development in the Belfast area.

3.iii. THE NORTH EAST

Unlike the rest of Ireland, industrialisation continued in the north east, with linen replacing cotton as the major mechanised industry after the 1820s. Belfast's population rose from under 20,000 in 1791 to 75,000 in 1841, and close to 400,000 by the 1900s. Industrialisation also affected some smaller towns in a district within about 30 miles of Belfast.

During the nineteenth century, the northern Irish linen industry gained markets rapidly from the British linen centres. This was probably mainly because British producers had made a slower start on a smaller scale in developing this sector. As the Irish industry grew, linen spinning began to decline before 1860 in England and by 1890 it had almost ceased there and was no longer a major industry in Scotland. But although Belfast linen prospered for a considerable period by capturing markets from others, the long-term prospects were not good. World demand for linen began to decline before the end of the nineteenth century, although Irish output continued to grow for several decades more.

Linkages with Engineering

Belfast's textile industries gave rise to many important branches of engineering, including steam engine construction. Until the late nineteenth century, the weight of this machinery combined with poor transport conditions encouraged its production near to where it would be used. Another advantage of such a location was the fact that for maximum efficiency steam engines had to be designed for the particular circumstances in which they would work. In the first half of the nineteenth century, too, 'any large engineering firm would have been prepared to undertake the construction of all types of machinery including steam engines, if they could secure designs or machinery to copy, for specialisation did not become general until the second half of the nineteenth century'. (Coe, 1969, p. 39). Thus it was possible for many non-specialised firms around Ireland to produce them if the demand arose locally. As late as 1838, two-thirds of the steam engines used in Irish industry were made and located outside Belfast. But because the number of new installations had been increasing fastest in Belfast since the early 1830s, as the linen industry grew and became mechanised, Belfast overtook Dublin as the main producer of engines during that decade. Belfast's dominance was already well established when specialisation became important later.

Part of steam engine manufacture was the construction of high-pressure boilers which were quite different to those used at atmospheric pressure in such processes as distilling (Coe, 1969, ch. 6). They also had to be replaced more frequently than engines and had other uses too, so that boilermaking became an important industry requiring many skilled men.

The growth of boilermaking in Belfast was a crucial initial step in the development of shipbuilding. For, as Coe (1969) points out, 'the building of iron ships was not a further extension of wooden shipbuilding, but a different craft, a development of boilermaking. Thus, the first iron vessel launched in Belfast was constructed, not in one of the existing shipbuilding yards, but in the engineering and boilermaking firm of Victor Coates & Co.' That was in 1838 when Belfast had just become the main producer of steam engines and boilers in Ireland. But iron shipbuilding remained a relatively small industry throughout the UK for some time, and when it began to expand decisively Belfast was clearly the one place in Ireland that offered the necessary conditions — i.e. the external economies, or the skills and related engineering industries, as well as a favourable physical setting — for a major shipbuilding industry.

The specific origins of the shipbuilding firm of Harland and Wolff support the view that Belfast was particularly suited for this industry, because of the fact that local demand had already given rise to the production of boilers from heavy iron plates. For the company, founded in 1851 by William Hickson, was actually a spin-off from what was originally an ironworks, making iron plates from the meagre supplies of Irish ore and coal. When the ironworks inevitably collapsed due to British competition, Hickson decided to make his unsold stocks into iron ships (Goldstrom, 1968). He had the right idea but he knew little about shipbuilding and the venture was saved only by the experienced shipbuilder he recruited from England, Edward Harland. Harland soon bought out the firm, took Wolff as a partner, and they went on to build up the company that became the second largest shipbuilder in the UK by the 1900s.

Another important industry which developed in the north east was the production of machinery for preparing and spinning flax (the raw material for linen), and later for other similar hard fibres such as hemp, jute and sisal. Again, there are good reasons why this industry developed there since there were significant external economies, in the form of a close association between machine-makers and users benefiting both parties. Coe (1969, ch. 5) quotes a commentator in 1874 who said that the Belfast machine-making establishments were 'surrounded by spinning mills and were visited almost daily by spinners, who thus were able to see the progress being made in the execution of their orders, and to point out their exact requirements and the defects of previous machines.' Machinery for preparing and spinning flax was also produced in British linen centres, but as they became eclipsed by the Belfast linen industry, the Belfast machine-makers grew more competitive and captured export markets from them. Because cotton machinery did not lend itself to preparing and spinning hard fibres such as flax, Belfast machine-makers were not in competition with the larger more advanced industry producing such machinery for cotton. Thus, the Belfast industry was able to become the largest and most advanced in the world in its own field.

Other industries arose later in the north east, not in response to local demand, but rather due to the availability of skills, marketing organisation and other advantages of a large manufacturing centre, which developed earlier due to local demand but could be turned to specialised manufacture of new products for other markets. One outstanding example of this was Davidson & Co., which was the first producer of tea-drying equipment in the 1880s and was supplying 70% of the world market for this equipment in the 1930s. Through their pioneering development of fans for this machinery, Davidson's came to be major producers of ventilating and heating equipment for ships, factories, mines, etc. (They even supplied most of the ventilating fans for the ships which made up the German navy in the First World War.) Although Davidson, who came from the north of Ireland, first designed his tea-drying equipment while working in India, Belfast was a more suitable location for his factory than India at the time. Probably similar factors — the existence of supporting engineering industries, skilled labour and advantages in the organisation of export trade — made the Belfast area a large centre of production and export of food, drink and tobacco (Cullen, 1976, p. 161).

To support the argument that significant industrial development was generally only possible, in a competitive environment, where particular industries were established relatively early and on a relatively large scale, it is useful to consider briefly some of the sectors which did *not* develop or succeed for long, even in Belfast. Thus, despite the existence of a cotton industry there until the 1820s and later, the manufacture of cotton spinning machinery never became important due to competition from larger more advanced specialists in Britain. Furthermore, because the power looms which were eventually developed for weaving linen were somewhat modified versions of those used for cotton, Belfast machine-makers were never major suppliers of power looms to the linen industry — again due to competition from British specialists in cotton looms (Coe, 1969, ch. 5).

The experience of Irish iron-founding is significant too. When general iron-founding, which was widespread throughout the island, suffered badly from increasingly specialised British competition in the later part of the nineteenth century, the industry in the north east declined in the same way, with the significant exceptions of firms specialising in parts for machinery being made locally. Part of this general decline was the drop in production of agricultural implements and machinery which was hastened by the relatively small size of Irish farms and the decrease in tillage. Again, firms in this industry in the north east fared no better, and in some cases worse, than in the south. Similar remarks about the failure of particular engineering industries in the north east, due to the absence of a sufficiently large local market and the existence of specialised producers elsewhere, apply to locomotives and most machine tools, as well as the new generation of consumer durables (Coe, 1969, chs. 7-9).

To conclude these remarks on the north east, the region became a closely integrated and highly developed part of the UK industrial economy, depending heavily on trade with Britain and the empire. By the late nineteenth century, on the other hand, the southern economy was already suffering visibly from political and economic integration with the UK. This situation, combined with the British roots and religious distinctiveness of the Protestant community of the north east, is an appropriate starting point for an understanding of the subsequent partition of Ireland, when most of the population of the north east demanded to remain in the UK while the rest of Ireland opted for independence. Seen in a socio-economic context, Ireland was not really the natural unit it seemed on geographic grounds.

The Role of 'Entrepreneurship'

We can now return to consider the argument that poor entrepreneurship was the main cause of industrial under-development in most of Ireland. Lee (1973) mentions the story, referred to above, of Hickson and Harland at the time of the foundation of Harland and Wolff as an example in support of this view, arguing that where Hickson failed the immigrant entrepreneur, Harland, showed what could be achieved. But this appears to overlook the point that, although Harland may have been the more talented of the two, both he and Hickson evidently agreed that the situation offered an excellent opportunity to build iron ships. And, as was argued above, conditions in the Belfast area were indeed exceptionally good for such a venture. Lee also points out that many other engineering industries were developed in the Belfast area by entrepreneurs who included many new British immigrants, with local businessmen becoming prominent only later. But these examples, like the case of Harland, do not prove the point that competent Irish businessmen could have fostered widespread industrialisation. Rather, they show that exceptional opportunities for profitable industrial development must have existed in the north east to attract such people, who might reasonably have been expected to perform a similar function, if possible, in the south. The reason why so many early industrial entrepreneurs in Belfast were immigrants was probably because they had greater engineering experience at an earlier date, due to the earlier and more extensive development of such industries in Britain arising from the earlier mechanisation of cotton and, perhaps, mining.

Lee (1968) also suggests that Irish capitalists showed examples of poor enterprise in not investing in railways and banks until after British capital bore the initial risks. But, concerning railways, it must be recognised that the period referred to was notable for the 'railway mania' rampant among British capitalists. Hobsbawm (1969) says that a great deal of English capital 'was sunk into railways, and much of it sank without trace, because by the 1830s there were vast accumulations of capital burning holes in their owners' pockets . . .'. In these circumstances, the relative slowness of Irish investment in railways does not necessarily indicate excessive caution. Furthermore, Hobsbawm could say of Europe as a whole 'inevitably we find the first railways — and often the bulk of railways — built by British contractors, with British locomotives, rails, technical staff and capital'. Ireland simply fitted into the general pattern. As regards the banks, it seems likely that the reluctance of Irish investors to take advantage immediately of the ending of the Bank of Ireland's monopoly of joint-stock banking in 1821 was related to the discouraging events of the Irish banking crisis of the previous year, in which a number of private banks failed.

That business enterprise was not generally absent when opportunities existed was suggested by the efficient reorganisation and growth of most non-textile industries, along lines similar to Britain's, after the 1770s and in the first half of the nineteenth century, as well as by the satisfactory development of distribution and transport. But whatever the quality of local business enterprise, the fact that British capital and capitalists did get involved in economic activity in Ireland, in some sectors, and in the north east in particular — but not on a broader scale — suggests that untapped profitable opportunities for wider industrialisation were not particularly evident to them either.

General Implications of Irish Industrial History
This account of Irish industry up to the 1920s can be concluded with a number of remarks relating to the main theoretical concerns of this book, as set out in chapters 1 and 2.

1. It is clear that this historical experience could not be understood by concentrating on conditions in the Irish economy alone. The external (mainly British) influence was very important from its first significant appearance in the phase of invasion and direct expropriation. This led on to the stage where it was principally the impersonal operation of market forces, heavily influenced by the dominant British economy, that played a leading role in shaping the Irish economy. In the

nineteenth century, these factors changed the pattern of agriculture leading to famine and heavy emigration, they contributed largely to the success of linen in the north east, and they led to widespread industrial decline in other areas in the face of larger and more advanced competitors.

2. This experience conflicts with the view that the attainment of favourable local conditions and reliance on free market forces is sufficient to generate industrial development. Considerable progress was being made before the Industrial Revolution began, and in many sectors for long afterwards, indicating that local conditions were not particularly adverse. It appears that the necessary conditions for industrialisation were rather more specific, including the early establishment of important, internationally competitive leading sectors. Sectors with this potential were limited in number and mostly already established more strongly elsewhere.

3. The development of external economies in large industrial centres and of economies of scale began in the very early stages of mechanisation and tended to cumulate, so that by the second generation smaller industries, like Belfast cotton-spinning, were in difficulties. Economies of scale and external economies continued to develop and technological specialisation began to grow increasingly important. Smaller, less advanced producers were thus continually edged out of a widening range of industries, as in the south in the 1870s and later. The barriers to entry for newcomers were simultaneously, through this process, continually raised. In the unprotected relatively less advanced economy of Ireland, the timing of phases of permanent decline coincided with depression, or crisis, in the more advanced British economy (1820s and 1870s).

4. The experience of most of Ireland in the nineteenth century shows that the free operation of market forces can have catastrophic results for large parts of a population and even for a national economy, for a very long period. The fact that emigration was always an option for many no doubt alleviated some of the potential effects.

4

Independence and Protection

When the Irish Free State was established in the early 1920s, its industry had been reduced to very small dimensions. In 1926, according to the Census of Industrial Production (CIP), only 7.8% of the labour force were engaged in industry, broadly defined,[1] and 4.3% (or 56,400) in manufacturing. Thus despite its earlier lengthy industrial history, the country was virtually in the same position as many other less-developed countries, in so far as it had to start almost from the beginning in a process of late industrialisation. The political system of the Free State was shaped to a great extent by the relationship with Britain, both through its basis in the economic structure which had been heavily influenced by Britain and through the effects of issues of Anglo-Irish relations in the political sphere. It has been argued by Garvin (1974 and 1977) that the party system which emerged, and which appears as a deviant case among Western European party systems (especially in lacking a clear left-right dimension), is best viewed in the perspective of decolonialising political systems. This again suggests that the country's experience — political and economic — is best understood when viewed as a post-colonial late-developer. Since some understanding of this political system is useful for an understanding of the economic policies which were applied, it is worthwhile to outline briefly the way it developed.

4.i. THE FIRST TEN YEARS

The Irish Free State was established, with Dominion status such as already existed in Canada or Australia, by the Anglo-Irish treaty of 1921.[2] This treaty was ratified by the Dail (the Free State's parliament) in 1922 and apparently accepted by the electorate when returning the pro-Treaty party to power later that year. But a substantial minority of the former united front independence party, Sinn Fein, with the backing of part of the IRA (the independence movement's military wing), rejected the Treaty. There followed a civil war between the anti-Treaty faction and the pro-Treaty government, which ended in victory for the government in 1923. Although it is commonly said that the civil war was fought mainly on the issue of the partition of Ireland which had been provided for in the Treaty, the Northern Ireland question in fact received relatively little attention in Dail debates. Rather there was a great deal of concern about the issue of the formal status of the Free State. The anti-Treaty side was determined to fight on for a fully sovereign republic while the pro-Treaty side accepted Dominion status, not necessarily as desirable in itself but at least as providing sufficient independence to allow further progress to be made towards a full republic. The difference in terms of substantive political independence was not very great although the symbolic difference, particularly concerning the oath of allegiance to Britain's constitutional monarch, was regarded by the anti-Treaty faction as important.

Meenan (1970, p. 31) expresses one fairly widely held view when he says 'It was a true division on a political issue, unaffected by social or economic factors. No doubt the propertied interests favoured acceptance of the Treaty: so did the Labour Party.' Some Marxist accounts, on the other hand, have regarded the civil war as a class struggle and its outcome as the victory of the bourgeoisie over progressive forces. (See, for example, Sinn Fein The Workers Party, 1978, ch. 3). In fact, however, the issue at stake was scarcely an important focus of class struggle, while the class basis of support of the two sides, although different, was also by no means clear cut. Certainly, the pro-Treaty government party, Cumann na nGaedheal, was largely based in the professional, property-owning and large farmer classes, but the Treaty was also accepted by the Labour Party which won a fairly substantial 21% of the vote in 1922, compared with Cumann na nGaedheal's 38%.[3] The anti-Treatyites, who took 22% of the vote, were mostly based among small farmers as well as some of the workers although, as is common in such circumstances, they also drew leadership from among the professional classes. The issue at stake and the rather ambiguous nature of the class composition of the two sides suggests that the civil war was not a clear-cut class struggle, at least not in the classic Marxist sense of a struggle between progressive and reactionary forces. Rather, it was a confrontation mainly concerned with degrees of nationalism.

The civil war was quite localised and brief but it did have important lasting effects on political alignments and hence on later economic policy. For it involved the immediate breakdown of the old Sinn Fein coalition along entrenched party lines, which contained principally a division between small farmers, on the one hand, versus big farmers and business people on the other, both groups of farmers being mostly owner-occupiers. Both sides also found support and leadership among professional people. The small industrial and agricultural working class was left somewhat divided, mainly between the Labour Party and the anti-Treaty faction, so that its rather limited potential as a distinctive political entity was further diminshed. The major political cleavage, therefore, was not to be the familiar European 'left-right' division. Instead it was based on the different interests and outlooks of the externally oriented commercial bourgeoisie and large commercial farmers, mainly located in the east and south, as against those of the small-scale farming communities mostly located in the less commercially developed west and north. The former of these two groups prevailed for the first ten years. But most of the anti-Treaty faction began to shed its militant nationalism and to work, as the Fianna Fail party, within the parliamentary system which commanded broad support. At the same time it succeeded in mobilising its potential support more fully. By 1932 its support had grown sufficiently to give it a general election victory, although the absolute level of Cumann na nGaedheal's electoral support did not decline.

The two major parties shared an antipathy to socialism, which was scarcely surprising since so many of their supporters were property-owners. For the base of the social pyramid, the labouring classes with no property, had been largely drained away by several generations of heavy emigration. These values were strengthened by the powerful influence of a rather conservative Catholic church (Catholicism being, for many, a part of the national identity), while the continuing issues of partition and Anglo-Irish relations further diverted attention from any potential confrontation between capital and labour. The two major parties also had common roots in Sinn Fein, whose economic policies, especially under the influence of Arthur Griffith as its president until 1917, had favoured protection for industry on a broad scale. But in view of the nature of its support following the split in Sinn Fein, the Cumann na nGaedheal government did not implement this policy with any great force. Many of its supporters had an interest in continuing their existing externally oriented activities which benefited from free trade.[4] However, a small number of fairly low tariffs were imposed selectively and this encouraged a modest expansion of industrial employment, which occurred particularly in the newly protected manufacturing industries. Lyons (1976, p. 601) says that over a hundred new factories had opened in the protected industries by 1930. And, according to the *Irish Trade Journal* of February 1928, the numbers employed in protected industries increased by 7,700 from the time of the introduction of the relevant tariffs up to September 1927. This increase in employment occurred mainly in clothing (2,700 jobs), confectionery (1,600 jobs), tobacco (1,400 jobs) and boots (700 jobs).

The growth of industrial employment at this time is illustrated in table 4.1.

Table 4.1: Industrial Employment, 1926-31 (thousands)

	1926	1929	1931
All Industries	102.5	108.9	110.6
Transportable Goods	61.3	67.9	66.5
Building, etc., and 'Service Industries'	41.2	41.0	44.1

Source: Census of Industrial Production, as adjusted by Kennedy (1971, table 2.2).

Note: Transportable Goods means manufacturing plus mining and peat, but manufacturing accounts for over 90% of this category. 'Service Industries' are electricity, gas, water, maintenance of canals and docks and the like.

Table 4.2 shows the sectoral composition of manufacturing and its degree of export-orientation in 1929.

Table 4.2: Sectoral Composition and Exports of Manufacturing, 1929

	Employ-ment ('000)	Employ-ment (%)	Gross Output (£m.)	Gross Output (%)	Exports (£m.)	Exports as % of Gross Output
Food	19.0	30.3	27.7	51.4	15.6	56.3
Drink & Tobacco	8.5	13.6	13.2	24.5	5.0	37.6
Textiles	5.4	8.7	1.6	3.0		
Clothing & Footwear	6.2	10.0	1.7	3.1		
Wood & Furniture	4.6	7.3	1.5	2.7		
Paper & Printing	6.0	9.6	2.0	3.7	3.5	26.8
Chemicals	1.7	2.7	1.2	2.3		
Bricks, etc.	0.9	1.4	0.2	0.4		
Metals & Engineering	6.9	11.1	2.5	4.6		
Other	3.4	5.5	2.3	4.2		
TOTAL	62.5	100.0	53.9	100.0	24.1	44.6

Sources: Census of Industrial Production for employment and gross output. *Trade and Shipping Statistics* for exports. (Food exports are taken as classes IIA, B and C, Drink and Tobacco as classes IID and E, and all other manufactured exports as the 'manufactured or prepared' sub-divisions of class III; these classifications correspond closely with SITC classifications 0 less 00, 1, and 5-8 respectively, when both classifications are available in 1951.)

As the table shows, manufacturing was heavily concentrated in food, drink and tobacco. Food was mainly quite basic, low value-added processing of local primary products — hence the much higher proportion of gross output than employment in food, since a high proportion of final output was accounted for by material inputs. Other sectors accounted for quite small fractions of a very small manufacturing sector. The overall proportion of output going for export was fairly high, mostly going to the nearby UK market which took 92.3% of the Free State's exports.

The very small overall scale of manufacturing and its structure could be understood as a reflection of the overwhelming competitive pressures, as outlined in section 2.ii, exerted by powerful advanced economies on a latecomer in a relationship of fairly free trade. These competitive pressures, emanating largely from the UK, would have ruled out most industries in Ireland so that the manufacturing sector was very small. The principal exceptions which could survive were naturally sheltered, local market-oriented activities such as printing, packaging, small-scale engineering repairs etc., and the basic processing of local primary products such as low value-added food processing, much of which could be for export. The very small number of unsheltered activities which survived, some examples of which occurred in textiles, clothing and footwear, would have had to be capable of meeting foreign competition and hence capable of exporting, so that a fairly high export-orientation among them was not surprising. But the very limited extent of manufactured exports other than food or drink, which came mostly from a small number of relatively large firms, is indicated by the fact that their production employed only about 9,400 or about 0.7% of the labour force.[5]

4.ii. THE PROTECTIONIST PHASE

Whereas the Cumann na nGaedheal government had been willing to water down Griffith's protectionist ideas substantially, the Fianna Fail government which came to power in 1932 was prepared to go even further than Griffith's plans for temporary protection for 'infant industries'. In 1928, Sean Lemass of Fianna Fail had said in the Dail 'we believe that Ireland can be made a self-contained unit, providing all the necessities of living in adequate quantities for the people residing in the island at the moment and probably for a much larger number' (quoted in Meenan, 1970, p. 319). Fianna Fail's commitment to a high degree of protection and self-sufficiency was partly a reflection of the rather isolationist nationalism of the party leadership and partly a reflection of the interests of their supporters. Protection for industry had obvious appeal for the industrial working class; and as regards the farmers, as Garvin (1977) puts it,

Cumann na nGaedheal's unapologetic favouring of commercial, export-oriented agriculture, a kind of Irish wager on the strong, was replaced under Fianna Fail by encouragement of tillage, protection of smaller agricultural producers by guaranteeing them unchallenged access to at least the home market, and a general national-populist encouragement of mixed farming so as to increase self-sufficiency and improve the lot of the small to medium farmer.

Fianna Fail moved quickly to impose protection so that between 1931 and 1936 the average nominal tariff rose from 9% to 45%, falling to 35% in 1938 (Ryan, 1949).[6] This was in addition to quota and licensing restrictions. As a result of protection, as well as the 'Economic War' with Britain, industries producing for the home market grew rapidly while agricultural and industrial exports fell. (The 'Economic War' began with the Irish government's refusal to transmit the remaining land annuities accruing under the Irish Land Acts to the UK government and it involved successive impositions of punitive tariffs by both governments.) With the ending of the international depression and of the 'Economic War' in 1938, the situation of agricultural exports was improved. But manufactured exports remained reduced, perhaps due to higher domestic costs for exporters as a result of protection or perhaps simply because markets, once lost, are not easily regained. The growth of industrial employment until 1951 is shown in table 4.3.

Table 4.3: Industrial Employment, 1929-51 (thousands)

	1929	1931	1938	1946	1951
All Industry	108.9	110.6	166.5	169.8	226.7
Transportable Goods	67.9	66.5	103.2	116.3	148.0
Building, etc., and 'Service Industries'	41.0	44.1	63.3	53.5	78.7

Source: Census of Industrial Production, as adjusted by Kennedy (1971), table 2.2).
Note: Transportable Goods and Service Industries are as defined in table 4.1. The data in the table probably overstate the rate of growth to some extent since the Census increased its coverage during this period.

The table shows a remarkably rapid increase in industrial employment once the free trade policy was abandoned, although there was a temporary halt caused by the difficulty of obtaining materials and fuel imports during the Second World War. In fact the level of All Industry employment fell as low as 143,500 in 1943. But apart from the war years, Transportable Goods employment grew at an average annual rate of 6.5% in 1931-38 and 4.9% in 1946-51. This experience of virtually unprecedented industrial growth during the international depression of the 1930s was obviously quite anomalous among European countries. But it corresponds quite well with the contemporary experience of some of the other less-developed countries (e.g. Argentina, Brazil, Chile, Mexico, South Africa), which resorted to protection during the depression. This experience of such countries indicates that barriers to entry for latecomers, arising from the competitive strength of advanced countries in a relationship of free trade, had been a serious constraint on their industrial development. Once the adoption of protection overcame these barriers for many activities in the home market, it released a latent potential to develop industry. But Ireland later differed from some of these other countries in so far as they continued the process of growth through the war, because the disruption caused to international trade had an effect comparable to protection for them. For Ireland, however, the disruption to trade caused by the war also cut off much of the supply of materials and fuel imports essential for industry.

By 1951, the industrial sector had become considerably more important in the national economy of the Republic of Ireland, but it remained quite small in relative size compared with most other European countries, especially the UK (table 4.4).

The sectoral composition and export-orientation of manufacturing in 1951 is shown in table 4.5, which may be compared with table 4.2 to see the changes which had occurred since 1929. The level of employment had increased in all 10 sectors since 1929 but the relative importance of Food, Drink & Tobacco was now considerably reduced. The greatest increase in relative size was in Clothing & Footwear, with lesser increases in Textiles, Clay, Glass & Cement, Metals & Engineering and 'Other' Manufacturing. More specifically, a number of activities had grown particularly rapidly or had been newly established. These included more processed foods, vehicle assembly, fertilisers, cement, glass, leather and steel. Thus the main emphasis in this expansion was on consumer goods and certain quite technically mature intermediate products, such as those mentioned above, with only a very limited range of capital goods which were generally particularly heavily protected. This pattern of industrial growth was quite typical of what is commonly called the 'easy' stage of import-substitution. It appears that protection proved adequate to overcome barriers to entry (in the *home* market) arising from the economies of scale and marketing strength of foreign competitors in the more technically mature industries, but little real progress was made in developing technologically demanding activities.[7]

Table 4.4: Percentage of Economically Active Population Engaged in Industry in Certain European Countries, 1951

England and Wales	46.2
Scotland	45.1
Switzerland	43.6
Northern Ireland	39.7
Luxembourg	39.7
West Germany	38.5
Sweden	37.9
Czechoslovakia	37.3
Netherlands	33.4
Austria	32.4
Denmark	30.7
France	29.7
Italy	27.5
Iceland	22.7
Portugal	20.7
Republic of Ireland	17.9
Yugoslavia	11.1
Rumania	7.2

Source: Report of the Commission on Emigration and Other Population Problems, 1948-1954, table 18.
Note: The figure for the Republic of Ireland is all Census of Industrial Production (CIP) industries as a percentage of the total labour force.

Table 4.5: Sectoral Composition and Exports of Manufacturing, 1951

	Employ-ment ('000)	Employ-ment (%)	Gross Output (£m.)	Gross Output (%)	Exports (£m.)	Exports as % of Gross Output
Food	31.4	22.4	96.0	35.9	29.2	30.4
Drink & Tobacco	10.6	7.6	39.5	14.8	5.3	13.5
Textiles	14.9	10.6	22.9	8.6		
Clothing & Footwear	22.7	16.2	18.6	7.0		
Wood & Furniture	8.8	6.2	11.1	4.2		
Paper & Printing	12.3	8.8	14.7	5.5	8.2	6.2
Chemicals	4.4	3.1	10.8	4.1		
Clay, Glass & Cement	5.0	3.6	5.9	2.2		
Metals & Engineering	18.0	12.8	28.2	10.6		
Other	12.1	8.6	19.5	7.3		
TOTAL	140.3	100.0	267.3	100.0	42.7	16.0

Source: as table 4.2
Note: Clay, Glass & Cement includes activities labelled Bricks, etc., in table 4.2.

Industrial expansion was focussed heavily on the protected home market as the export figures show, suggesting that most of the 'infant industries' remained too small and too weak in marketing by international standards. The proportion of manufacturing output going for export was now at a very low level, especially in sectors other than Food and Drink & Tobacco. In these other sectors, only about 6,100 people were employed in export manufacturing which was even less than the small corresponding figure for 1929. Thus little progress had been made in breaking into competition with advanced industrial countries. Also there had been little diversification of export markets, since 84.8% of all exports still went to the UK in 1951.

Industrialisation since the early 1930s had been subject to the Control of Manufactures Acts of 1932-34, which required that Irish citizens had to hold a majority of assets, voting shares and votes on the board of directors in new manufacturing companies starting operations. However, this did not prevent the involvement of many foreign companies, especially British ones, in the industrial growth of this time, since joint ownership arrangements and manufacturing under foreign licence were common, probably quite often involving restrictions on exporting by the Irish plant. There are few firm figures on the extent of foreign involvement at this time, but there are some indications. For instance, the Committee on Industrial Organisation's survey in 1960/61 found that five out of 22 sectors surveyed were mostly under foreign control (Brock, 1963/64). Also, Sweeney (1973) found that, by the end of 1972, over 50% of fixed assets of Irish-registered industrial and service companies were owned by foreign companies. Of these foreign-owned assets only just over 45% were in manufacturing firms which had started up with the New Industry grants available since the 1950s, the rest being in older manufacturing companies and in service companies. Sweeney found also that, in 1973, two-thirds of Britain's 100 largest industrial companies had one or more subsidiaries in Ireland. Of the total of 310 such subsidiaries, only 25 had received the New Industry grants available since the 1950s, whereas 70 had received grants for re-equipment of longer established industries.

One could conclude, first, that protection must have provided a considerable inducement to foreign-based companies to get involved in production in Ireland. And second, despite persistent references to a critical lack of enterprise, there was not only a considerable movement of foreign industrial enterprise into Ireland but also a rapid emergence of Irish entrepreneurs willing to get involved in industry, whether alone or in association with foreign companies.

Balance of Payments Crises and Recession in the 1950s

The 1950s saw the end of the period of sustained industrial expansion (apart from the war years) which had begun some 20 years before. Industrial production faltered in 1952 then increased until 1955 before falling again until 1957 (table 4.6). Output was little higher in 1958, the year when industrial employment reached its lowest level of the decade, but after that a sustained recovery began.

Table 4.6: Volume of Industrial Production Indices, 1951-60

	1951	1952	1953	1954	1955	1956	1957	1958	1959	1960
All Industries	93.4	93.5	100	105.0	107.8	104.0	99.0	101.9	110.9	118.7
Transportable Goods	94.0	91.6	100	103.3	107.5	105.3	104.5	106.5	117.5	126.0

Source: Census of Industrial Production, as adjusted by Kennedy (1971, table 2.2).
Note: Manufacturing accounted for about 93-95% of the Transportable Goods category in this period.

The average annual rate of growth for 1951-58 was thus reduced to 1.8% for Transportable Goods and 1.3% for all industry, compared with 9.1% and 10.7% respectively for 1946-51 or 4.0% and 4.2% for the whole quarter century 1926-51. As output per worker continued to increase, total industrial employment declined and did not regain its 1951 level until 1961, while employment in Transportable Goods showed virtually no growth between 1951 and 1958 (table 4.7).

Table 4.7: Employment, 1951-61 (thousands)

	1951	1952	1954	1958	1960	1961
All Industries	226.7	221.8	233.4	210.3	221.5	230.6
Transportable Goods	148.0	144.0	153.9	150.3	160.0	167.3
Labour Force	1261.9	1254.0	1228.0	1141.0	1118.0	1108.1

Source: Economic Statistics, Budget 1964, for total Labour Force. Other data from *Census of Industrial Production*, as adjusted by Kennedy (1971, table 2.2).

Since the recession in industry occurred while the large agricultural labour force continued to decline, as it had been doing for a century past, the total labour force fell dramatically — by more in one decade than in the previous three. Emigration, mainly to the UK now, rose to levels unseen for 70 years, regularly exceeding 40,000 people per year — a figure which may be compared with about 55,000 per year reaching the age of 15.

The sense of national crisis at this time was expressed frankly in the report *Economic Development* (1958):

> It is apparent that we have come to a critical and decisive point in our economic affairs. The policies hitherto followed, though given a fair trial, have not resulted in a viable economy. We have power, transport facilities, public services, houses, hospitals and a general 'infrastructure' on a scale which is reasonable by Western European standards, yet large-scale emigration and unemployment still persist. The population is falling, the national income rising more slowly than in the rest of Europe.

This report went on to mention the 'all-too-prevalent mood of despondency about the country's future' and a justified anxiety which

> can too easily degenerate into feelings of frustration and despair. After 35 years of native government people are asking whether we can achieve an acceptable degree of economic progress. The common talk amongst parents in the towns, as in rural Ireland, is of their children having to emigrate as soon as their education is completed in order to be sure of a reasonable livelihood.

The difficulties of the 1950s were mainly due to the emergence of a chronic balance of payments crisis. This arose partly from the near exhaustion of the 'easy' stage of import-substituting industrialisation, which meant that there was relatively little further replacement of imports by new domestic production. At the same time, imports of goods which had *not* been replaced by domestic production, including many capital goods and material inputs, had to continue to grow as long as the economy was growing. Thus the import bill for goods which had not been substituted by domestic production eventually grew to exceed the cost of imports before the process of import-substitution began. Since there was a continuing failure to achieve significant growth of exports, serious balance of trade deficits became inevitable, leading to a chronic balance of payments crisis.

Table 4.8: Exports and Imports, Selected Years 1924-51, in Constant 1953 Prices (£ million)

Year	Exports	Imports	Balance of Trade
1924	136.5	154.7	—18.2
1929	131.9	157.6	—25.7
1931	118.0	166.8	—48.8
1938	83.0	129.9	—46.9
1943	46.7	38.6	+ 8.1
1948	60.8	165.1	—104.3
1951	82.2	194.0	—111.8

Source: Trade and Shipping Statistics, 1961.

The background to the development of this balance of payments crisis is shown in table 4.8 which outlines the record of exports and imports and the balance of trade in constant prices, leading up to the recessions of the 1950s. Trade was at a relatively high level in the free-trading 1920s, normally resulting in a fairly modest deficit. But in the next decade exports declined due to depression in the UK and the 'Economic War'. At the same time imports declined too, although to a lesser extent, in the first phase of rapid import-substituting industrialisation. Thus the trade deficits were somewhat higher in the 1930s, until the difficulties of conducting trade during the war reduced imports especially and resulted in some small surpluses. Then in the years after the war, the deficits rose to new heights as there were record levels of imports, mainly of inputs for renewed economic growth. Exports, however, only just regained their pre-war level. Thus the nature of industrialisation had produced economic growth, and hence ultimately a rising demand for imports despite an initial decline, but no expansion of exports.[8]

The continual trade deficits could only have been sustained for so long due to large external assets which were mainly accumulated at the time of the First World War as a result of high prices for agricultural exports, and external assets accumulated again during the Second World War due to the unobtainability of imports. But eventually the deficits, particularly that of 1951, and the reduction of external assets, caused great concern to the government. Deflationary measures were taken in order to reduce demand and cut imports, and this precipitated the recession of 1952. Table 4.9 shows subsequent trends in trade during the 1950s.

Table 4.9: Exports and Imports, 1951-60, in Constant 1953 Prices (£ million)

Year	Exports	Imports	Balance of Trade
1951	82.2	194.0	—111.8
1952	99.9	161.7	—61.8
1953	111.5	182.5	— 71.0
1954	113.5	178.7	—65.2
1955	105.4	196.3	—90.9
1956	108.7	172.3	—63.6
1957	130.2	164.6	—34.4
1958	126.6	185.9	—59.3
1959	121.7	203.2	—81.5
1960	144.9	212.2	—67.3

Source: Trade and Shipping Statistics, 1961.

The reduction of imports in 1952 and some growth of exports (especially of food to the UK, which still had some shortages since the war) reduced the deficit for a time. But it rose again in 1955 as imports regained their 1951 level and exports faltered again. The deflationary measures which followed led to the second and more severe recession. The later recovery was made possible by more positive export growth as well as capital inflows arising from increasing foreign direct investment in export-oriented industry.

Export Growth in the 1950s
The sectoral composition and export-orientation of industry near the end of the protectionist period in 1960 is shown in table 4.10, which again may be compared with tables 4.5 and 4.2. Compared

with 1951 (table 4.5), Food, Drink & Tobacco retain about the same importance, but a number of sectors had grown in relative size, especially Textiles and Metals & Engineering, the latter now being the second largest employer in this 10 sector classification. More notably, however, the proportion of output going for export in sectors other than Food, Drink & Tobacco had more than doubled from 6.2% in 1951 to 14.7% in 1960. Manufactured goods other than Food, Drink & Tobacco now accounted for 21.2% of all exports compared with 10.2% in 1951, and the proportion of all exports going to the UK was down from 84.8% to 75%. These trends in exports were of some significance since they represent the start of what were to become important features of the 1960s and 1970s.

It is also important to note, however, that this shift towards greater export-orientation of manufacturing in the 1950s does not indicate any great improvement in the competitive ability of indigenous, or native, industry. For most of the increase in export-orientation (i.e. the increase in the ratio of exports to gross output) was simply due to the combination of rapid growth in foreign demand and slow growth in home demand. Thus the mere maintenance of constant market shares at home and abroad would have meant a substantial increase in export-orientation — without requiring any improvement in international competitive ability. Probably about two-thirds or more of the growth of manufactured exports in the 1950s (excluding Food, Drink & Tobacco) would have resulted simply from maintaining constant shares of growing export markets, and one-third or less from increasing foreign market shares.[9] In addition, it may be noted that the absolute level of non-Food, Drink & Tobacco manufacturing for export was still very small by 1960. To express it in terms of employment, for the purpose of illustration, such export manufacturing employed about 15,600 people (or only 1.4% of the total labour force in 1960), which was an increase of about 9,500 since 1951. Finally, part of the rise in manufactured exports was due to the inflow of new, highly export-oriented *foreign* firms, which started in the 1950s. Although no definite figures are available on the new foreign firms at this time, it can be estimated that they employed about 2,300-2,700 people in export-oriented manufacturing in 1960 (excluding those in the Shannon estate, which is not included in the other national statistics quoted in this chapter).[10] They were mainly engaged in Textiles, Clothing, Metals & Engineering, and 'Other' Manufacturing. ('Other' Manufacturing includes plastics, leather products, rubber products, toys and scientific instruments.)

Table 4.10: Sectoral Composition and Exports of Manufacturing, 1960

	Employment ('000s)	Employment (%)	Gross Output (£m.)	Gross Output (%)	Exports (£m)	Exports as % of Gross Output
Food	34.9	23.1	161.7	37.2	44.9	27.8
Drink & Tobacco	9.8	6.5	58.9	13.6	7.9	13.4
Textiles	20.5	13.6	39.2	9.0	4.8	12.3
Clothing & Footwear	21.4	14.2	24.9	5.7	4.4	17.7
Wood & Furniture	6.8	4.5	9.1	2.1	0.6	6.6
Paper & Printing	14.4	9.5	24.5	5.7	3.9	15.9
Chemicals	5.4	3.6	18.0	4.2	0.9	5.0
Clay, Glass & Cement	5.6	3.7	10.3	2.4	1.6	15.5
Metals & Engineering	24.1	16.0	57.4	13.2	7.1	12.4
Other	7.8	5.2	30.3	7.0	8.1	26.8
TOTAL	150.7	100.0	434.2	100.0	84.2	19.4

(Textiles through Other grouped: 14.7)

Source: Census of Industrial Production for Employment and Gross Output. Exports from table (i), *Review of 1973 and Outlook for 1974.* All figures exclude the duty-free export-processing zone at Shannon.

To summarise, it can be estimated that (a) the increase in non-Food, Drink & Tobacco export manufacturing in 1951-60 amounted, in terms of employment, to about an extra 9,500 jobs; (b) that only about one-third of this, amounting to about the equivalent of 3,200 jobs, was attributable to increased shares of export markets (or an improved ability to compete internationally); and (c) that new foreign firms *first* set up during the 1950s, whose exports therefore all contributed to raising foreign market shares, accounted for about 2,300-2,700 of such jobs. One is therefore left with the conclusion that the improvement, during the 1950s, of the ability of *indigenous* manufacturing industry to compete internationally was rather minor, amounting to an increase of probably no more than 500-900 in employment terms.[11] This relatively weak performance of indigenous manufactured exports remained consistent with the view that considerable difficulties impede the indigenous industry of latecomers from competing in open international markets.

General Conclusions on the Protectionist Period
Let us conclude with some reflections on the relevance of the experience of the 1920s-1950s for the general issues raised in chapter 2. The Republic of Ireland experienced in the 1950s a fairly typical conclusion to a process of import-substituting industrialisation, where rather indiscriminate protection was the main instrument used, unaccompanied by the type of systematic and selective intervention which later came to be used in Japan or South Korea for example (see chapter 8). Protection, it seems, enabled industries to develop particularly in technically mature activities and particularly where the entry barriers were not very great. But it did not prove adequate to gain entry to more technologically demanding industries. It is worth emphasising, too, that neither a shortage of capital nor a shortage of enterprise proved to be a binding constraint on industrial development, as indicated by rapid growth once protection was introduced. Thus the previous failure of industrial development could not be attributed to the supposed capital constraint or lack of enterprise which the conventional view tends to emphasise as prevailing major constraints on development.

The general absence of technologically demanding and highly skilled activities meant, crucially, that machinery and other capital goods, as well as many materials, still had to be imported — in increasing quantities as industry grew. At the same time, the small size of the domestic market and the fact that protection did little to develop an export marketing capability meant that, with few exceptions, the new infant industries did not develop the scale and capability to compete internationally and develop exports. The combination of these two factors ultimately led to chronic balance of payments crises — a fairly typical conclusion to a process of protected industrialisation by latecomers.[12]

Of course, the conventional economic analysis of the causes of such problems in developing countries which have adopted protection tends to conclude that protection itself is the basic cause of the problem. Protection is said to create inefficiency, whereas outward-looking policies and reliance on market forces would solve the problem. The experience of Ireland, however, when viewed in a long-term perspective, casts considerable doubt on this analysis. What were effectively outward-looking policies and reliance on market forces for more than a century before the 1930s had already produced very poor results. This was before protection was introduced and ultimately proved unsatisfactory, so protection cannot be regarded as the *original* cause of industrial stagnation. Rather it may be concluded that protection, for a time, probably generated greater industrial growth than would have occurred under continuing free trade and reliance on market forces. But protection alone was ultimately incapable of creating efficient industries which could compete internationally, in view of the level to which barriers to entry into international competition had been raised by the mid-twentieth century.

It may be noted, too, that the issue of rejection or implementation of protection — the major economic policy issue in the new Free State — was decided not simply by 'objective' economic analysis, but by political conflict between two groups whose economic interests differed. The two groups had been formed by a division over an issue of external relations with the dominant advanced country, which is a theme of the Dependency views referred to in section 2.ii. This underlines the need to take account of political considerations and external influences in considering what economic policy options are realistically available. The next chapter discusses the change of economic strategy which occurred in the 1950s, in the context of a changed basis of political party support and a changed international environment.

5

Outward-looking Policies and Industrial Growth

5.i. THE INTRODUCTION OF OUTWARD-LOOKING POLICIES

In this book, the term 'outward-looking' policies means, as was said in chapter 2, (a) policies to give particular encouragement to exports, (b) encouragement of foreign direct investment, and (c) free trade with other countries. The introduction of these policies began in Ireland in the 1950s and all three aspects involved a substantial change from existing policies. The first section of this chapter outlines the steps by which the new policies were introduced, then considers the political and economic reasons why the change occurred, and finally refers to some other aspects of economic policy.

Policy Changes

The first step, which could only with the benefit of hindsight be recognised as the beginning of a major policy re-orientation, was the establishment in 1949 (legally enacted in 1950) of the Industrial Development Authority (IDA) within the Department of Industry and Commerce. The IDA's main functions included the initiation of proposals for the creation of new industries and, more relevant to our concern here, the attraction of foreign industrialists to the country, but not the power to give grants. This was followed in 1952 by the establishment of Coras Trachtala (the Irish Export Board), a promotional and advisory body concerned with assisting firms attempting to develop exports.

In the same year, under the Undeveloped Areas Act, 1952, a Grants Board (An Foras Tionscal) was established to administer a scheme of non-repayable grants for new industries in Designated (underdeveloped) Areas, which included most of the western half of the country. The Industrial Grants Act, 1956, extended the area eligible for new industry grants to the whole country. Under this Act the IDA could give grants towards the cost of industrial buildings and land in the non-designated areas. Three years later the IDA's grant-giving function in these areas was transferred to An Foras Tionscal under the Industrial Grants Act, 1959, which also allowed major expansions of existing plants to qualify for grant assistance. According to McAleese (1971a, ch. 2), although an ability to export was not a legal pre-condition for receiving grants,

> it almost invariably happened that only export-oriented firms were able to satisfy the government's requirements that grant-aided firms should be internationally competitive, and have favourable growth prospects. Furthermore, a clause in the 1956 Industrial Grants Act explicitly mentioned the development of an export trade (along with the provision of employment and favourable growth prospects) as a desirable attribute to any firm seeking a grant.

By 1959, therefore, grants were available mainly for export-oriented new industries or major expansions, at the maximum rates of 50% of plant and machinery costs and 100% of buildings and land costs in the Designated Areas. Elsewhere, grants were at the maximum rate of one-third of plant and machinery costs, and two-thirds of building and land costs. The second half of the 1950s also saw the introduction of Export Profits Tax Relief (EPTR) and the easing of restrictions on foreign direct investment. The Finance Act of 1956 granted 50% tax remission on profits earned from increases in export sales over the 1956 (or 1955) level, and in 1958 the proportion of tax remission was raised to 100%. Since this tax relief was on *increases* in profits arising from exports since 1956, it applied to *all* exports of firms starting up since that date. The Finance Act of 1960 extended the period of tax relief from 10 to 15 years and diminishing concessions for a further five years were also granted. Foreign investment in export-oriented industry was encouraged by the Industrial Development (Encouragement of External Investment) Act, 1958, which allowed the provisions of the Control of Manufactures Acts to be waived, by Ministerial order, for new, predominantly export-oriented, foreign investment. The Control of Manufactures Acts were repealed completely by an Act of 1964 which provided that they would cease to operate in 1968. There has been no restriction on foreign ownership or control since that time and no restriction on the repatriation of profits.

By 1959 the main elements of the policy package to promote exports and to encourage new foreign direct investment for that purpose were thus already in place. As regards official expectations in the late 1950s, it was apparently expected that export development would occur at least partly, and perhaps mainly, through a re-orientation of existing industries towards export markets, with new export-oriented foreign firms supplementing this effort. This view is implicit in the discussion of the effects of protection in chapter 2 of *Economic Development* (1958) — the first full-scale re-evaluation of earlier economic policies. It was argued that 'the danger has always been apparent that protection might impair the incentive to reduce costs and increase efficiency'. The degree of development of exports is then treated as an indication of prevailing levels of efficiency. 'A number of the protected industries have reduced production costs sufficiently to compete successsfully in export markets but in many productivity remains below the British level. This is partly a reflection of the problem of catering for a small home market which yet demands a considerable range of products.' The implication of this discussion is that rationalisation, under free trade and export-promoting policies, would promote greater efficiency and make possible the growth of exports from existing industries. A number of specific examples of existing industries which were considered capable of developing exports are discussed later in chapter 17 of the same document. By 1960 no steps had yet been taken to dismantle protection and to introduce freer trade. Before going into the introduction of free trade, the development of other aspects of policy up to the early 1980s will be outlined first.[1]

A number of detailed amendments to the grant scheme were made in the 1960s. In addition, An Foras Tionscal was empowered in 1966 to set up several industrial estates with advance factories, and the IDA was given responsibility for the more intensive promotion of small Irish-based industries, employing less than 50 people initially. The Industrial Development Act, 1969 merged An Foras Tionscal and the IDA in one body, called the IDA, which was given greater autonomy from the civil service but is still accountable to the Minister for Industry and Commerce. The IDA now was responsible for all grant-giving and promotional functions for the whole country, except for the activities of the Shannon Free Airport Development Company (SFADCO) which performed a similar function for the free trade zone at Shannon and the surrounding mid-west region, and Gaeltarra Eireann which was responsible for the small Irish-speaking areas in the west (the Gaeltacht). The 1969 Act set the legal limit for new industry grants at 60% of all capital costs in the Designated Areas and 45% elsewhere, but the IDA generally implemented a somewhat lower 'administrative' limit. New industries are also offered grants towards the training of workers and managers and for research and development, as well as industrial housing for workers, advance factories at selected centres and after-care advisory service. The IDA is also empowered, at its own discretion, to contribute to the equity of new enterprises, but this power has been used relatively little.

Apart from its main grants programme, called the New Industry programme, the IDA introduced a number of other programmes such as one for Small Industries which was started on a pilot basis in 1967 and extended throughout the country in 1969. And the Enterprise Development programme, which started in 1978, aims to encourage first-time Irish entrepreneurs. These programmes are aimed particularly at Irish-owned industries and the rate of grants and other incentives available is somewhat higher than for New Industries. According to the IDA (1978), these

> are medium-term development programmes which should result in major job creation over time. At present they absorb substantially more IDA staff resources per manufacturing job provided than New Industry. This is because of the considerable individual attention given to projects which, on average, yield a small number of jobs in the short term. However, the grant cost per job is approximately half the cost under the New Industry Programme.

A related development was the change in SFADCO's role in 1978, whereby it handed over its broader activities to the IDA in order to concentrate intensively on the promotion of small indigenous industry in the mid-west region; a decade later, however, SFADCO again took on responsibility for promotion of all industries in that region.

There have also been some further changes in tax incentives

for industry. Export Profits Tax Relief (EPTR), which was originally intended to terminate in 1979-80, was extended to 1989-90. Then, under pressure from the EEC against this discrimination in favour of exports, the government in 1978 announced the abolition of EPTR and its simultaneous replacement with a new low rate of corporation tax of only 10% for *all* manufacturing in 1981-2000 inclusive. But full EPTR continued to apply to firms which qualified for it before 1981, until 1990. The attraction of Irish tax relief to foreign investors was enhanced by double taxation agreements with many countries, eliminating or limiting taxes in their parent countries on profits of Irish branches of foreign companies. These countries include Austria, Belgium, Canada, Cyprus, Denmark, Finland, France, Germany, Italy, Japan, Luxembourg, Netherlands, Norway, Pakistan, Sweden, Switzerland, UK, USA and Zambia. In addition, after 1967, free depreciation on investments in manufacturing was allowed, with slightly more attractive terms for the Designated Areas. The effect of these measures has been that most new exporting firms established since the late 1950s have had little or no tax to pay on profits, and tax bills for all manufacturing are now very small under the 10% rate combined with other allowances.

The overall attractiveness of the package of industrial incentives was indicated by the Economic Commission for Europe's judgement in the early 1970s that the Irish measures go 'further than those of any other country in Europe in encouraging export industries and in attracting private capital for this purpose' (quoted in Schaffer, 1979). More recently Telesis (1982, ch. 6) compared the value of Irish incentives for new foreign investors with those of five other countries, in the case of a typical small labour-intensive project and a larger more capital-intensive one. Telesis concluded that '. . . Ireland is always the most competitive. For the large project, its package is comparable to Northern Ireland, though substantially larger than for other countries. For the smaller project, Ireland is considerably higher than all other countries.' A number of studies have also suggested that Ireland (meaning the IDA and SFADCO in particular) ranks first or second among countries competing for foreign investment in the speed and efficiency of dissemination of accurate information on investment opportunities to foreign industrialists (Teeling, 1975, ch. 3). Thus one gains the impression that the incentive package for investment in industry and in exports particularly, and the scale and efficiency of the effort to attract foreign investment, amount to one of the most highly intensive and effective of the kind among competing countries.

The question of returning to freer trade first arose in Ireland in the late 1950s when negotiations were in progress among the members of the Organisation for European Economic Co-operation (a forerunner of the OECD) to establish an industrial Free Trade Area. Both *Economic Development* (1958) and the first *Programme for Economic Expansion* (1958) assumed that this Free Trade Area would go ahead and that Ireland would be included. But Ireland, according to Whitaker (1973), was pressing in the negotiations for a lengthy transition period for the elimination of industrial protection over about 25 years, claiming the same derogations as Greece and Turkey. The whole project, however, eventually collapsed due to French opposition because of the absence of an agricultural dimension which was resisted principally by the UK. When the UK and six smaller countries went on to set up their own industrial European Free Trade Area (EFTA), Ireland did not join because it offered little improvement over Ireland's existing virtually free access for manufactures to the UK market, which was by far the largest one concerned.

The first definite decision to move to free trade was Ireland's subsequent application to join the EEC together with the UK in 1961. But when de Gaulle vetoed the British application in 1963, Ireland also withdrew voluntarily due to her heavy dependence on trade with Britain. In the belief that trade liberalisation was coming eventually, however, the government made two small unilateral 'across the board' tariff reductions by 10% (of existing tariff rates) in 1963 and 1964. This was intended 'to encourage industries to undertake measures necessary for reorganisation and adaptation so that they might achieve the level of competitiveness necessary for survival in conditions of freer trade.' (*Irish Statistical Bulletin*, March 1964). This was followed by the signing in December 1965 of the Anglo-Irish Free Trade Area (AIFTA) agreement, which removed the few remaining UK tariffs on Irish manufactures (mainly on synthetic textiles) and the more severe restrictions on imports into Britain of Irish agricultural products and some processed food. In return, Ireland was to remove all protection against imports of British manufactures by ten annual reductions of 10% each. When Ireland and the UK, together with Denmark, joined the EEC in January 1973, Ireland agreed to remove protection against other EEC manufactures by five annual tariff reductions of 20% each. The level of industrial protection thus fell from an average nominal tariff of 25% and an average effective tariff of 79% in 1966 (much higher rates than were then prevalent in the UK or the EEC) to one-fifth of this level within 10 years (McAleese, 1971b and 1978).

To begin preparations for freer trade, the government set up the Committee on Industrial Organisation (CIO) in 1961, with members drawn from employers, trade unions and the public service. Its brief was to assess the state of Irish industry and to recommend measures necessary for adaptation to more intense competition. The Committee concluded that quite extensive adaptation was required, noting widespread problems such as poor management, shortages of skilled labour, old buildings and equipment, small scale and short production runs due to small market size and a wide diversity of products; these features led to relatively high production costs (CIO, 1965; and Brock 1963/64 and 1965). It was thought that, in the absence of adaptation measures, 21 out of 22 sectors surveyed would experience some loss of production and employment under free trade, but most sectors were considered to be basically capable of adapting quite successfully.[2]

The principal adaptation measures recommended included the formation of Adaptation Councils for each industry which would encourage co-operation in purchasing materials, marketing, selecting areas for specialisation and promoting the amalgamation of firms. In addition, an adaptation grants scheme began in 1963 in order to help meet the costs of structural change. These grants, payable at a rate of up to 25% of adaptation costs, were approved for firms accounting for at least 75% of manufacturing output and employment by 1968, when they were replaced by the IDA's re-equipment grants programme.

Causes of the Change of Policy
A number of different factors combined to bring about this change of industrial development strategy. To start with, there was an obvious motivation for some sort of policy change arising from the prolonged economic crisis in the 1950s, and this motivation was heightened by an awareness of the far more favourable situation in other countries. Thus, *Economic Development* (1958, pp. 10, 11) mentions that the average income in Ireland in 1956 was

roughly one-half of that in Denmark and Britain, one-third of that in Canada and one-fifth of that in the United States . . . between 1949 and 1956 the volume of gross national product increased by 8% as compared with 21% for Britain and 42% for OEEC countries generally . . . The increase in the volume of industrial output between 1949 and 1956 was 30% as compared with 62% for OEEC countries.

In the circumstances, the existence of a widespread mood receptive to changes in policy was not surprising. The need for new solutions was given political urgency by the succession of defeats of outgoing governments in the general elections of 1948, 1951, 1954 and 1957, which followed after 16 years of continuous Fianna Fail government from 1932 to 1948.

The introduction of the whole package of outward-looking policies has often been associated with Sean Lemass's period as Minister for Industry and Commerce in the Fianna Fail government which won the 1957 election, with 1958 being seen as the turning point since that was the year of publication of both *Economic Development* and the *Programme for Economic Expansion*. But, as mentioned above, several important measures had already been taken before then. Of these, the establishment of the IDA, the extension of the grants scheme and the introduction of EPTR took place under the Inter-Party governments (of 1948-51 and 1954-57) led by Fine Gael, the descendant mainly of the pro-Treaty Cumann na nGaedheal party of the 1920s combined with some smaller groups.

Thus the idea of seeking to attract more foreign investment and the introduction of the major export incentive arose under the Inter-Party governments. The relaxation and repeal of the Control of Manufactures Acts was carried out by Fianna Fail alone, but there was obviously little disagreement about this among the other parties. Speaking in 1957, a leading opposition spokesman on these matters, William Norton, said in the Dail

It is not very important what the Minister does at the moment with regard to the Control of Manufactures Act. Speaking for my own [Labour] Party I should like to say that we recognise it is out of date, that it has lost its early significance, that there is a change in the whole industrial and economic situation and that in contemplation of these circumstances the Act should be modified, if not in fact abolished altogether. Except for the purpose of the directional powers it gives the Minister it has little or no value in the present circumstances (quoted in Whitaker, 1973).

The introduction of free trade was also carried out entirely under Fianna Fail who remained in office from 1957 until 1973. But again, there was no very strong political opposition to this move. Garret FitzGerald, who was later to be leader of Fine Gael, expressed his approval of the government's decision to publish *Economic Development* (1958) as a report from civil servants rather than as a government paper, suggesting that one reason for the decision was 'a desire to secure the most widespread acceptance of these new policies by making it as clear as possible that they are not party political policies, but national policies, which, the government might hope, could in large measure be kept out of the arena of party politics by thus revealing their impeccably non-political origin'. FitzGerald found such an approach quite plausible: 'the break with the past, implied in all these documents,[3] is in tune with a widespread public mood'.

It is thus quite striking that the introduction of outward-looking policies was not done by any single party, and no important aspect of it was strongly resisted by either side. (The Labour Party, however, did oppose EEC membership in 1973, mainly because by that time it meant a large rise in food prices due to the Common Agricultural Policy, with no corresponding increase in incomes for their supporters such as the farmers could expect.) Such a measure of political consensus contrasted noticeably with the previous party differences over the introduction of protection and the Control of Manufactures Acts in the early 1930s.

This new consensus arose partly from the fact that the two major parties, Fianna Fail and Fine Gael, had moved much closer together with the decline in importance of the civil war issues and the changing basis of support of Fianna Fail in particular. With the exception of partition, the civil war issues had by now been gradually resolved to Fianna Fail's satisfaction, without any necessity for further armed conflict with the UK — as the supporters of the Treaty, in fact, had believed could be done. De Valera's Fianna Fail governments had abolished the Oath of Allegiance to the British monarch, introduced a new constitution and reached a settlement with Britain on the land annuities issue. The process had been concluded by the declaration of the Republic of Ireland and withdrawal from the British Commonwealth by the Inter-Party government in 1949.[4] The result of these events was a decline in the nationalistic feeling which had initially helped to encourage the adoption of protection and the Control of Manufactures Acts. The issue of Northern Ireland remained, but it had tended to become something of a side issue. The three main parties in principle favoured a united Ireland but did little of practical consequence to pursue it. All governments had taken a similar firm line against illegal IRA activities, while none since the 1920s had made important efforts to pursue the alternative line of closer contacts and friendly relations with the North.

The change in the nature of Fianna Fail's support, which was already evident by 1943, has been described by Garvin (1974) as Fianna Fail's 'invasion of commercialised and urban Ireland, joining a cross-class eastern support to its small-farm western base'. The reasons why this occurred included migration to urban areas, the party's capturing of much support from industrialists who had been helped by their protectionist policies, and the inroads they made on Labour support through their being a more successful party which also favoured welfarist and nationalist protest policies. The party thus shed much of its distinctive regional, agrarian-populist character and began to draw more support in areas other than its original northern and western small-farm base, including Dublin, and among business people and workers as well as small farmers. The effect of this change was that Fianna Fail became a centrist or 'catch-all' party. As such it was less and less distinguishable in matters of policy from the only plausible alternative government — a 'catch-all' alliance involving the more conservative Fine Gael party and the Labour party. 'Electoral politics, because of the divorce of "politics" from policy formation, evolved towards trivial, parish-pump issues and an all-pervading "brokerage" style, while bureaucratic administration shielded from politics, tended to be more and more divorced from public political life' (Garvin, 1977). Thus, since there was little consistent difference between the main alignments on substantive policy matters, 'politics' mostly revolved around local or personal matters and the nuances of nationalist rhetoric, while the public service effectively formed policy — subject to a certain minimum consensus.[5]

The adoption of outward-looking policies which evolved in these circumstances was quite a natural response to the country's economic difficulties and a changing international economy. It was natural, at least, in the sense that it was the technically correct solution according to orthodox economic theory, which was therefore favoured by the leading economic advisers in the public service. It was natural also in the sense that it took advantage of *newly emerging* opportunities — both to secure more satisfactory export markets for the country's important agricultural sector, and to attract export-oriented foreign direct investment which was a phenomenon that first became significant in the world economy in the 1950s. Apart from some positive attractions of the new policy, there was also felt to be some necessity to follow Britain into the EEC in view of Ireland's still overwhelming dependence on British markets for exports. And finally, there was less resistance than might have been expected to free trade — potentially the most contentious element of the new strategy — since it was considered that most of the existing protected industries could be prepared successfully over a long adjustment period to meet the challenge. The bigger industrial capitalists themselves accepted this view (see Federation of Irish Industries, 1968). No doubt it was felt, too, that faster economic growth in services (helped by the effects of new foreign manufacturing investment) and in agriculture would benefit Irish capital generally, even if Irish manufacturing firms came under some pressure.[6]

Stanton (1979) has argued that the adoption of outward-looking policies involved two distinct decisions, the first being the decision to integrate with the European market which 'was fundamental, the authentic choice of Ireland's dominant, agricultural exporting class'. The second decision, he says, which was complementary to the first, was to start 'industrialisation-by-invitation' in order to alleviate the already serious employment problem which would be exacerbated by free trade, causing more serious unrest. It is certainly true that the AIFTA agreement and EEC membership greatly benefited the externally oriented farmers, but it is not so clear that this factor was the first cause of the overall shift in policy or that it forced changes which would not otherwise have been made on other classes. There was a wider range of interests which stood to benefit from more export-oriented foreign investment, and few which objected to it, whether or not closer economic integration with other European countries went ahead. And in fact, moves were made in this direction several years before freer trade was introduced.

Other Aspects of Economic Policy

Before concluding this section it will be convenient to mention briefly here some other aspects of economic policy, namely budget management, management of the balance of payments, planning and the role of state enterprises. Up to the mid-1950s, the prevailing attitude to the management of the public finances was the orthodox conservative approach. It was clearly articulated by Whitaker (1953), referring to the role of the Department of Finance: 'our function is not to select the most meritorious [departmental proposals] and clap them on the taxpayer's back but, rather, to see that as few as possible emerge as new burdens on the community.' As Chubb and Lynch (1969) commented, his article 'revealed little appreciation of the role of the State (or of the Department as its instrument) in stimulating and guiding growth or as an architect of community welfare'.

From the late 1950s, however, this attitude changed somewhat and public expenditure, particularly capital expenditure, became more expansionary and tolerant of a growing public debt. This not only directly contributed to a higher rate of investment, but also meant long-term additional expansion of domestic demand, which was important for that large portion of Irish industry which sells almost exclusively to the home market. During the 1970s, the expansionary trend was accelerated considerably, involving large current budget deficits too, so that both the total public debt and the public foreign debt in relation to GNP were far higher than the levels prevailing elsewhere in western Europe by the early 1980s.

In a small and open economy which has come to spend more than half of its income (and an even higher marginal percentage) on imports, the management of demand via the public finances has an important impact on the balance of payments. The persistence (and intensification) of deficit financing since the 1950s has generated strong demand for imports, to a degree which, for most of the period, was not matched even by the rapid growth of exports. Thus the pursuit of an expansionary public spending policy necessarily involved a more liberal attitude to tolerating current balance of payments deficits. Since a fixed exchange rate policy was always pursued (linked rigidly to sterling until 1979 and a little more flexibly to the European Monetary System since then), capital inflows have been necessary to cover current deficits and maintain the value of the currency. Particularly since the second half of the 1970s, a substantial part of the required capital inflows was achieved by foreign borrowing by the public sector.[7]

Economic 'planning' began with the first *Programme for Economic Expansion* in 1958 and was followed by two others which covered the period until 1972. The Coalition government of 1973-77, however, dropped this type of formal planning or programming, producing only a Green Paper on *Economic and Social Development, 1976-80*. But a number of further planning documents have been produced since 1977. Thus there has been some type of formal 'plan' or programme in existence for much of the period since 1958. What was attempted, however, was a very mild form of 'indicative' planning. According to the First Programme 'the programme should be read as an *outline* of the more important contributions, direct and indirect, which the Government propose to make to economic development'. The private sector was left to itself to respond as it saw fit to the beneficial environment which the government aimed to create for investment. The general philosophy of planning adopted by successive governments was expressed thus by Whitaker (1976b): 'a plan indicates objectives, it specifies an agenda, but it does not guarantee fulfilment. . . . Detailed prescriptions for constituent sectors of the economy are, therefore, not appropriate; rather, must attention be focussed on creating an environment and an institutional framework in which the myriad of individual decisions will tend to accord in general direction and effect.'

A similar wariness of very specific interventions by the state in the structure of production has generally been evident in the limited use made of state enterprise as an instrument of development since the 1950s. Although commercial state enterprises had always been rather more widely acceptable in Ireland than, say, the USA or among Conservatives in Britain, they have always been considered very much secondary to the private sector, and to a great extent at the service of the private sector. Many of them began under Sean Lemass, Minister for Industry and Commerce in much of the 1930s-1950s, who has consequently been regarded as relatively favourably disposed towards the concept of commercial state enterprise. But even his view of its limited role is clear from the following:

In contrast to many countries where similar State-sponsored organisations have been created as part of a deliberate policy of State socialism, they developed in this country in a more haphazard way to meet particular needs and opportunities as they arose, when no other course appeared to be practicable. Industrial development in Ireland is based on private enterprise and profit motive: State-financed industries have been set up only where considerations of national policy were involved or where the projects were beyond the scope of, or unlikely to be undertaken by, private enterprise. As set out in the Government White Paper on Economic Expansion, the Government favour the system of private ownership of industry and will not be disposed to enter any manufacturing field in which private enterprise is already operating successfully. (Lemass, 1959).

Most of the Irish commercial state enterprises are of the type familiar in other western European countries, being either public utilities or formerly ailing private companies taken over to preserve employment and services. But there are also a few industrial companies which were initiated by the state for such purposes as the promotion of self-sufficiency (e.g. Bord na Mona, which produces various forms of peat for domestic fuel, electricity generation, etc.), or the provision of outlets for agricultural produce (e.g. Comhlucht Siuicre Eireann which processes sugar beet and a range of vegetables). An impression of the scale of industrial state enterprises in the 1950s is given in *Economic Development* (1958) which said (while total CIP employment in 1956 was 228,000), that employment in those industrial enterprises *initiated* by the state was 15,300 in 1956-57 — including 8,500 in the Electricity Supply Board, 4,900 in Bord na Mona, and 1,900 in Comhlucht Siuicre Eireann. As well as the enterprises started by the state, a further 8,350 *industrial* personnel were employed by formerly private companies taken over by the state — including 6,200 in CIE (national rail and road transport, including building and maintenance of buses, rolling stock and railways), 1,700 in Great Northern Railways, and 450 in Irish Steel Holdings. Thus altogether there were almost 24,000 people, or just over 10% of the industrial labour force, employed in industrial activity by commercial state enterprises in 1956-57.

The relative importance of state enterprises in industry declined somewhat after the 1950s and they accounted for 8% of industrial employment in 1983. This was in line with the intention of the First Programme, which was 'based on the principle that, in the future, as in the past, the private sector will be the principal source of new productive projects'.

It may be concluded that the policies adopted since the 1950s have been close to those recommended by the conventional, neo-classical view discussed in section 2.i. Protection was dismantled and replaced by grant incentives and tax concessions, for exports particularly. Foreign direct investment was welcomed. The role of state enterprise was slightly reduced and confined mainly to the limited functions which private capitalists desired. Other forms of government activity related to industry were mostly confined to servicing the needs of private capital, providing advice and information on matters such as export marketing, investment opportunities and the expenditure plans of the public sector. Thus, outward-looking policies and a general reliance on market forces with little detailed or selective state intervention have prevailed, as recommended by the conventional view.

One possible qualification to this conclusion is that the system of grants and tax concessions used to encourage industry was biased in favour of *export* industries, and to this extent distorted the profit criteria thrown up by the market. But this seems to be in accord at least with the spirit of the conventional recommendation for 'export-oriented' industrialisation, and so long as such a bias is 'stable and automatic' there would be little objection to it from the conventional view. But while the general shape of the incentive package was fairly stable for over two decades, and the tax concessions have been automatic, the grants do not quite appear to have been automatic since the grant level as a percentage of capital investment (subject to a maximum limit) is at the discretion of the IDA or SFADCO, subject to negotiation in each case. This would be acceptable to the conventional view if variations in grants awarded were based on consistent specified criteria, and thus automatic given the nature of the project concerned. But it is clear that this has not been the practice, since the IDA's discretionary powers are used at least partly as a bargaining device (which makes the grant level uncertain *a priori*) in order to attempt to minimise the expenditure necessary to attract projects, *in competition* with alternative sites such as the various regions of the UK (see McKeon, 1980). Thus, the level of grants on offer has not been fully automatic as the conventional view would recommend so that some distortion of the profit criteria thrown up by the market could result. But this arises mainly from conditions of uncertainty in multiple bargaining situations, and as such may be about as close to the conventionally recommended strategy as could realistically be expected. At any rate, few late-industrialising countries have adopted a strategy which is in most respects quite so close to it, so that Irish industrial policy since the 1950s is one of the best examples of the conventional strategy one is likely to find.

Admittedly, in the 1980s particularly, a certain amount of attention has been focussed on a number of ways in which the government is said to distort market forces and to impede private industry, e.g. by pushing up labour costs by high taxation, or by providing incentives for investment in property and government bonds which diverts resources from industrial development. The stress on these arguments is a recent phenomenon which seems to follow from a growing realisation that Irish indigenous industry has not performed as well as was once thought. Since an explanation is now needed for this, the conventional economic approach naturally looks for distortions to the market caused by government, because the possibility of basic defects or 'imperfections' in the market itself has been assumed away from the start. These supposed distortions and impediments caused by the government were apparently not so evident when Irish industry was thought to be performing quite well up to about 1980, and indeed the conventional view seemed to be that the perceived strong performance was due to broadly correct market-oriented policies.

This book takes the view that, by any reasonable standard of international comparison, policies have in fact generally been market-oriented over the past two or three decades. Irish indigenous industry never performed well under these policies, and the cause lies not primarily in government impediments and distortions but in widespread market imperfections which create entry barriers for late-developers. However, more detailed consideration of the recent arguments mentioned above, which claim that government impediments and distortions are at fault, will have to wait until chapter 9, after first examining the pattern of change and development in Irish industry. For the nature of this pattern itself provides the basis for a refutation of the main arguments concerning government impediments and distortions.

5.ii. THE SCALE OF INDUSTRIAL GROWTH SINCE THE 1950s

Ten years have passed since the Government published their first programme for economic expansion. In that period the nation has made substantial advances in material prosperity. The gross national product . . . has during those ten years grown by nearly 4% a year — three times as fast as during the preceding decade. *Third Programme: Economic and Social Development 1969-72* (1969)

There was a sharp contrast between the history of stagnation and failure throughout most of the 1950s and the record of steady progress achieved in the years immediately after 1958 under conditions which were unchanged so far as basic economic resources were concerned . . . . What was achieved after 1958 could have been secured a decade earlier with a better organisation of the economy, a greater will to develop its potentialities, sounder economic policies and adequate leadership. Garret FitzGerald (1968).

The pervading thread of the evidence is that outward-looking policies laid the basis for substantial economic growth . . . . The growth rate increased fourfold after 1958, the industrial drive took on depth, and a variety of industries developed their size and importance in the economy . . . . The diversification and fast growth of exports was an outstanding achievement of the period. Noel J. J. Farley (1973).

One can safely assert that this pragmatic nationalist [Sean Lemass] who had erected the high tariff wall in the nineteen thirties to shelter Ireland's infant industry, would have been happy to see it razed to the ground in return for the benefits to Ireland of membership of the [European Economic] Community . . . . We can salute Sean Lemass for having so effectively pursued policies which have taken Ireland from the embattled and impoverished protectionism of the nineteen thirties into the more exposed but also better-off nineteen seventies. T. K. Whitaker (1973).

Over the past 25 years Ireland has undergone a 'crash course' in industrial development. We have had to go through this process to ensure the foundation for the stable development of our society. Sean Lemass saw this need and began the highly successful programme of planned growth, based on rapid export development, a high level of investment and selective attraction of foreign enterprise to strengthen the industrial base. This period has seen a dramatic growth and broadening of employment opportunities and a steady rise in the country's living standards. We have today the fastest growing industrial sector in the European Economic Community. Desmond O'Malley (Fianna Fail), Minister for Industry, Commerce and Tourism, 1980.

The extracts quoted above indicate that the Republic of Ireland experienced considerable industrial and economic development, as measured by the conventional indicators, after the introduction of outward-looking policies. They show too that these policies were widely regarded as highly satisfactory, at least until the early 1980s, by people whose views command some respect.[8] While it would not be reasonable to suggest that all these people naively regarded the country's development problems as finally solved, there was certainly a tendency to believe that the country made a basic breakthrough after the 1950s. This section outlines the economic trends, at the aggregate level, which gave rise to this view. The following chapters examine the record in more detail and show that the change was rather less profound than it appeared on the surface.

Table 5.1 shows average annual rates of growth of the volume of industrial output and employment for various periods between 1951 and 1987.

Table 5.1: Average Annual Percentage Growth in Industry, Various Periods, 1951-87

	Volume of Output, All CIP Industry	Volume of Output, CIP Manufacturing	Employment, Manufacturing
1951-58	1.3	1.7	0.2
1958-73	6.7	6.7	2.4
1973-76	1.2	1.6	—1.0
1976-79	9.1	7.6	3.2
1979-82	1.5	1.5	—2.1
1982-87	6.3	6.9	—3.0

Sources: Census of Industrial Production, and *Quarterly Inquiries* for 1987.

As the table shows, following the recession of 1951-58, the rate of growth of industrial output and employment rose very substantially for a period of 15 years. This was interrupted by the international recession of the mid-1970s, which hit Ireland during 1974 and lasted until 1976, but after that growth rates rose again to new heights. In 1979, the IDA was able to say: 'manufacturing industry in Ireland expanded faster in the past three years than in any other country in the EEC, with annual average increases of output of +9%, exports +13%, and net employment +2%' (IDA, 1979). Although growth rates in the 1960s and early 1970s were perhaps not as spectacular as in some other newly industrialising countries, they represented a great improvement over Ireland's own experience in the 1950s. And although Irish industrial growth rates in the 1960s and early 1970s were not extraordinarily high for western Europe, the return to high growth in the late 1970s was quite exceptional.

As table 5.1 also shows, however, industrial expansion was virtually halted again in the international recession of the early 1980s, and manufacturing employment fell. This was followed, in 1982-87, by a resumption of quite strong growth in output, but this was coupled with a continuing decline in employment. By 1987, manufacturing employment had fallen by almost 20% from the peak level reached in 1979, despite the fact that Ireland had the fastest rate of growth of industrial output in the OECD for much of that period. Such a decline in manufacturing employment was unprecedented in the history of Ireland as an independent state.

The main cause of these apparently paradoxical trends in the 1980s was a very high rate of output growth in a small number of sectors with exceptionally high productivity, while the rest of industry experienced little or no growth in output and a decline in employment. In the high-growth sectors, namely Pharmaceuticals, Office & Data Processing Machinery, Electrical Engineering, Instrument Engineering and 'Other' Foods, the volume of output grew by 14.7% per annum in 1980-86, while in the rest of industry there was no growth at all in the volume of output. The high-growth sectors accounted for just 15% of manufacturing employment in 1980.

For most of Irish industry, therefore, the 1980s has been a period of serious and prolonged recession. It has also become increasingly recognised that the high-growth sectors, being mainly foreign-owned, import most of their inputs and repatriate substantial amounts of profits, thus leaving a relatively low proportion of their recorded output as a contribution to the Irish economy. Consequently it would be fair to say that overall industrial performance weakened very substantially in the 1980s compared with the 1960s and 1970s.

Table 5.2 shows the change in the relative importance of industrial employment as a share of total employment.

Table 5.2: Sectoral Distribution of Employment, 1960-86 (%)

	1960	1970	1979	1986
Agriculture	37	27	19	16
Industry	23	30	32	28
(of which,				
Manufacturing)	(16)	(20)	(21)	(19)
Services	40	43	49	56
	100	100	100	100

Sources: Trend in Employment and Unemployment and Economic Review and Outlook, 1987.

The growth in industry's share of employment was fairly substantial up to 1979, with agriculture showing a large decline. Most of this change occurred before the early 1970s since agriculture got quite a boost from EEC membership after 1973, and since service employment, too, was boosted particularly by expansionary government fiscal policies after the early 1970s.

Unemployment, however, remained relatively high by European standards at about 6-8% of the labour force throughout most of the 1960s and 1970s, although this was far below the level reached in the 1980s in a time of severe recession when the unemployment rate rose from 10% in 1981 to over 17% by 1985. Industrial employment was hit relatively hard in this recession, as reflected in table 5.2. Despite the difficulties of the 1980s, a novel feature for Ireland was the fact that the total labour force actually grew in the 1960s and 1970s, from 1,108,000 in 1961 to over 1,200,000 by 1979. Although emigration was quite high compared with most other countries, it was much reduced in the 1960s compared with the 1950s, and net immigration, largely of former emigrants, occurred during the 1970s. There was a return to continuous net emigration in the 1980s, however, as total employment began to decline.

The sectoral composition and export-orientation of manufacturing industry in 1978 is shown in table 5.3, which may be compared with table 4.10 to see the changes since 1960.

Table 5.3: Sectoral Composition and Exports of Manufacturing, 1978

	Employment ('000)	Employment (%)	Gross Output (£m.)	Gross Output (%)	Exports (£m.)	Exports as % of Gross Output
Food	42.0	20.9	2,444	40.8	891	36.5
Drink & Tobacco	10.3	5.1	408	6.8	52	12.7
Textiles	20.0	9.9	365	6.1	235	64.4
Clothing & Footwear	15.8	7.9	152	2.5	64	42.1
Wood & Furniture	7.3	3.6	92	1.5	23	25.0
Paper & Printing	15.7	7.8	225	3.8	50	22.2
Chemicals	10.5	5.2	530	8.9	328	61.9
Clay, Glass & Cement	12.6	6.3	309	5.2	51	16.5
Metals & Engineering	46.5	23.1	954	15.9	500	52.4
Other	20.4	10.1	507	8.5	262	51.7
TOTAL	201.1	100.0	5,986	100.0	2,456	41.0

(Textiles through Other bracketed: 48.3)

Source: Employment from *Review and Outlook, 1979*. Gross Output and Exports figures as supplied by the Department of Industry, Commerce and Tourism for the National Economic and Social Council's study of job losses in manufacturing. All figures are based on the CIP, and Shannon is excluded.

Comparing the sectoral composition with 1960, there was a decline in the relative importance of the 'traditional' sectors like Textiles, Clothing & Footwear, Wood & Furniture and Paper & Printing, although Food changed little. And there was a corresponding growth in the share of 'modern' activities which have usually been (not necessarily correctly, as is shown later) assumed to be more technically advanced, in sectors like Metals & Engineering, Chemicals and Other Manufacturing. A more noticeable feature of the change since 1960, however, is seen in the export figures. The overall proportion of output going for export more than doubled, with nearly all sectors showing a large change in this direction — the only exceptions being Drink & Tobacco, and Clay, Glass & Cement. In view of the nature of the difficulties of the 1950s, and the aims of policy since that time, this feature was generally regarded as a particularly valuable success. The growth of manufactured exports is also reflected in the fact that manufactured goods including Food made up 76% of exports in 1979 compared with 50% in 1960, and manufactured goods excluding Food made up 57% of exports in 1979 compared with 27% in 1960. It may be estimated that about 72,000 people were employed in non-Food, Drink & Tobacco manufacturing for export in 1978, a very substantial rise from less than 16,000 in 1960.

The growth of Irish manufactured exports was partly an effect of the growth of foreign demand but a very large part of

Table 5.4: Irish Exports' Share of Foreign Imports of Manufactures — UK, 1966 and 1978; Rest of OECD, 1966 and 1977 (%)

	UK		Rest of OECD	
	1966	1978	1966	1977
Food	3.60	9.07	0.28	0.76
Drink & Tobacco	12.87	8.17	0.14	0.38
Textiles	5.34	8.29	0.13	0.31
Clothing & Footwear	10.49	6.10	0.17	0.18
Wood & Furniture	0.48	1.39	0.03	0.02
Paper & Printing	1.98	2.32	0.02	0.12
Chemicals	0.67	3.27	0.15	0.55
Clay, Glass & Cement	1.53	0.71	0.21	0.24
Metals & Engineering	0.80	1.58	0.09	0.19
Other Manufacturing	1.59	2.72	0.06	0.22
TOTAL	2.38	3.50	0.13	0.30

Source: Blackwell, Danaher and O'Malley (1983), table 7.5.

it, too, was due to an increase in Irish exports' share of foreign markets. Such an increase in market shares was recorded in most sectors in Ireland's main export markets. Table 5.4 shows the change in Irish exports' share of the UK market in 1966-78, and in the rest of the OECD countries in 1966-77.

The table shows that the increase in Irish manufactured exports' shares of foreign imports was not only large, but also widely spread across the sectors; an increase occurred in seven out of ten sectors in the UK market, and nine out of ten in the rest of the OECD. Table 5.5 breaks down the growth of Irish manufactured exports to the UK and the rest of the OECD into components due to the growth of foreign demand, changes in the composition of foreign import demand, and changes in Irish exports' share of these markets. This table shows the important effect of the increase in Ireland's share of foreign markets, which in the two markets combined accounted for more than half the growth.

Table 5.5: Source of Changes in Irish Manufacturing Exports

Source of Change	UK, 1966-78		Rest of OECD, 1966-77	
	($m, current values)			
Growth of Foreign Imports	1,224	(63.1%)	526.8	(37.6%)
Changes in Composition of Foreign Imports	−188.9	(−9.7%)	3.7	(0.3%)
Changes in Ireland's Market Shares	903.7	(46.6%)	868.2	(62.1%)
TOTAL CHANGE	1,938.9	(100.0%)	1,398.7	(100.0%)

Source: Blackwell, Danaher and O'Malley (1983), tables 7.1 and 7.2.

The growth of industry in Ireland was accompanied by relatively rapid growth of incomes, which was also a policy goal, so that Irish wage levels moved closer to those in the UK. Between 1963 and 1978, average hourly nominal earnings in manufacturing grew at an average annual rate of 14.3% in Ireland, compared with 11.8% in the UK, and average weekly earnings in manufacturing in Ireland rose from 65% of the UK level in 1963 to 84% in 1973 and 93% in 1978.[9] Then when

Ireland joined the European Monetary System in 1979, while the UK did not join it, the Irish pound soon fell below its former parity with sterling — or rather, sterling rose in relation to the other western European currencies. Consequently, Irish wages fell further below the British levels in the first half of the 1980s, when measured in a common currency.

Although average manufacturing earnings in Ireland rose to almost the same level as UK rates, GDP per head remained a good deal lower, due to the larger proportionate size of the Irish agricultural sector which had lower than average incomes, and to the considerably lower proportion of the Irish population at work. In 1985, Irish GDP per head was US$5,123 compared with US$7,943 in the UK. The Irish GDP per head was still one of the lowest in the OECD, ranking above only Turkey, Portugal, Greece, Spain and Yugoslavia.[10]

Finally another notable apparent success of industrial policy was the considerable decentralisation of industry, which had long been a stated aim of policy. There had been very little change in the geographical concentration of industry between 1931 and 1961, but table 5.6 shows that industry became noticeably more decentralised between then and 1981.

Table 5.6: Industrial Location — Percentage Distribution of Industrial Employment by Area, 1961, 1973 and 1981

Location	1961	1973	1981
	%	%	%
Main Urban Areas			
Dublin City and County	46.5	39.0	33.1
Cork, Limerick, Waterford Cities	10.7	10.0	9.3
Other Areas			
Rest of Leinster	18.1	20.0	22.8
Rest of Munster	14.6	19.4	20.1
Connaught	6.0	6.6	8.9
Ulster (3 counties)	4.2	5.0	5.8
TOTAL	100.0	100.0	100.0

Source: *Statistical Abstract* for 1961 and 1973, *Census of Population* for 1981.
Note: The 1961 figures include Building, unlike those for 1973 and 1981. Since Building is probably relatively highly dispersed, the effect is probably to understate a little the degree of relative decentralisation which occurred.

The decentralisation of industry was due to the establishment of a high proportion of new foreign-owned industries outside the main urban areas, combined with the decline of older indigenous industry which was quite heavily concentrated in the towns, especially Dublin. Further comments will be made on both of these developments later.

To conclude, this section has shown that up to the end of the 1970s at least, policies adopted since the 1950s met with considerable success in most respects, as judged by the conventional indicators. It appears there was a profound change for the better in Irish industry. The next two chapters, however, examine the record in more detail and show that this change was not so profound as it appears. There were fundamental weaknesses in the nature of this industrialisation, some of which have become far more evident in the 1980s.

6

Irish Indigenous Industry

It has been shown in chapter 5 that the introduction of policies which corresponded closely with the conventionally recommended strategy was followed by a marked improvement in the performance of industry in Ireland in several respects. This experience might therefore appear to offer support for the conventional view outlined in section 2.i and to cast doubt on the alternative view put forward in section 2.ii. The alternative view did note, however, that there are *exceptional* circumstances in which a small number of latecomers might experience good results for some time with the conventional strategy. Thus it was suggested that latecomers adopting this strategy could have only very limited success in developing *indigenous* industry. But it was also recognised that a few exceptional countries among them might be able to attract a greatly disproportionate share of the limited amount of foreign direct manufacturing investment which is willing to go to late-industrialising countries. By this means, quite rapid industrial growth might be attained, for a time at least, despite a poor performance by indigenous firms. The question therefore arises whether Ireland's experience has been an exceptional case of this type, and in order to assess this it is necessary to examine the record of indigenous and foreign industries separately. This chapter deals with indigenous industry and chapter 7 deals with foreign industry.

To clarify the implications of the issue raised here, if Ireland's experience can be explained as an *exceptional* case of the type suggested above, it offers no *general* support for the conventional view on the appropriate strategy for most latecomers. In fact — given the relative scarcity of sufficiently mobile foreign investment worldwide — a poor performance by the country's indigenous industry would cast doubt on the general validity of the conventional view. It would also tend to support the conclusions of the alternative view that there are serious constraints on the development of latecomers which cannot generally be overcome by reliance on the conventionally recommended policies. For Ireland itself, the fact of being an exceptional 'success' of the type suggested might also have important implications. For it would mean both that future development is rather precariously dependent on foreign investment, and that policies were not well designed to encourage the development of the important indigenous sector which still accounts for the dominant share of manufacturing employment.

6.i. THE OVERALL SCALE OF GROWTH IN IRISH INDIGENOUS INDUSTRY

The first section of this chapter outlines the overall scale of growth in Irish indigenous industry, and the rest of the chapter goes on to analyse the record in greater detail. But first it is necessary to deal with the problems of definition and data availability which arise when one seeks to distinguish 'indigenous' from 'foreign' firms.

Definitions and Data Constraints

In principle, the appropriate definition of indigenous industry, which is relevant to the theoretical discussion in chapter 2 concerning barriers to entry for newcomers in a late-industrialising country, would be firms which first arose in the country concerned, as opposed to those first established there as subsidiaries of companies already in existence elsewhere. Thus Irish 'indigenous' firms could differ from Irish-owned firms, since they could include some which later passed into majority foreign ownership after originating independently in Ireland. A further complication which must be considered is the fact that indigenous firms defined in this way, even if majority native-owned, could be effectively controlled in some important respects by foreign firms if, say, they are using the foreign firms' patented processes, products or trade marks under licence, or if they sell their output to one dominant foreign buyer. It is not uncommon to find, for example, that licensing agreements include constraints on exports from the licensee. For some purposes this consideration could mean that such a licensee firm should be regarded as an arm of the dominant foreign enterprise — an aspect of its operations which should be considered in examining its international activities, for example, if such is the focus of interest.

For the purpose of this book, however, this consideration does not mean that such dominated Irish firms should be excluded from 'indigenous' industry. Given our focus of interest, which is the constraints on, and opportunities for, the development of latecomer industry originating locally, this type of influence or control from abroad may be regarded as *one form* of constraint on, or opportunity for, indigenous development. Presumably the indigenous firm enters into a foreign licensing or trading agreement because it judges that this will enable it to operate more effectively than without it — to overcome to some extent, in fact, technological or marketing barriers to entry. The constraints which also go with such an agreement, then, are one form in which barriers to entry into wider markets or other activities are experienced. For our purposes, therefore, such a licensee or sub-contractor firm should be included as indigenous, and indeed to exclude it could be effectively to prejudge as invalid one possible way around barriers to entry.

For this analysis, then, the ideal definition of Irish indigenous industry is considered to be industrial firms which originated in Ireland (rather than first appearing there as subsidiaries of existing foreign companies), including those which subsequently passed into majority foreign ownership and those which may be effectively dominated in important respects by foreign firms. But although this is the definition in principle, it must be modified in practice for empirical study due to data constraints. The way in which the available data are defined in effect imposes definitions on the content of this chapter, and as it happens these definitions are not unacceptable.

Rather than go into a full explanation in the main text of the derivation of the data, an account is provided in appendix I. But to make a few general comments, the distinction between Irish indigenous and foreign industry is in fact defined here by nationality of ownership (the country of incorporation of the ultimate parent company, or the nationality of the ultimate individual owner). So the data presented here for Irish indigenous industry differ from the preferred definition in excluding indigenous firms which have passed into foreign ownership. It is often possible, however, to include Guinness, which is by far the largest of these companies, so that this is not considered to be a very serious defect.[1] As regards the issue of foreign influence or control in Irish-owned companies, it may be borne in mind that there has been little or no legal restriction on foreign ownership since 1958 so that the typical form of new foreign involvement in industry in Ireland is the openly owned subsidiary. There would thus be much less of a distinction between control and ownership among new industries established in the period of outward-looking policies than among those established during the previous period when the Control of Manufactures Acts were in force.

Besides the distinction between Irish indigenous and foreign industry, some of the tables below also refer to a distinction between 'New' or 'New and Small' industry on the one hand, and 'Old' or the 'Rest of' industry on the other. New and Small industries are those which have received the grants payable since 1952 (in the Designated Areas) or 1956 (in other areas) for the establishment of new projects. The vast majority of foreign-owned projects established since that time (with over 90% of their employment) have received these grants so that foreign New and Small industry is virtually synonymous with foreign industries set up under outward-looking policies. It is necessary to use these categories in some tables because some of the data are available only for foreign and Irish New and Small industries and for all industry, not for all foreign and all Irish. This means that in many cases the closest available approximation to data on Irish indigenous industry is to subtract the figures for foreign 'New' or 'New and Small' from the total for all industry, leaving figures for Irish indigenous *plus* 'Old' foreign industry. While this is not fully satisfactory, the relatively small size of 'Old' foreign industry means that these data are still useful as indicators of the performance of indigenous industry, particularly if one concentrates on trends over time rather than absolute numbers. What these data do bring out most clearly is the extent to which industrial expansion has depended on new foreign projects.

Principal Trends in Indigenous Industry

Table 6.1 shows manufacturing employment in 1960, 1966 and 1973, distinguishing between New and Small foreign industry and the rest of industry.

Table 6.1: Manufacturing Employment in New and Small Foreign Industry and the Rest of Industry, 1960-73 (thousands)

	1960	1966	1973
New and Small Foreign	3	10	36
Rest of Industry	169	188	186
TOTAL	172	198	222

Source: Derived from *Trend in Employment and Unemployment, Survey of Grant-Aided Industry* (1967), *IDA Employment Survey*, as explained in appendix 1.

For a later period, 1973-87, it is possible to break down fully the figures for industrial employment into Irish indigenous and foreign components, as is done in table 6.2.[2] The trends outlined in table 6.2 are charted in figure 6.1 for greater clarity.

Table 6.2: Manufacturing Employment in Foreign Industry and Irish Indigenous Industry, 1973-87 (thousands)

	1973	1975	1977	1979	1981	1983	1985	1987
Irish Indigenous	149	154	147	152	148	132	122	114
Foreign	66	71	76	84	91	84	81	80
TOTAL	215	226	222	236	239	216	203	193

Source: IDA Employment Survey.
Notes: Guinness brewery has been included as Irish indigenous rather than foreign here. Some totals may not add due to rounding. Data for 1973 to 1981 are from surveys done in January, whereas those for 1983 to 1987 are from surveys done in November.

Apart from the recession of 1974-76, total manufacturing employment showed quite a strong growth trend from 1960 to 1980, although it later fell rapidly in the 1980s. In industries other than New and Small Foreign industry, however, the experience was rather different. Table 6.1 shows that employment in these industries grew by almost 20,000 in 1960-66 while protection still remained, but showed no further growth in 1966-73. Similarly in 1973-80, indigenous industry, which accounts for the bulk of industries other than New Foreign ones, experienced little employment growth — with an increase of under 7,000 compared with 24,000 in foreign firms.[3] The decline in employment in 1980-87 occurred mainly in indigenous firms, which lost 42,000 jobs (27% of their 1980 employment), although the decline of 10,000 jobs (11% of 1980 employment) in the foreign sector was also quite severe. It is very likely that by 1985 indigenous industrial employment was below its 1960 level. Indeed, since manufacturing employment scarcely grew at all in the 1950s, the level of employment in indigenous industry by 1985 was probably lower than at any time since the 1940s.

Data on industrial output distinguishing between foreign and Irish firms are scarcer than those on employment but some estimates are shown in table 6.3.

Table 6.3: Gross Output of Foreign New Industry and the Rest of Industry, Selected Years 1960-85, £ million, Current Prices

	1960	1966	1973	1976	1985
New Foreign	10	35	306	858	5,763
The Rest	424	661	1,619	3,144	8,672
All Industry	434	696	1,925	4,002	14,435

Source: Derived from *Census of Industrial Production, Survey of Grant-Aided Industry* (1967), *O'Loughlin* (1978), and *McAleese* (1977), as explained in appendix 1.

Table 6.3 is in current prices. To express the data in constant prices it is necessary to use the deflator for all manufacturing which is implicit in the official indices of volume of gross output, i.e. it is assumed that the same deflator applies for both categories in the table (which may not be quite the case, so some margin of error exists). Table 6.4 is derived in this way.

Figure 6.1: Manufacturing Employment (Thousands), 1973-87

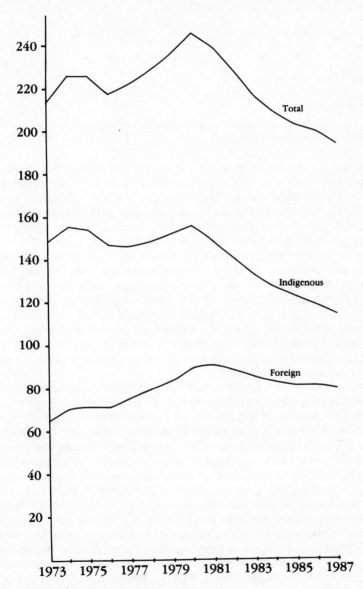

Source: IDA Employment Survey.

Table 6.4: Estimated Gross Output of Foreign New Industry and the Rest of Industry, 1960-85, £ million, Constant Prices

	1960	1966	1973	1976	1985
New Foreign	10	31	157	222	677
The Rest	424	582	831	814	1,020
All Industry	434	613	988	1,036	1,697

Source: as explained in the text.

It can be estimated from table 6.4 that the average annual real growth rates for 1960-85 were about 5.6% for all industry, 18.4% for New Foreign and 3.6% for the rest. Although New Foreign industry still accounted for just 40% of total gross output by 1985, it had accounted for about 60% of real growth in 1966-85 and about 69% in 1976-85.[4] The figure of 3.6% growth p.a. for all industries except New Foreign industry would represent a distinct improvement over the 1950s, but this fact alone does not necessarily indicate a good performance. For much of this improvement after the 1950s could be due simply to stronger growth of domestic demand. It was possible for domestic demand to grow faster when the balance of payments constraint was relaxed, and the easing of this constraint apparently owed little to the contribution of indigenous industry itself.

To assess the performance of industries other than New Foreign industry, a useful criterion is to compare the growth of their output with the growth of demand. Their output in fact grew more slowly than demand, as indicated by their declining share of the home market while their exports remained of lesser importance and were also rather unimpressive. Information on their declining position in the home market comes from statistics on the growing share of 'competing' manufactured imports. (The classification of imports as 'competing' with domestic producers was done by the Department of Industry and Commerce in consultation with business interests, and official data on such 'competing' imports used to be published regularly. Because there is an element of subjective judgement in making this classification, the data should not be regarded as precise.) Since New Foreign industries have always been very highly export oriented, the effects of any increase in 'competing' imports are felt almost exclusively by other industries.[5]

The data on 'competing' imports are contained in three different series for three different periods, rather than one continuous series, and these three series involve somewhat different classifications (see appendix 1 for sources). In order to illustrate clearly the trends over time, however, the three series have been joined together in figure 6.2 which shows the increase in the share of 'competing' imports in the home market.[6] 'Competing' imports' share of home consumption grew slowly and erratically from 1960 to 1967, gaining only an extra 0.2% of the market per annum, on average.[7] But after that their share of the market grew continuously and at a faster rate — with an average annual gain of 1.5% in 1967-73, 0.6% in 1973-77 and 2% in 1977-79. While one should not place great confidence in the precision of these figures, it is clear at least that import penetration increased markedly and continuously after 1967. The timing of this increase is not surprising in view of the first small steps that were taken to reduce protection unilaterally in 1963 and 1964, followed by the start of the implementation of the Anglo-Irish Free Trade Agreement in 1966. The sustained increase in import penetration after 1967 meant that the sales of industry other than New Foreign industry to the home market were enabled to grow only because of strong market growth up to 1973, while their relative position declined. The interruption of market growth in the 1974-76 recession led to a decline in output for these industries (table 6.4), as well as a decline in employment — an experience repeated with greater severity in the years after 1980. The poor record of indigenous employment is thus partly a reflection of the continuous erosion of market shares.

Part of the problem for indigenous industries, too, was that they not only lost domestic market shares for goods which they did produce, but also that they seem to have been largely confined to producing goods for which domestic demand grew relatively slowly. Thus domestic demand for goods produced by Irish industry (defined as industrial gross output minus exports plus 'competing' imports) grew by 13.7% per annum, in current values, in 1967-73. But in the same period, domestic demand for *all* manufactured goods (defined as industrial gross output minus exports plus *all* manufactured imports) grew by 15.1% per annum.

Figure 6.2: Competing Imports' Share of Home Consumption

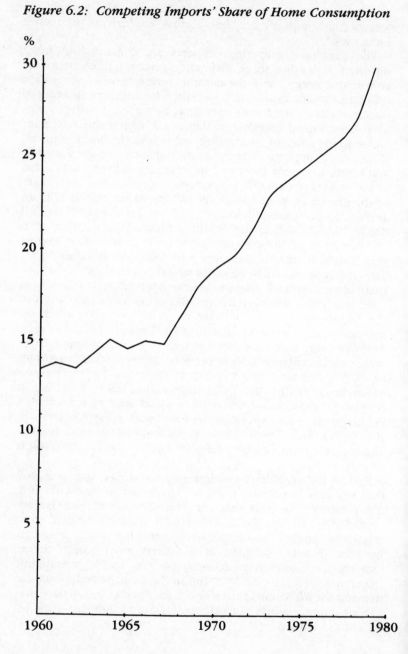

It might be felt, of course, that some loss of home market shares was only to be expected under freer trade, but that the accompanying gain in export market shares would compensate (or more than compensate) for this. In fact, however, Irish industries other than New Foreign industry showed little overall gain in export market shares. Table 6.5 presents some estimates of exports, distinguishing between New Foreign and the Rest of Industry.

Table 6.5: Exports of New Foreign Industry and the Rest of Industry, 1960-76, £ million, Current Prices

	1960	1966	1973	1976
Total Manufactured Exports	84	154	684	1,581
New Foreign Industry	9	31	268	743
Rest of Industry	75	123	416	838
Exports of 'Rest of Industry' as % of their Gross Output	18%	19%	26%	27%

Sources: Various sources, as explained in appendix 1. The figures in this table (except for 1973) involve some estimation and should not be regarded as exact, though it is most unlikely that they seriously misrepresent the facts.

New Foreign firms obviously played a major part in the overall growth of exports. They accounted for only about 10% of manufactured exports in 1960, rising to about 47% by 1976. These proportions are considerably greater if Food is excluded. For example, in 1966 New Foreign industry accounted for about 19% of all manufactured exports but 36% of non-Food manufactured exports, rising to 39% and 53% respectively by 1973. By 1976 they probably accounted for something over 60% of non-Food manufactured exports. Using more recent survey data, the Telesis Report (1982, exhibit 3.2) finds that foreign firms (New *and* Old) accounted for about 70% of manufactured exports by 1979.

Despite this dominance of New Foreign industry in export growth, the last row of table 6.5 might appear at first sight to point to a reasonably strong export performance in the rest of industry too, since the proportion of their output going for export rose quite noticeably after 1966. However, this was mainly a reflection of relatively slow growth of sales on the home market, due to a declining home market share and to slower growth of home than foreign demand. These factors, rather than a rising share of export markets, explain the rise in the export-gross output ratio of the 'Rest of Industry'. The exports of these industries amounted to 0.26% of manufactured exports of all developed market economies in 1966 and just the same percentage in 1976, showing no overall gain.

As an indication of more recent developments, Foley (1987) estimates that Irish indigenous industry exported about 31% of its output in 1984. This is not precisely comparable with the data in table 6.5 for the 'Rest of Industry', which includes some old foreign firms. But since indigenous industry accounts for a large majority of this group, it does suggest that there was no major change in the export propensity of indigenous firms between 1976 and 1984 although there probably was some increase. If we accept Foley's figure of 31% of output of Irish indigenous firms being exported in 1984 as reasonably representative of all industry other than New Foreign industry, this allows us to estimate the exports of industry other than New Foreign industry at about £2,800 million in 1984 (using output data for this group of industries from the CIP 1984). This would amount to 0.29% of manufactured exports of all developed market economies in 1984, which represents a modest increase over the figure of 0.26% in 1966 and 1976.

This gain in export market share between 1966 and 1984 meant that exports of industries other than New Foreign industry were about 11.5% higher by 1984 than they would have been with a constant market share. Or, since their exports were about 31% of their sales, the gain in export market share accounted for about 3.6% of their total sales by 1984. On the other hand, the rising domestic market share of competing imports had already cost them about 15% of the home market between 1966 and 1979, which was equivalent to about 15% of their total sales. Thus, even allowing for a considerable margin of error in these estimates, the sales lost due to their falling share of the home market greatly outweighed the sales gained by their rising share of export markets.

It might be suggested, as was noted earlier with respect to sales in the domestic market, that the exports of Irish indigenous industry suffered from being concentrated in products for which demand grew relatively slowly. If so, their export market share performance in their own particular sectors might be rather stronger than it appears from the aggregate market share. Although the data are inadequate to investigate this fully, there appears to be some truth in this in the sense that Food, for which demand generally grows relatively slowly, has been the dominant component of indigenous industry's exports.[8] And Irish Food exports, which come very largely from indigenous firms, substantially increased their share of UK Food imports from 3.6% to 9.1%, and their share of the rest of the OECD's Food imports from 0.3% to 0.8%, between 1966 and 1978. This strong market share peformance by Food exports would be consistent with the suggestions made about the constraints on indigenous industrial development by latecomers in section 2.ii. For it was mentioned there that basic processing of local primary resources would be one type in a limited range of industries which could be relatively easily developed by them, and most Irish indigenous Food exports involve only very low value-added, basic processing, as will be seen below in section 6.ii. Since there was a strong market share performance by Food exports, but not by total indigenous manufactured exports, there probably was not a strong export market share performance by most other branches of indigenous industry.

It may be concluded, therefore, that (apart from Food) industries other than New Foreign industry did not show a strong improvement in their ability to compete in export markets, in terms of gaining larger export market shares. The substantial improvement in this regard seen earlier in tables 5.4 and 5.5 was, therefore, an effect of the growth of export-oriented New Foreign industry.

To conclude this section, the greatly improved overall performance of industry in Ireland in the 1960s and 1970s was very largely due to the inflow of new export-oriented foreign industries. It owed little to the development of indigenous industry. What occurred was essentially the successful development of Ireland as a site for mobile foreign investment. Industries other than new foreign ones have had a decline in employment since the mid-1960s, declining shares of the home market and (apart from Food) little increase in their shares of foreign markets. These trends are consistent with the view that the indigenous industry of a late-industrialising country faces great difficulties in breaking into open international competition, or even maintaining a position built up under protection once freer trade is introduced.

The remainder of this chapter examines the performance of

indigenous industry in more detail. To do this, use is made of various data broken down by industrial sector in section 6.ii, and section 6.iii examines the largest indigenous manufacturing firms. The main objective of this more detailed review of the experience of indigenous industry is to assess the validity of the 'alternative' view put forward in section 2.ii. It was suggested there that the indigenous industry of latecomers relying on the conventional strategy would tend to be excluded from internationally traded sectors with significant barriers to entry, although able to operate in the limited range of other sectors, especially sheltered non-traded activities and limited processing of local primary resources.

6.ii. SECTORAL TRENDS IN INDIGENOUS INDUSTRY

The Impact of Free Trade — 1960s and 1970s

There was considerable variation in the impact of import penetration since the mid-1960s on different sectors of indigenous industry. Table 6.6 shows the increase in import penetration, by sector, together with the change in employment in indigenous firms which had been set up before 1973. In this table the sectors are ranked so that those which suffered least import penetration are at the top while those with the greatest increases in competing imports are at the bottom. There was evidently a close relationship between the extent of increased import competition and employment decline in companies already existing as the free trade policy was coming into effect. For it can be seen in table 6.6 that sectors which resisted import penetration relatively well tended to have the strongest employment performance in established firms, while those hit most by competing imports showed the greatest decline in employment.

Table 6.6 shows an above average performance on both indicators for Clay, Glass & Cement, Drink & Tobacco and Food, with Paper & Printing also looking relatively strong. In contrast, Clothing & Footwear, Textiles and Chemicals stand out as the weakest sectors. However, if one looks at changes in *total* employment, taking into account new firms starting up under free trade conditions after 1973, there are some differences. In table 6.7, which shows total employment by sector, Textiles, Clothing & Footwear and Chemicals again stand out as the weakest sectors. And Clay, Glass & Cement, Paper & Printing, Food and Drink & Tobacco still look fairly strong since they all have positive employment growth. But Metals & Engineering in particular, and Wood & Furniture and Other Manufacturing to a lesser extent, now appear stronger than in table 6.6 since the establishment of many new firms after 1973 gave these sectors overall employment growth as well.

Table 6.6: Import Penetration and Employment Change in Established Indigenous Firms, by Sector

	Increase in in Competing Imports' Market Share, 1967-79 (% p.a.)	Employment Change (%), 1973-80, in Firms Established before 1973
Clay, Glass & Cement	0.2	6.5
Drink & Tobacco	0.3	1.1
Food	0.5	—2.1
Paper & Printing	1.4	—2.0
Other Manufacturing	1.4	—14.2
Wood & Furniture	2.0	—16.0
Metals & Engineering	2.3	—8.7
Chemicals	2.3	—27.1
Textiles	2.8	—39.9
Clothing & Footwear	4.6	—36.3
TOTAL	1.2	—12.8

Sources: Competing imports are derived from the annual *Review and Outlook* for 1960-73, *Trade Statistics of Ireland* for 1973-77, Department of Industry, Commerce and Tourism for 1977-79, as explained in appendix 1. Employment data are from the *IDA Employment Survey*.

Notes: Column 1 shows the average gain per annum in competing imports' percentage share of the Irish market; e.g. an increase from a 20% market share for competing imports to 44% twelve years later would appear in column 1 as a 2% gain per annum. Column 2 shows the percentage change in employment in firms already existing in 1973, leaving out new companies established after that date.

Table 6.7: Employment, by Sector, in Indigenous Industry (thousands), 1973-80

	1973	1980	Per-centage Change
Metals & Engineering	22.3	27.6	23.9
Clay, Glass & Cement	13.6	15.8	16.4
Paper & Printing	13.4	15.6	16.0
Wood & Furniture	9.6	10.3	6.8
Other Manufacturing	8.7	9.1	5.2
Food	40.0	42.0	4.9
Drink & Tobacco	9.4	9.5	1.6
Chemicals	5.2	4.8	—9.1
Clothing & Footwear	21.2	16.0	—24.6
Textiles	16.3	10.8	—33.4
TOTAL	159.6	161.4	1.1

Source: IDA Employment Survey.
Notes: Guinness brewery is included here as indigenous. The totals here differ from table 6.2 because the classification system used in this table, and in table 6.6, is the Standard Industrial Classification (SIC) system, which is comparable with the competing imports data. In table 6.2, however, the EEC's NACE system is used.

To fill out the picture a little further, trends in exports by sector can be examined, although the available data on this are unfortunately rather limited. The data on exports refer not to Irish indigenous industry alone, but to all industries except New Foreign industry — i.e. they include 'old' foreign firms and a small group of new foreign 'Small' industries. Table 6.8 shows estimates for 1960 and 1973.

A notable feature of the estimates in table 6.8 is the very large share of the exports of these industries held by the Food sector, accounting for 53% in both years and undoubtedly an even higher proportion of foreign exchange earnings due to its low import content. With relatively low import penetration and quite a high export-orientation, the Food sector has shown the greatest ability to compete internationally. Two of the other three sectors which emerged earlier as being relatively strongly resistant to competing imports, viz. Paper & Printing and Clay, Glass & Cement, exported low proportions of output, by contrast, below average in both years and apparently declining. Although Drink & Tobacco cannot be shown separately in the table, it is clear enough that it too exported rather little.[9] Thus, unlike Food, the competitive strength of these three sectors appears to be largely confined to the domestic market. Metals & Engineering which showed particularly rapid employment growth, also had low exports. Since import penetration in this sector was well above average, it seems that its growth was largely due to rapid growth of domestic demand, which was sufficient to allow it to expand despite falling market shares at home and little or no increase in export orientation.

Table 6.8: Estimated Exports of Industries Other Than New Foreign Industry, 1960 and 1973

	1960 Exports (£m.)	1973 Exports (£m.)	Exports as % of Gross Output 1960	Exports as % of Gross Output 1973
Food	44.9	224.8	28	35
Textiles	4.8	46.4	12	35
Other/Drink & Tobacco	16.0	67.9	18	25
Chemicals	0.9	16.9	5	21
Clothing & Footwear	4.4	9.2	18	16
Clay, Glass & Cement	1.6	10.3	16	15
Metals & Engineering	7.1	28.8	12	13
Paper & Printing	3.9	11.6	16	13
Wood & Furniture	0.6	4.9	7	11
TOTAL	84.2	420.3	19	26

Sources: Trade Statistics of Ireland, the *Census of Industrial Production*, and McAleese (1977), as explained in appendix 1.
Note: Figures for 1960 refer to *all* industry (except those at Shannon) and thus include a small number of New Foreign firms.

As well as Food, Textiles and Chemicals also showed a marked increase in export-orientation. In the case of Chemicals, however, this is likely to be mainly an effect of the behaviour of the 'old' foreign firms included here, rather than of indigenous industry. The 'old' foreign firms account for a large share of this sector, one-third of its employment in Irish and old foreign firms combined. Furthermore, among Irish indigenous firms in the sector, the largest ones, which would be most likely to engage in exporting significantly, were mostly producers of fertilisers; almost two-thirds of employment in indigenous Chemical firms with over 100 employees in 1973 was accounted for by fertiliser producers. The fact that fertiliser exports in 1973 were only £2 million, compared with £17 million for Chemicals in table 6.8, suggests that Irish indigenous firms probably did not play a very large part in this export growth. In Textiles, however, it seems that indigenous firms did increase their export-orientation considerably, behaving as the conventional theory would have predicted. But, contrary to the predictions of that theory, the expansion of exports was far from sufficient to compensate for major losses in the home market, resulting in sharp employment decline in indigenous Textiles.

Explanation of the Trends
To move on to some discussion of how the trends outlined in this section so far might be explained, they would appear to be generally consistent with the theoretical discussion in section 2.ii. According to the 'alternative' view put forward there, the indigenous industry of latecomers adopting the conventional strategy would tend to experience great difficulty in competing successfully in internationally traded activities with substantial barriers to entry. But they could operate more easily in a limited range of other activities — sheltered or non-traded industries, basic processing of local primary products, and 'easily entered' traded activities with low entry barriers. It was suggested, too, that confinement to this range of activities would result in persistent unemployment, since continuing diversification or 'upgrading' of the industrial structure would generally be required to provide sufficient employment. In Ireland unemployment and/or emigration have, in fact, continuously been symptoms of a failure to mobilise productive resources fully, so the question is whether the suggested constraints on latecomers explain this failure. This view would be supported if

the varying experiences of the different industrial sectors have been consistent with the suggestions made about the type of sectors which are most open or closed to latecomers.

It must be remembered, too, that Ireland introduced outward-looking policies after a period of sustained protection, during which some industries had developed, producing for the protected home market, in activities with quite substantial entry barriers. The 'alternative' view, stressing the constraints on latecomers, would suggest that, following the introduction of outward-looking policies, many of such industries would be overwhelmed by competition from more advanced countries, unlike the non-traded or basic processing industries. A further possibility mentioned in chapter 2 is that even some of the 'easily entered' traded industries with low entry barriers would also tend to be undermined in conditions of free trade, by new low-wage countries entering the market.

It can be shown that in general the strongest performances in indigenous industry occurred in activities which are *not* subject to the constraints imposed on latecomers by barriers to entry. The three main categories of such activities are (a) low value-added processing of local primary products, (b) the few exceptional industries which are very long established in Ireland and therefore have not had to overcome entry barriers *as newcomers*, and (c) virtually 'non-traded' industries which enjoy a degree of natural protection in local markets.

Thus the indigenous Food sector, which fared relatively well, consists quite largely of low value-added basic processing of local primary products. Although data on output and value-added were not available until quite recently for indigenous as distinct from foreign firms in the industry, over 80% of employment in the Food sector as a whole is in Irish-owned companies so that data for the whole sector are of some use as indicators of the nature of indigenous Food enterprises. In 1973, value-added to materials in this sector was exceptionally low at 21% of gross output rising only slightly to 23.4% in 1985. By comparison, value-added in non-Food manufacturing was 44% in 1973. The CIP for 1985 distinguishes indigenous from foreign firms and reports that value-added was just 17.7% of gross output in the indigenous branch of the Food industry.

Low value-added basic processing activities, which use locally supplied inputs, have an important natural competitive advantage which makes them relatively easy for latecomers to develop. This is because transport or logistical costs would generally be large in relation to value-added, even if they represent only a small fraction of the value of final output. If, for example, logistical costs for imports amount to 5% of a product's value, and the value-added to materials in processing the product is low at say 10%, then logistical costs for imports would represent 50% of value-added. This means that a local producer with a ready supply of inputs can run a processing operation for the domestic market competitively even if its processing costs are up to 50% higher than for foreign competitors.[10]

Even in the case of low value-added processing for export, there is a strong competitive advantage for processors which are close to a source of material inputs, so long as transport costs for the final product are significantly less than for the raw material. And this is frequently the case if the inputs are bulky or perishable compared with the final product — e.g. milk, live animals or felled trees as compared with butter, meat or sawn timber. Thus it is no accident that the branches of the Irish Food industry with lowest value-added — meat-processing and dairy products — have accounted for most of indigenous Food exports.

The indigenous Drink & Tobacco sector also fared relatively well in the transition to free trade, at least in resisting import penetration and maintaining employment, although there was no significant increase in export-orientation. The main explanation for this sector's relatively strong competitive performance is probably that the bulk of its output is produced by a few large, long-established firms which survived the general decline of the nineteenth century. The very long-established position of these big companies — notably Guinness, Carroll Industries and Irish Distillers — is quite exceptional in Ireland since the newest of them, Carroll's, was founded in 1824. This means that they have not had to overcome, *as newcomers*, the entry barriers arising from economies of scale, product differentiation and capital requirements which are now quite substantial in their main activities of brewing, tobacco products and distilling.

Because successful Irish indigenous involvement in such industries with significant entry barriers is largely due to these very long-established firms, they are exceptions which in a sense underline the general rule that newcomers cannot easily compete in this type of activity. But even for such large established companies, product differentiation or marketing probably pose significant entry barriers in new export markets, so that there was little sign of a major increase in export-orientation during the transition to free trade.

The relatively strong performance of a number of other branches of indigenous industry can be largely explained by the fact that they are naturally protected or virtually non-traded industries.[11] Such industries can be protected in two different ways. First, there may be natural protection from import competition due to transport costs for products with a low value in relation to their weight, as in most building materials for example. And second, there may be protection against imports due to the need for flexibility of response to local demand, for local knowledge and close contact with customers, as in much of Printing & Packaging.

The quite strong performance of the indigenous Clay, Glass & Cement sector can be largely understood as the performance of a virtually non-traded industry. Competing imports in this sector scarcely increased their market share since the beginning of freer trade in the mid-1960s, while *at the same time* the sector exported a small proportion of its output, showing little or no sign of increasing its export-orientation. Such dominance of the local market combined with such low exports are the hallmarks of a non-traded industry. Within Clay, Glass & Cement, however, some activities fit this description better than others. Although more detailed data are not available for Irish as distinct from foreign firms, the data for the whole sector give a useful indication of the nature of Irish indigenous activities since Irish firms account for most of its employment (91.4% in 1980). The sector is broken down into two parts, of which 'Glass and Glassware, Pottery, China and Earthenware' is more highly traded than 'Structural Clay Products, Asbestos, Plaster, Gypsum etc. and Cement'. In 1965-73 only 5.5% of the increase in domestic demand for Structural Clay etc. was met by competing imports, compared with 86% in Glass etc. (Blackwell, Danaher and O'Malley, 1983, table 6.1). Structural Clay etc. was thus the more resistant of the two to competing imports, but at the same time the much lower proportion of its output going for export — at 10% in 1973 compared with 51% for Glass etc. — identifies it as an essentially non-traded industry.[12] Structural Clay etc. (which is mostly building materials) would be sheltered due to transport costs for heavy products of low value, though parts of Glass etc., such as glass bottles, are probably comparable. Structural Clay etc. is also the larger of the two, with 77% of the whole sector's gross output in 1973, while the foreign firms in the sector seem to be mostly concentrated in Glass etc., to judge by company names in the *IDA Employment Survey.*

While most indigenous activities in Clay, Glass & Cement could thus be regarded as sheltered, and consequently not subject to the general constraints on latecomers, one of the largest Irish indigenous firms is involved in production of high quality glassware, largely for export. This firm, Waterford Glass, is clearly not sheltered, but it has had certain special advantages (see section 6.iii). In contrast, an even larger firm in the Structural Clay etc. branch, Cement Roadstone, exemplifies the predominantly sheltered nature of its sector by its dominance of the domestic market combined with a very low export-orientation (see section 6.iii).

Paper & Printing is also quite sheltered, though it too contains some activities which are not. As in Clay, Glass & Cement, employment in this sector is very largely in indigenous firms (90.2% in 1980), so that statistics for the sector as a whole are a useful indication of indigenous activities. The Standard Industrial Classification breaks this sector down into 'Paper & Paper Products' and 'Printing, Publishing & Allied Trades'. The Printing & Publishing branch was more resistant to competing imports, since only 21% of the increase in home demand in 1965-73 in Printing & Publishing was met by competing imports, compared with 44% in Paper & Paper Products. At the same time, Printing & Publishing exported only 14% of its output in 1973, compared with 21% for Paper & Paper Products. So Printing & Publishing appears to be largely non-traded while this is not so much the case in the other branch. Printing & Publishing would probably be sheltered mainly by the importance of local knowledge, close local contacts and the need for flexibility of response to local demand, since the bulk of its output is newspapers, magazines, and job and general printing. Paper & Paper Products also contains some quite sheltered activities, especially in packaging, but the manufacture of paper itself is a large-scale activity without comparable natural protection, and it has declined to the point of virtual extinction in Ireland under free trade.

The general experience of this sector, then, shows Irish industry prospering in relatively sheltered areas, and being squeezed out of traded activities characterised by significant economies of scale in advanced countries. The largest Irish indigenous firm, the Smurfit Group, is involved mainly in Printing & Packaging, and its dominance of the home market combined with a very low export-orientation exemplifies the sheltered, non-traded nature of much of indigenous industry in this sector (see section 6.iii).

Virtually non-traded industries which fared quite well are also found among the *small-scale* firms in Metals & Engineering, Wood & Furniture and Other Manufacturing. Small non-traded activities in these sectors include, for example, carpentry workshops, simple metal fabrication, structural steel, some plastic moulding and tyre remoulds. These would be naturally protected by transport costs and/or the advantages of proximity to the market for activities in which frequent local contact and flexibility of response is important. Due to the combination of internationally traded and non-traded activities in each of these three sectors, their rate of import penetration and job loss was in the intermediate range in table 6.6.

As a result of rising import penetration, employment declined quite markedly in firms set up before 1973 in Metals & Engineering, Wood & Furniture and 'Other' Manufacturing. Yet total employment growth in these three sectors was relatively strong, especially in Metals & Engineering, since a good deal of employment was generated in *new* firms set up after the early 1970s. These trends were due, first, to the rapid decline of a number of relatively *large* firms in internationally tradeable activities, which had been previously established behind protectionist barriers. And, second, this was combined with rapid growth of the *small-scale* non-traded activities, mainly through the establishment of many new small firms, in response to growing domestic demand for their products. (See Kennedy and Healy, 1985, for a detailed review of small-scale industry in Ireland.)

Table 6.9 shows that employment decline among firms aleady set up before 1973 was most makred in the larger-size categories, while growth occurred only in the smallest (mainly non-traded) category. Similarly, the establishment of many new firms after 1973 in these sectors was even more concentrated in the relatively small-size categories; of the 11,100 jobs existing in 1980 in such new firms, none were in establishments employing over 500 people, and less than 10% were in plants employing over 200. In total, employment in establishments with over 200 workers fell by 30% in 1973-80 in these three sectors, while it grew by 32% in smaller establishments.

Table 6.9: Employment by Plant Size, in Irish Indigenous Metals & Engineering, Wood & Furniture and Other Manufacturing

Employment Size	Plants Established Before 1973		
	1973	1980	% Change
Over 500	2,263	923	−59.2
201-500	7,351	4,772	−35.1
101-200	8,226	7,615	−7.4
51-100	5,584	5,102	−8.6
Under 50	17,155	17,451	+ 1.7
	40,579	35,863	−11.6

Source: Derived from *IDA Employment Survey.*

Generally, the larger firms would have been involved in activities with significant economies of scale, as indicated by their own relatively large size by Irish standards. For example, relatively large Irish companies were involved in making or assembling vehicles, telecommunications equipment, agricultural machinery, radios and televisions. As was seen in table 2.1, such industries tend to be characterised by very substantial economies of scale in advanced countries such as the USA. So the Irish firms, although large by Irish standards, would probably have been too small and/or too weak in marketing and technology to survive in open international competition following the introduction of freer trade.[13]

There are a number of strong indications that the small firms in Metals & Engineering, Wood & Furniture and Other Manufacturing, by contrast, were generally in non-traded activities. Thus despite their rapid growth in employment, which suggests they were thriving, table 6.8 showed little indication of strong export development in these sectors up to the early 1970s. Furthermore, the Telesis Report (1982) found that over 600 new, mainly small firms were established since 1967 in Metals & Engineering, but their total exports by 1979 were only £11 million — about 2% of all indigenous manufacturing exports. Only two of these firms exported a significant amount (over £1 million worth in 1980). Their growth, Telesis suggests, was largely linked to the Irish agricultural and construction booms of the 1970s, since many of these small firms supplied equipment and materials to these sectors in a limited local area. Thus, of the 60 firms making agricultural machinery and equipment, for example, only three exported anything beyond Northern Ireland. Telesis also reported that not one exporter had evolved out of supplying inputs to New Foreign Industry.

Textiles, Clothing & Footwear and Chemicals emerged earlier as the three sectors showing the severest signs of decline and the greatest rates of increase in import penetration, among indigenous industries. In Textiles and Clothing & Footwear, there are activities in which barriers to entry for latecomers are not particularly great, as evidenced by the success of many NICs in developing these industries. Consequently, it is not surprising to find among Irish indigenous industries quite a number of firms in these sectors which export substantially. This is true of the Textiles sector generally, as was shown in table 6.8, and also of the largest Irish Clothing firms. The particularly rapid growth of competing imports in these sectors, therefore, could not simply be put down to Irish firms having virtually no hope of competing internationally. Rather it should be seen more as an effect of the general increase in import penetration under freer trade, which looks particularly severe in these two sectors because they contain little or no sheltered activities — unlike other sectors of indigenous industry. In other words, their experience with competing imports is probably more a reflection of the experience of the internationally traded sections of indigenous industry generally, rather than something which is peculiar to these two sectors.

Competitive production in these two sectors, particularly in Textiles, often depends on developing fairly long runs of production, so that economies of scale do exist. But an efficient scale is often not so great as to be unattainable by Irish firms, provided they specialise in areas of particular strength and manage to break into export markets, as some of them succeeded in doing. Those which failed to do so would have declined fairly quickly in the face of imports, while the specialisation in a narrower range of products required under freer trade would have opened the way for more imports. The adverse balance of competing imports and exports has been such as to lead to a substantial net decline in employment in these sectors. But the fact that the decline has been greatest here, in sectors with relatively low barriers to entry, need not cast doubt on the suggestion that the scale of barriers to entry is a major determinant of the opportunities available to latecomers. For an exceptional number of indigenous firms did in fact develop quite substantial exports, in unsheltered activities, in these sectors unlike most other sectors.

Another factor in the decline of these two sectors is the fact that they tend to be relatively easily entered and they are rather more labour-intensive than most, so that some activities suffered from competition from low-wage LDCs, to an extent which is difficult to determine precisely. According to the official trade statistics, imports from the less-developed countries accounted for only 6.8% of Textile imports and 8.8% of Clothing imports in 1979. But in some subdivisions of these sectors, the importance of imports from LDCs was far greater. In Textiles, in 1978, these accounted for 24% of cotton yarn imports and 19% of cotton fabrics; and in Clothing, imports from LDCs accounted for 75% of gloves, 73% of jerseys and cardigans, 55% of men's cotton trousers, 40% of women's cotton outerwear, and 26% of both knitted and cotton shirts (Fitzpatrick, 1981). It is possible, too, that competition from LDCs in export markets in Europe may be more serious than is suggested by the Irish import figures. And it is also possible, as is often claimed, that official statistics understate imports to Ireland from LDCs since they often pass through the UK or other European countries and may be recorded as originating there.

The indigenous Chemicals sector, which is very small, has also shown signs of significant decline. This is consistent with the fact that the Chemicals industry in advanced countries tends to be highly concentrated in large firms due to economies of scale in production, research and development and marketing, which creates high barriers to entry for latecomers in most important divisions. The decline in employment was listed as —9% in 1973-80 in table 6.7, but the sector contains one large state enterprise producing nitrogenous fertilisers, Nitrigin Eireann Teoranta (NET), which grew considerably. In view of this company's substantial losses, it would probably have closed or declined if it had not been heavily subsidised. Excluding NET, Irish indigenous Chemicals employment actually declined by 26% in 1973-80, which is greater than the figure of 25% in Clothing & Footwear. If NET is included for 1973, but excluded in 1980 on the grounds that it would probably have closed in the interval if subject to market forces, indigenous Chemicals employment would have declined by as much as 38% in 1973-80.

A further notable feature of structural change in indigenous industry was a general change in size structure. It was suggested in chapter 2 that one of the major factors creating barriers to entry for newcomers is the competitive advantage of large established firms in advanced countries arising from economies of scale. Consequently, in a small late-developing country returning to free trade after a period of protection, one would expect to observe a particularly marked decline in the largest indigenous manufacturing firms. For they would be engaged in activities characterised by significant economies of scale, but they would generally not be as large as competitors in advanced countries which would therefore have the advantage of superior economies of scale.

It was noted already, however, that some sectors have special advantages such as natural protection against foreign competition. For this reason they would be expected to show relatively little sign of such a decline due to superior foreign competition, while the more exposed sectors should show it most clearly. In table 6.10, the ten sectors are divided into a relatively sheltered group of four — Food, Drink & Tobacco, Paper & Printing and Clay, Glass & Cement — and a relatively exposed group consisting of the other six.

Table 6.10: Employment Change in 'Sheltered' and 'Exposed' Indigenous Industries Established Prior to 1973, by Establishment Size

Employment Size	'Sheltered'			'Exposed'		
	1973	1980	% Change	1973	1980	% Change
Over 500	19,421	18,564	−4.4	9,639	5,206	−46.0
201-500	17,733	16,552	−6.7	18,614	11,738	−36.9
101-200	10,061	10,582	+5.2	16,561	12,297	−25.7
51-100	10,097	10,459	+3.6	12,780	10,075	−21.2
Under 50	19,027	20,065	+5.5	25,703	23,662	−7.9
	76,339	76,222	−0.2	83,297	62,978	−24.4

Source: IDA Employment Survey.

The table shows that the overall decline in industries established before 1973 occurred primarily in the more 'exposed' sectors. It suggests, too, that there was some relationship between establishment size and adverse employment change in the more 'sheltered' sectors, but this relationship was relatively weak. In the more 'exposed' sectors, however, the relationship was clear-cut and much stronger. In fact, 55% of the whole employment decline in these established industries occurred in plants employing over 200 people in the 'exposed' sectors, although they accounted for less than 18% of indigenous employment in 1973.[14] As a result of this pattern of decline in large *established* plants, and the emergence of quite a large number of *new* small establishments, but few large ones in the 'exposed' sectors especially, the distribution of total employment by establishment size shifted noticeably from large to small establishments. This shift was not in evidence, however, in the 'sheltered' sectors, and was very marked in the 'exposed' ones (table 6.11).

Table 6.11: Percentage Distribution of Employment by Establishment Size in Indigenous Industry, 1973 and 1980

Employment Size	All Sectors		'Sheltered'		'Exposed'	
	1973	1980	1973	1980	1973	1980
Over 500	18.2	16.6	25.4	26.0	11.6	6.7
201-500	22.8	19.2	23.2	22.1	22.3	16.1
101-200	16.7	18.5	13.2	15.7	19.9	21.4
51-100	14.3	15.9	13.2	13.4	15.3	18.4
Under 50	28.0	29.9	24.9	22.8	30.9	37.3
	100.0	100.0	100.0	100.0	100.0	100.0

Source: IDA Employment Survey.

The growth of small industries which is reflected in this table appears to be mostly in sheltered activities (although there are exceptions), even in those sectors referred to here as 'exposed'. This finding of the Telesis study with respect to the particularly rapid growth of new small firms in Metals & Engineering was referred to above. In addition, table 6.12 shows the degree of export-orientation, by size category, of firms in Irish indigenous manufacturing. For example, the table shows that 29% of indigenous firms employing 31-40 people export nothing and a further 38% of firms of that size export under 25% of their output. It is clear that a majority of small firms with under 100 employees export little or nothing, suggesting that they tend to be local market-oriented and frequently engaged in sheltered or non-traded activities.

Table 6.12: Percentage Distribution of Indigenous Firms by Export Propensity and Size Category, 1984

Employment Size	Exports as % of Sales			
	0	0-25	25-50	Over 50
	Percentage of Firms			
Over 500	9	27	18	45
201-500	12	36	16	36
101-200	18	32	16	34
51-100	19	39	14	27
41-50	27	35	10	27
31-40	29	38	14	19

Source: Foley (1987), table 7.

Since Irish small industries could grow quite rapidly in the 1970s by selling mainly to the home market, while at the same time their export performance was below average, they must have had advantages in local markets which did not apply elsewhere. In other words, they must have been quite largely engaged in sheltered non-traded activities for which there was strong domestic demand.

The available evidence suggests, too, that few indigenous firms became involved in technologically demanding activities, so that one could conclude that they also had little success in overcoming technological barriers to entry. *Science and Irish Economic Development* (1966) reported its findings in the mid-1960s that 'industrial research is relatively non-existent' and much of what was done was 'plant and process adaptation development and barely merited the title research and development'.

Cooper and Whelan (1973) again pointed out that, in the early 1970s, expenditure on R & D in Ireland was close to the lowest among OECD countries, whether as a percentage of GNP or in terms of expenditure per capita. Furthermore, compared with other OECD countries, R & D expenditure in the industrial sector was a relatively low proportion of this relatively small total. And a large proportion of industrial R & D was concentrated in the Food and Drink industries, which are certainly not particularly technology-intensive industries elsewhere. So truly technology-intensive industries, which would require significant R & D expenditure, must have been very weak indeed. Cooper and Whelan also noted that R & D expenditure was highly concentrated in a small number of firms, so that most companies had little contact with R & D done in Ireland. Similar conclusions on the low level and the nature of Irish industrial R & D were reported at about the same time by the OECD (1974). For purposes of international comparison, Maguire (1979) finds that the R & D intensity of manufacturing (R & D as a percentage of output) in 1975 was only about one-quarter of the average for the EEC countries and one-sixth of that in the USA.

R & D expenditure is admittedly far from perfect as an indicator of trends in the development of technologically demanding industries, since advanced technology may be imported. But R & D expenditure is widely regarded as a necessary complement to the development of technologically advanced industries, even if the principal method of acquiring technology is through importing it from abroad. For the development of technologically demanding activities usually requires R & D expenditure on at least some technical adaptation and development of imported technology.[15] Consequently, it is safe to assume that persistently low R & D expenditure, starting from an initially low base, would be a fair indication that there has been little progress in developing technologically demanding industries.

In the period 1971-79, real R & D expenditure by all (i.e. Irish and foreign) business enterprises in Ireland increased by 3.7% p.a. (NBST statistics), which was less than the rate of growth of manufacturing output at 5.5% p.a. in the same period. This implies that there was some *reduction* in R & D intensity during the 1970s. Since many new, generally somewhat more R & D intensive foreign firms were established in Ireland during the 1970s, it seems reasonable to conclude that indigenous industry must have made little or no progress in shifting into technologically demanding activities. In 1979-84, however, real R & D expenditure increased by 12.8% p.a. while industrial output grew by just 4.1% p.a. This probably reflects some increase in R & D intensity in indigenous industry, but much of the increase would be due to foreign firms, which accounted for 67% of manufacturing R & D by 1984 although they had less than 40% of manufacturing employment. The indications are, then, that indigenous firms were very slow to become involved in industries where a strong technological capability is important for competitive success. And the extent of their involvement in such industries is still very limited.

To sum up this section so far, it appears that the constraints on late-developers arising from barriers to entry, as outlined in section 2.ii, are broadly consistent with the experience of Irish indigenous industry in the 1960s and 1970s. Little progress was made in developing technologically advanced industries or large internationally traded industries characterised by economies of scale, and indeed the latter category declined markedly after the removal of protection. Sheltered, virtually non-traded industries (many of them very small in scale) and basic processing of local primary products were the main sources of growth in indigenous industry, and neither of these are subject to the suggested constraints on latecomers. A small number of large indigenous firms were quite successfully engaged in traded activities with substantial entry barriers, however, but these are generally exceptional in being very long-established and hence do not refute the suggested difficulties for *newcomers* (these firms are referred to in more detail in the next section). It appears, too, that Irish industry experienced difficulties in some of the 'easily entered' traded sectors due to low-wage competition from NICs, which can also easily enter the same limited range of sectors.

It is worth stressing that many internationally traded indigenous industries were losing market shares since the mid-1960s and declining in terms of employment since the early 1970s, despite the fact that *overall* employment in indigenous industry held up fairly well until 1980. The growth of domestic demand led to growth in non-traded industries, which tended to conceal the decline in traded activities. This is important because it indicates that the sharp overall decline in indigenous industry which followed in the 1980s was not merely a temporary cyclical decline, from which recovery could be confidently expected. Rather, as is shown below, it represented *continuing long-term* decline in many traded activities, combined with a downturn in non-traded industries in conditions of weaker domestic demand.

Trends in the 1980s in Context

The most useful series of data on Irish indigenous industry in the 1980s relates to employment. The data concerned are classified according to the EEC's NACE system, following reclassification of the IDA's employment survey, rather than the SIC system. This means that they are comparable with other EEC countries and they are also more disaggregated than the SIC employment data used so far. Furthermore, since the IDA has reclassified all its employment survey data going back to 1973 according to NACE, there is a continuous disaggregated NACE employment series for indigenous industry covering the period 1973-87. This provides further insights on developments in Irish industry in the 1970s as well as in the 1980s. (But the NACE employment data are not comparable with the competing imports, exports or output figures referred to already in this chapter, which is the reason why SIC employment data have been used so far in examining developments in the 1970s.)

Table 6.13 compares the structure of employment in Irish indigenous industry at the end of the 1970s with the EEC countries, which may be taken as fairly representative of advanced industrial economies in general. Column 1 of table 6.13 shows the percentage of EEC manufacturing employment in each industry, and column 2 shows the percentage distribution in Irish indigenous industry.

The third column of table 6.13, by dividing column 2 by column 1, shows an index of relative concentration in each sector in Irish indigenous industry compared with the EEC. Thus an index greater than 1 means that the sector concerned accounted for a larger proportion of Irish indigenous manufacturing employment than of EEC manufacturing employment, and conversely for indices less than 1. Sectors are ranked in table 6.13 in order of this index. It should be pointed out that an index greater than 1 does *not* necessarily mean that the Irish industry is stronger, more developed or more competitive than in the EEC, in any absolute sense. For EEC industry as a whole is obviously more highly developed and more competitive than Irish indigenous industry, so the average Irish industry (with an index of 1) would actually be considerably weaker than its EEC

Table 6.13: Sectoral Distribution of Employment in Irish Indigenous and EEC Industry, 1978

NACE Code	Industry	(1) Employment (%) EEC	(2) Employment (%) Irish Indigenous	(3) Irish/EEC Relative Size (2) ÷ (1)
412-423	Food	6.9	28.4	4.1
44	Leather Products	.5	1.5	3.0
424-428	Drink	1.5	3.7	2.5
247	Glass, Glassware	1.1	2.8	2.5
241-246	Cement, Concrete	2.3	5.3	2.3
45	Footwear, Clothing	5.3	10.9	2.1
46	Wood, Furniture	3.6	7.0	1.9
47	Paper, Printing	5.7	9.7	1.7
429	Tobacco	.5	.7	1.4
49	Miscellaneous	1.1	1.1	1.0
43	Textiles	6.0	5.5	.9
31	Metal Articles	8.8	8.4	.9
48	Rubber, Plastics	4.0	1.9	.5
25	Chemicals	7.1	2.9	.4
36	Other Means of Transport	3.8	1.4	.4
34	Electrical Engineering	11.3	3.0	.3
35	Motor Vehicles	8.4	1.6	.2
32	Mechanical Engineering	10.9	2.6	.2
37	Instrument Engineering	1.6	.3	.2
22	Metals	6.3	1.0	.2
248	Ceramic Goods	1.1	.1	.1
33	Office & Data Processing Machinery	.8	.05	.1
26	Man-Made Fibres	.5	.02	.04
		100.0	100.0	100.0

Sources: Eurostat, *Structure and Activity of Industry 1978* (1983) for column 1. *IDA Employment Survey* for column 2. Column 3 is derived by dividing column 2 by column 1.
Notes: Totals do not add due to rounding. Some NACE industries have to be grouped in this table since the Eurostat sources are not fully disaggregated.

counterpart. For example, the index for Manufacture of Metal Articles (NACE 31) is .9, but Ireland would have to be regarded as quite weak by international comparison in this industry since its imports of products of the industry were more than double its exports in 1979. In general, the index would have to be considerably greater than 1 before one might consider the possibility that the Irish industry is more highly developed or more competitive than in the other EEC countries.

One could say with some confidence, however, that a *low* index in column 3 of table 6.13 means that the Irish industry was distinctly weak and undeveloped compared with advanced industrial economies, as represented by the EEC countries. A further purpose of the index is to indicate the *relative* strengths and weaknesses within Irish indigenous industry, compared with the standards established by advanced economies. Thus, for example, column 3 of table 6.13 provides an objective standard of international comparison to justify the statement that Irish indigenous industry was more developed in Food or Cement & Concrete Products than in Mechanical Engineering or Metals. Table 6.13 shows, therefore, that in the late 1970s Irish indigenous industry was relatively well developed in sectors ranked towards the top of the table — sectors such as Food, Drink, Clothing & Footwear, Leather Products, Cement & Concrete, Paper & Printing. It was weak and undeveloped in industries such as Metals, Motor Vehicles and Other Transport Equipment, Chemicals and Man-Made Fibres, and Electrical, Electronic, Mechanical and Instrument Engineering. By the late 1970s, therefore, native Irish industry still had the sort of structure associated more with LDCs than with advanced industrial economies.

The weakness of the advanced industries in the bottom half of table 6.13 would go a long way towards explaining the higher unemployment and lower incomes in Ireland than in the rest of the EEC. For the industries listed below Rubber & Plastics in the table, with an index of .5 or less, accounted for 56% of manufacturing employment in the EEC but only 15% in Irish indigenous industry. If Irish industry were to maintain about the same level of employment in its relatively strong sectors, and were to increase employment in its relatively weak sectors until they accounted for 56% of the total, as in the EEC, its total employment would double and (together with extra spin-off jobs in services), this would be sufficient to eliminate unemployment. And since the new industries would tend to have relatively high value-added and to be internationally traded, incomes would be a good deal higher with no balance of payments difficulties. Of course, such a scenario is too simplistic since it ignores inevitable secondary effects such as a possible loss of employment in some labour-intensive industries and a possible loss of new foreign investment requiring cheap labour. Nevertheless there remains the fundamental point that the weakness of Irish indigenous industry in sectors in the bottom half of table 6.13 is a major part of the explanation of Ireland's overall economic weakness relative to advanced industrial countries.

The low level of development of Irish industry in these advanced sectors can mostly be explained by the entry barriers for newcomers which characterise such activities. To take economies of scale alone, which is a widespread source of barriers to entry, it can be shown that the sectors in which native Irish industry is least developed tend to have significant economies of scale in advanced countries. This would make it difficult for latecomers, such as native Irish firms, to compete successfully. Table 6.14 ranks sectors according to the percentage of employment in each industry in the United Kingdom which is in large establishments employing over 500 people. This is presented as an indicator of the relative importance of economies of scale in each industry in advanced industrial countries. (The UK is chosen for comparison here both because it is Ireland's main trading partner, with which many Irish firms must compete, and because the overall degree of concentration in large establishments in the UK is about average for EEC countries, so it is fairly representative in this respect.) The second column of the table shows the same index of relative concentration in Irish indigenous industries compared with the EEC that was used in table 6.13, column 3. Thus this index shows which industries are most and least developed by Irish firms.

It can be seen that, for the most part, industries characterised by significant economies of scale in the UK are those in which Irish firms are particularly weak, whereas Irish companies have developed the smaller-scale industries to a much greater degree. This suggests that entry barriers arising from economies of scale in established competitors is a major cause of the underdevelopment of Irish industry. The most extreme exception to this general pattern is Tobacco, which is very highly concentrated in large establishments in the UK (and in

Table 6.14: Industrial Concentration, by Sector, and Relative Strength of Irish Indigenous Industry, 1978

NACE Code	Industry	% of UK Employment in Large Establishments*	Irish/EEC Relative Size Index
429	Tobacco	88 +	1.4
26	Man-Made Fibres	84.1	.04
36	Other Means of Transport	82.6	.4
35	Motor Vehicles	80.3	.2
22	Metals	65.3	.2
34	Electrical Engineering	56.8	.3
33	Office & Data Processing Machinery	55.6	.1
247	Glass, Glassware	54.4	2.5
25	Chemicals	48.4	.4
424-428	Drink	47.8	2.5
248	Ceramic Goods	46.1	.1
48	Rubber, Plastics	39.7	.5
412-423	Food	39.1	4.1
37	Instrument Engineering	38.8	.2
32	Mechanical Engineering	37.2	.2
47	Paper, Printing	32.5	1.7
31	Metal Articles	28.5	.9
49	Miscellaneous	22.2	1.0
43	Textiles	21.8	.9
241-246	Cement, Concrete	16.1	2.3
45	Footwear, Clothing	11.0	2.1
46	Wood, Furniture	7.5	1.9
44	Leather Products	3.4	3.0
	TOTAL	43.0	1.0

Source: Eurostat, *Labour Costs 1978, Volume 2* (1983) for column 1. Column 2 is taken from table 6.13, column 3.
*Large establishments are those employing over 500 people.

the USA — see table 2.1), yet it is relatively well developed in native Irish industry. This exception can be explained, however, by the fact that the Irish indigenous Tobacco industry consists largely of one big company which was established as long ago as the 1820s, so it has not had to overcome entry barriers as a newcomer — an exception which supports the general rule. Similarly, the relatively large size of the Irish Drink industry, despite the fact that economies of scale appear to be of slightly above average importance in the UK, is largely due to the presence of two big Irish companies which were established before the industrial revolution began.

Other industries which are somewhat out of line with the generally inverse relationship between economies of scale in the UK and the level of development in Ireland are Glass & Glassware, Food, and Instrument and Mechanical Engineering. The Irish Glass & Glassware industry is mainly involved in skilled labour-intensive manufacture of hand-cut glassware, rather than mass-produced glassware or flat glass which are probably the branches of the sector most characterised by economies of scale. Hence the Irish industry's strength is not in the type of activity where the most significant economies of scale probably occur.

The Irish Food industry largely consists of basic processing of local agricultural produce and there are natural advantages for such industries, as discussed above, which mean that entry barriers are not a decisive constraint on late-developers. The Food sector is not really very well developed in Ireland as an *industrial* activity. Rather its large weight in Irish industry, compared with its importance in other EEC countries, is simply a reflection of the country's large agricultural area in relation to the small size of its population and industrial sector. For this reason, Food accounts for a greater proportion of industry in Ireland than in other European countries which are more densely populated and more highly industrialised.

Mechanical and Instrument Engineering are also somewhat out of line with the general pattern in table 6.14, since economies of scale in these industries are of slightly less than average significance in the UK but they are still particularly weak and undeveloped by Irish firms. This can be explained by the role of *other* types of barriers to entry which have impeded their development in Ireland. Both of these industries are highly concentrated geographically within the advanced industrial countries, so that established competitors have significant advantages of external economies over late-developers. Efficiency and quality in both industries also generally depend on manual and/or engineering skills perfected through practical on-the-job experience. Hence established, experienced firms have the advantage of having already progressed along the 'learning curve', whereas new entrants would be deterred by the prospect of losses while they are trying to gain experience and develop skills (see O'Malley, 1987, pp. 81-83).

Tables 6.13 and 6.14 present a picture of native Irish industry at the end of the 1970s, giving an impression of an industrial sector still underdeveloped and especially weak in activities where entry barriers for late-developers prevail. It is also possible to examine trends in employment in the various industries from 1973 to 1987, to see how this picture might be changing. Table 6.15 shows the change in employment in 12 sectors of indigenous industry in which employment increased between the early 1970s and 1986-87. And table 6.16 shows the change in 29 industries which experienced employment decline in that period.

For the most part, the 1970s was a period of fairly strong growth in the Irish economy and also of a slight increase in indigenous industrial employment, which peaked in 1980. But the subsequent period since 1980 was one of continuous decline in industrial employment. Tables 6.15 and 6.16, therefore, show indices of employment in each sector for 1979-80 and 1986-87 (to the base 1973-74 = 100), in order to distinguish the trend in the earlier period of growth from the subsequent period of decline. (The average of two years is used in calculating these indices because some industries peaked in 1979 rather than 1980 and it is desired to compare them on a similar basis in relation to the cycle.)

Of the 43 industries, 41 can be classified in one of four categories. There are eight 'secular growth' industries, with employment increasing in both periods; four 'cyclical growth' industries, with growth in the first period followed by decline, but still remaining above the 1973-74 level; 13 industries showing 'cyclical decline', with employment growth followed by decline to below the 1973-74 level; and 16 sectors in 'secular decline', with decline already under way in the 1970s and continuing in the 1980s. The remaining two industries are small exceptions which followed an unusual anti-cyclical pattern, with employment decline in the 1970s followed by growth in the 1980s, and they are not included in table 6.15 or 6.16;

Paints, Varnishes & Inks accounted for 0.3% of indigenous industrial employment in 1986-87 and had an employment index of 134 by then, and Pharmaceutical Products accounted for 0.86% of employment by 1986-87 with an index of 111.

Table 6.15: Growth Sectors of Indigenous Industry, 1973-74 — 1986-87

NACE Code	Industry	Employment Index (1973-74 = 100)		Employment 1986-87	
		1979-80	1986-87	Number	% of Total In- digenous
SECULAR GROWTH:					
33	Office & Data Processing Machinery	194	913	955	.82
248	Ceramic Goods	134	247	449	.39
415	Seafood Processing	129	217	2,129	1.83
37	Instrument Engineering	118	201	712	.61
256	'Other' Chemical Products	167	172	241	.21
49	Miscellaneous	122	149	2,166	1.86
483	Plastic Processing	116	147	3,106	2.67
36	Other Means of Transport	109	139	2,542	2.19
				12,300	10.58
CYCLICAL GROWTH:					
26	Man-Made Fibres	160	157	28	.02
32	Mechanical Engineering	146	117	3,565	3.07
429	Tobacco	147	109	733	.63
247	Glass, Glassware	127	107	3,769	3.24
				8,095	6.96

Source: Derived from *IDA Employment Survey.*

Table 6.16: Declining Sectors of Indigenous Industry, 1973-74 — 1986-87

NACE Code	Industry	Employment Index (1973-74 = 100)		Employment 1986-87	
		1979-80	1986-87	Number	% of Total Indigenous
CYCLICAL DECLINE:					
473, 474	Printing & Publishing	109	97	9,116	7.84
464-467	Wood Products & Furniture	108	96	5,294	4.55
31	Metal Articles	132	94	10,275	8.84
259	House/Office Chemicals	104	94	278	0.24
413	Dairy Products	109	93	7,053	6.07
412	Meat Processing	112	81	8,369	7.20
461-463	Timber Processing	110	81	3,821	3.29
416, 422	Grain Milling, Animal Feed	105	78	5,298	4.56
455	Household Textiles	105	71	648	.56
22	Metals	101	69	1,197	1.03
241-246	Cement, Concrete	113	64	4,856	4.18
420, 421	Sugar, Sugar Confectionery	102	59	1,560	1.34
35	Motor Vehicles	104	58	1,357	1.17
				59,122	50.87
SECULAR DECLINE:					
411, 417, 418, 423	'Other' Food	87	82	1,920	1.65
34	Electrical Engineering	94	79	3,941	3.39
419	Bread, Flour Confectionery	97	71	6,339	5.45
428	Soft Drinks	91	60	1,329	1.14
471, 472	Paper Products	94	58	2,650	2.28
424, 426/7	Alcoholic Drinks	90	57	2,365	2.03
453, 456	Clothing	88	57	8,497	7.31
14, 251	Oil, Basic Chemicals	87	56	1,587	1.37
436	Knitting, Knitwear	59	47	1,946	1.67
414	Fruit & Vegetable Processing	69	37	709	.61
451	Footwear	67	34	1,027	.88
44	Leather Products	83	33	755	.65
481, 482	Rubber Products	81	33	210	.18
258	Soaps, Detergents etc.	44	27	241	.21
431, 432, 437, 439	Textiles	60	25	1,645	1.42
438	Carpets & Floorcoverings	86	16	200	.17
				35,361	30.41

Source: Derived from *IDA Employment Survey.*

The eight *secular growth* industries in table 6.15 represent the most positive feature of indigenous industrial development, the sort of results which advocates of the conventional development strategy might have expected to occur much more commonly. Four of them, however — Seafood Processing, Plastic Processing, Miscellaneous and Ceramic Goods — are fairly clearly the type of industry which the 'alternative' view outlined in section 2.ii would have expected to do well in a late-developer, since they are generally relatively small scale and easily entered or involved in basic processing of local primary produce. The largest Irish company in these four sectors employed just over 200 people by 1985 and there were only five others with between 100 and 200 workers.

Office & Data Processing Machinery, Instrument Engineering, Other Chemical Products and Other Means of Transport, however, might appear to be rather different, since economies of scale, proprietary technology or other barriers to entry are common features of these industries in advanced industrial countries. But what Irish firms have succeeded in doing here was mainly to move into certain very small-scale niches which exist within these industries. Also, four-fifths of employment in Other Means of Transport (and almost half of employment in these four sectors combined) is in the overhaul and maintenance of transport equipment on quite a large scale in a *state* enterprise, so this is a development resulting from state initiative rather than private enterprise and free market forces. The largest Irish private company in these four industries employed less than 100 people in 1985, and indeed only three private companies employed more than 50. While the growth of private firms in these industries is a positive development, it has thus been limited to certain very small-scale niches and it had little overall impact. It can scarcely continue, so as to develop these industries to levels comparable with advanced countries, unless the barriers to entry into somewhat larger scale activities can be overcome.

Among the four *cyclical growth* industries in table 6.15, similar remarks apply to Mechanical Engineering. In this industry the two largest establishments are state-owned, no Irish private firm employed over 100 people in 1985 and only six employed over 50. Most of the industry makes parts, tools or sub-assemblies on a small scale for local customers, rather than producing internationally traded machinery which is the dominant activity in advanced economies. Its local market orientation is reflected in the cyclical downturn in the 1980s. The tobacco industry has a special advantage which freed it from the constraints on late-developers, since it consists mainly of a large very long-established company. And Man-Made Fibres is a very small industry of little consequence. Glass & Glassware, however, is a sector where Irish firms, since the 1950s, have developed a fairly substantial internationally traded niche industry producing hand-made glassware. It is one of the more positive developments in indigenous industry. The cyclical downturn here in the 1980s was influenced by the inclusion in the sector of glass bottles and containers — a virtually non-traded industry due to the cost of transporting such bulky low-value objects which were also increasingly being replaced by plastic containers.

Among the sectors in *cyclical decline* in table 6.16, some of the largest — such as Dairy Products, Meat and Timber Processing — are low value-added basic processing industries which have natural advantages, as was already discussed. Printing & Publishing and Cement & Concrete Products, as was also discussed above, are virtually non-traded sectors which therefore followed a cyclical pattern in line with domestic demand. And many activities in Metal Articles are also naturally protected and largely non-traded. An indication of this is the fact that in 1979 Metal Articles accounted for 22% of output, but only 11% of exports and 10% of imports of all Metals & Engineering products. This sector grew rapidly in the 1970s, largely in supplying structural metal products and fabricated equipment to the booming agricultural and building sectors, but it inevitably declined following the downturn in local demand and investment. Motor Vehicles, which also followed a trend of cyclical decline, would probably have been in secular decline since the 1960s but for the fact that continuing protection until the early 1980s retarded the inevitable trend.

Sixteen industries are listed as being in *secular decline* in table 6.16 — a description which seems accurate for most of them but perhaps not for all. Near the top of this list, the decline was least severe in Other Food, Electrical Engineering, Bread & Flour Confectionery, Soft Drinks, Paper Products and Alcoholic Drinks. These industries may not necessarily *continue* to decline, although they certainly show no sign of positive growth. In particular, Bread & Flour Confectionery and Soft Drinks are mostly non-traded industries due, respectively, to perishability of the product and transport costs for bulky low-value goods, so they should at least maintain a level of activity commensurate with domestic demand. Decline in employment, however, could still occur gradually due to greater automation.

After a shake-out of big firms, Electrical Engineering by now consists very largely of small-scale local market-oriented activities which may also have a degree of natural protection due to an element of customer service and a need to respond flexibly to varying local demand. It contains practically none of the large-scale internationally traded activities which dominate this sector in advanced countries; one medium-size establishment employed over 400 people in 1985, but only three others had over 100 and three-quarters of employment was in smaller establishments. So this sector may behave in the future more like a non-traded industry. And Alcoholic Drinks consists mainly of two big long-established companies, as was already mentioned, which have scarcely shown a sparkling growth performance in recent years but at least seem to be in no immediate danger of continuous secular decline. Their fall in employment was more an effect of labour-saving investment and weak demand while their market-share performance was not very weak.

The rest of the industries in secular decline in table 6.16, however, do seem to exhibit serious weaknesses, with a continuous rapid fall in employment which almost certainly reflects falling market shares and competitive inadequacy. The process of secular decline may well continue in these industries. A common feature of these ten industries in serious secular decline is that they are internationally traded activities with no special advantages. They cover quite a broad spectrum of industries with little else in common, and they include sectors from five of the ten major Industry Groups. There are three each from Textiles and Clothing, Footwear & Leather, two from Chemicals, and one each from Food and Miscellaneous Manufacturing.

In view of the disaggregated trends discussed in this section, the decline of indigenous industry in the 1980s looks rather more lasting than a temporary cyclical downturn. There can be no confident expectation of a recovery sufficient to restore the employment lost, since it is difficult to see where such a major recovery would come from. In all, 13 internationally traded industries could be regarded as showing serious secular decline, so that they are unlikely to contribute much to recovery. These 13 industries — the ten at the bottom of table 6.16 as well as

Household Textiles, Sugar & Sugar Confectionery and Motor Vehicles — still accounted for 18% of indigenous industrial employment by 1986-87, after falling from 29% in 1973-74. If their decline continues, they are large enough to exert quite a significant drag on any overall recovery.

Furthermore, as these internationally traded industries have declined, the proportion of virtually non-traded industries which almost exclusively serve the domestic market has grown. Such industries are mainly represented by Printing & Publishing, Manufacture of Metal Articles, Cement & Concrete, Paper Products, Bread & Flour Confectionery and Soft Drinks, as well as, say, half each of Mechanical Engineering, Electrical Engineering, Wood Products & Furniture and Plastic Processing. This gives a rough estimate of about 37% of indigenous industrial employment in sheltered, virtually non-traded activities. These industries are not likely to make much of an independent contribution to recovery since their performance to date has largely tended to reflect the trend in domestic demand.

In the 1970s they grew quite quickly, but domestic demand was stimulated then by three rather exceptional factors. For there was a boom in agriculture during the initial transition to EEC membership; new foreign industrial investment accelerated to take advantage of Ireland's new access to EEC markets; and government expenditure grew rapidly, largely financed by a growing debt. Each of these three factors also brought in foreign exchange which facilitated demand expansion. To the extent that their stimulus to growth has been weaker in the 1980s and will probably continue to be relatively weak for some time, the outlook for growth of domestic demand does not look particularly bright.

Alcoholic Drinks and Other Food are two further sectors which seem unlikely to do any more than hold their own. The same seems to apply to the remaining half of Electrical Engineering (the proportion assumed to be traded). So here is another 5% of employment in industries which appear to be stagnant, at best, or perhaps in slow long-term decline.

Judging by the long-run trends, therefore, the prospects for a significant contribution to recovery and development are mainly focussed on 18 industries (and three halves of industries assumed to be internationally traded). These account for just 39% of indigenous industrial employment, 18% being in the basic processing activities in Seafood, Dairy Products, Meat and

Timber. Unless these four can move into higher value-added activities, which they have been rather slow to do so far, their growth will be largely dictated by growth in the domestic supply of primary produce. Progress here has been quite difficult and slow in recent years except in seafood, and financial constraints on the European Community's Common Agricultural Policy will not help the expansion of Dairy Products and Meat to resume in the manner of the 1970s.

All things considered, native industry appears to be facing significant long-term difficulties which are not merely of a temporary cyclical nature. As was noted in chapter 3, earlier phases of permanent decline in Irish industry, in the 1820s and 1870s, took the form of sharp decline during a period of recession from which there was no subsequent recovery. History does not necessarily repeat itself in precisely the same way, but there is a warning here of what may have been happening in the 1980s since an illusion of temporary recession has been known to mask a long-run trend of decline in the past.

To conclude this section, the experience of Irish indigenous industry since the 1950s is consistent with the argument outlined in section 2.ii which says that there are serious constraints on late-developers, which the orthodox free market strategy is inadequate to overcome. Many internationally traded industries have declined continuously under this policy, with a particularly rapid fall in large-scale industries characterised by barriers to entry for late-developers. The principal success stories were in basic processing and non-traded industries and in small-scale easily entered activities. The structure of Irish indigenous industry remains more typical of a less-developed economy than an advanced industrial country. There have been some positive aspects in its development, however, such as would have been expected by advocates of the conventional free market strategy introduced in the 1950s and 1960s. For example, certain industries began to export more and new industries were established and grew quite fast in certain small internationally traded niches. But these developments have had only a marginal overall impact which was outweighed, on balance, by the prevailing decline.

6.iii. THE LARGEST IRISH INDIGENOUS FIRMS

This section looks at the activities of the largest Irish indigenous manufacturing firms. The main reason for this focus on large companies arises from the discussion in chapter 2 concerning the problems confronting latecomers to industrial development. It was pointed out that some of the principal barriers to entry for latecomers arise from much the same causes that have given rise to the development of large firms and the common occurrence of oligopoly in the advanced countries. Factors such as economies of scale in production, and advantages of large firm size with regard to finance, marketing or research and development, have encouraged this prevalence of large firms and oligopolistic structures. At the same time they have created barriers to entry for latecomers into the industries where they are important. If this is so, it follows that it is primarily among the largest firms in Ireland too that one should look to find examples of companies which have succeeded in developing industries where barriers to entry prevail. For the largest Irish firms would be the ones with the greatest capacity to enter industries where there are special competitive advantages associated with large size. And if and when they have done so successfully, they would have to be quite large by Irish standards. Thus inspection of the activities of the *largest* Irish firms should be quite a good test of whether *any* Irish firms have successfully engaged in activities with substantial entry barriers.

It follows, too, however, from the general emphasis of the argument in section 2.ii that one should not expect to find many of such examples. If indigenous industries in Ireland generally face great difficulties in breaking into sectors dominated by large foreign firms and having high barriers to entry, the largest Irish firms would mostly not be found in these sectors. Rather, large Irish firms would simply not exist in these sectors, and the largest Irish companies would be the major ones involved in activities sheltered from foreign competition, basic processing of local primary products and others with low barriers to entry. In view of Ireland's long industrial history (see chapter 3), however, there could also be a few exceptional cases of very long-established firms, which survived the general decline in the last century; since these are not subject to the constraints on *newcomers*, they could be engaged in activities where barriers to entry for newcomers would be significant.

The table in appendix 2 lists 100 Irish indigenous, private-sector manufacturing companies which are thought to have been the largest of such firms in terms of sales in the mid-1980s. Details of the derivation of the list are given in that appendix, so just a few

brief remarks are made here on its composition. The list is supposed to contain the top 100 of such firms in terms of sales in the
most recent financial year up to January 1985, provided that they
employ at least 100 people. It is possible that some companies have
been omitted, although omissions are unlikely among larger firms
that should be included towards the top end of the list. A number
of firms engage in some manufacturing combined with some non-
manufacturing activities, and these are included only if the scale of
their manufacturing is believed to exceed that of the smallest firms
in the list. They are excluded otherwise, even if their total size
exceeds the minimum. For firms of this type which are included,
sales and employment are for the whole firm. 'Irish indigenous' is
defined, as in the rest of this chapter, by nationality of majority
ownership, plus some majority foreign-owned firms which are
known to have been originally Irish. There may be a few misclassifications in this regard but the large majority of cases are
fairly clear cut. Finally, the list excludes state enterprises, since we
are mainly concerned with the effects of outward-looking free
market policies, without specific state intervention, as a strategy
for late industrialisation.

In examining this list, the main objective is to assess to what
extent the firms involved are engaged in activities with significant
entry barriers for newcomers. As a first general impression, it may
be noted that the top end of the list has very few firms mainly
engaged in Metals & Engineering, Chemicals or 'Other'
Manufacturing. A similar list of the biggest firms in advanced
industrial countries would be largely made up of firms from these
sectors — in branches such as transport equipment, metals,
electrical and electronic engineering, machinery, pharmaceuticals,
toiletries, industrial chemicals and petroleum products. These are
industries which tend to be characterised by entry barriers of some
sort. Thus referring back to table 2.1 and table 6.14 it can be seen
that these types of industry, as well as tobacco products, tend to be
the most highly concentrated in large firms in the USA and the UK.
This indicates that economies of scale would create serious barriers
to entry for newcomers in these industries. Of course, the USA and
the UK are much larger than Ireland, but the small advanced
countries also have many sizeable companies in these industries.
Belgium and Denmark, for example, both have 17 indigenous
engineering firms employing over 1,000 people (Telesis, 1982, p.
349). In the Irish list, none of the top 20 companies come from
Metals & Engineering, Chemicals or 'Other' Manufacturing. For a
further general impression, tables 6.17 and 6.18 show the

distribution, by main manufacturing sector, of the whole group of 100 largest companies.

Table   6.17:   Sectoral   Distribution   of   the   Largest   Irish Manufacturing Firms, 1983-84

	Companies	Sales (£m.)	Employment	Sales per Worker (£'000)
Food	50	2,990.9	23,426	127
Drink & Tobacco	9	1,137.7	11,223	101
Textiles	3	95.1	3,528	27
Clothing & Footwear	1	12.5	722	17
Wood & Furniture	2	47.0	600	78
Paper & Printing	11	880.2	17,209	51
Chemicals	3	119.3	551	217
Clay, Glass & Cement	6	750.5	15,827	47
Metals & Engineering	10	187.8	3,751	50
Other Manufacturing	3	37.8	820	46
Multi-Sectoral(*)	2	60.1	494	122
	100	6,318.9	78,151	81

Source: See appendix 2. (*) 'Multi-Sectoral' firms are those whose manufacturing activities are not *predominantly* in one sector.

The Food sector emerges as by far the most important sector of activity of the largest Irish manufacturing firms, in terms of its share of companies and sales. It is also, by a lesser but still substantial margin, the largest sector in terms of employment, with the difference arising from the sector's concentration in very basic processing which results in low levels of employment in relation to sales. Metals & Engineering, which would be the main sector of activity for large firms in advanced economies, is third largest in terms of the number of companies, but ranks only fifth in terms of sales and employment. This is due to the relatively small size of the companies concerned, since eight of the ten rank below 60 on the list of 100. Apart from Food, the three sectors which are by far the most important in terms of sales and employment are Drink & Tobacco, Paper & Printing and Clay, Glass & Cement. These three, together with Food, account for 91% of sales and 87% of employment in the largest firms, (compared with 50% of employment in all indigenous industry in 1983). Thus these four sectors could be said to account for a disproportionately large part of the activity of the biggest Irish firms.[16] They are the same sectors which emerged in section 6.ii as being largely composed of non-traded or basic processing activities, and also containing some long-established firms in less sheltered activities with significant entry barriers. Food, Drink & Tobacco, Paper & Printing and Clay, Glass & Cement had also been growing in importance among the top 100 firms, since their share of sales and employment was 85% and 79% respectively in 1979-80.

Table 6.18: Percentage Distribution by Sector of the Largest Irish Manufacturing Firms, 1983-84

	Companies	Sales	Employ-ment
Food	50	47.3	30.0
Drink & Tobacco	9	18.0	14.4
Textiles	3	1.5	4.5
Clothing & Footwear	1	0.2	0.9
Wood & Furniture	2	0.7	0.8
Paper & Printing	11	13.9	22.0
Chemicals	3	1.9	0.7
Clay, Glass & Cement	6	11.9	20.3
Metals & Engineering	10	3.0	4.8
Other Manufacturing	3	0.6	1.0
Multi-Sectoral	2	1.0	0.6
	100	100	100

Source: Derived from table 6.17.

Referring back again to table 2.1, it can be seen that the four sectors mentioned as predominating among large Irish firms generally tend to have only low to medium degrees of concentration in large firms in the USA. The relevant industries in table 2.1 are Printing & Publishing, Paper & Allied Products, Food & Kindred Products (which includes Drink) and Stone, Clay & Glass Products. The US data suggest that barriers to entry due to economies of scale are not very severe in these industries, whereas large Irish firms are virtually absent from the more highly concentrated industries. There is one large Irish firm in Tobacco Products, however, which is a very highly concentrated industry in the USA, but this exception has already been explained as a very long-established firm.

Activities of the Large Firms

Since the Food sector is so dominant among large Irish firms, it will be useful to begin by considering that sector on its own. The largest firms in the Food sector are nearly all producers' (i.e. farmers') co-operative societies or meat processors. And the manufacturing activities of the co-ops are primarily in dairy products, and in meat processing to a lesser extent. Irish indigenous firms in the meat and dairy products divisions of the Food Sector are mostly engaged in basic processing activities with low value-added; their value-added to material inputs was just 14.3% and 13.5% of gross output, respectively, in 1985. This is consistent with the high sales per worker (or low employment in relation to sales) in the large Food firms — shown in table 6.17. Sales per worker in the large Food firms are, in fact, twice as high as in large firms in all other sectors combined. A further indication of the generally low level of value-added is the fact that the highest level of value-added as a percentage of sales among the 30 largest Co-ops in 1977-78 was 15%. ('Irish Times Top 30 Co-operatives', *The Irish Times,* 1 & 2/1/79). So, in general, the largest Food firms are in the basic processing activities, sheltered to a great extent from foreign competition by the advantage of proximity to the source of supply of inputs for low value-added processing. It is a reflection of this feature of these industries that there are so many relatively large firms, none very much larger than the next largest, widely spread throughout the country so that each can have its own catchment area for primary inputs. A few relatively small exceptions to this general picture are bakeries which are, however, sheltered from foreign competition by the perishability of the product although the value-added is higher.

One notable exception to the prevalence of basic low value-added processing is W. & R. Jacob (ranked 29 in the list of 100), which makes biscuits. Jacob's is a very long-established firm, founded in 1851, and was one of the largest manufacturing firms in the country at the time of the foundation of the state. As such it has not had to overcome, as a newcomer, the marketing and economies of scale barriers to entry which are probably important in this relatively high value-added activity. It has a long-established export trade, accounting for 21% of sales in 1978.

In contrast to the scarcity of higher value-added Food processing among large Irish firms, there are quite a number of foreign subsidiaries in such activities. These include (with an indication of how they would rank if included in the list of 100 large Irish firms): Cadbury (16), Carberry Milk Products (32), Rowntree Mackintosh (35), Virginia Milk Products (36), Batchelors (42), Reckitt's (49), and CPC Ireland (67). These companies make products such as chocolate, confectionery, processed dairy products, canned vegetables and sauces. Thus although it is often said that the lack of high value-added food processing by Irish firms is due to poor quality and seasonal irregularity in the supply of material inputs, the presence of these foreign firms suggests that this alone is not an adequate explanation. Very likely, barriers to entry in marketing play a major role in inhibiting the Irish firms.

Apart from Food, most of the other large indigenous firms are involved in sheltered, virtually non-traded activities, basic processing industries, or internationally traded activities with low entry barriers. The few exceptions involved in traded activities with more substantial entry barriers can generally be explained on the grounds that they are very long established and consequently have not had to overcome barriers to entry for newcomers.

Sheltered, non-traded businesses include the Smurfit Group (ranked No. 1) which is mainly in Printing & Packaging. The non-traded nature of its business is shown by its great success in the home market combined with a very low export-orientation — with 4% of its sales going for export in 1978-79).[17] Cement Roadstone (No. 2), which makes cement, concrete and other building materials, is also largely a non-traded business, as shown by its success in the home market combined with exports amounting to only 4.3% of sales in

1978.[18] This company did, however, make a substantial attempt at diversification into a traded area of manufacturing — with a 51% share, with a British partner, in a £38 million plant to produce seawater magnesia for export. But this project made considerable losses after its establishment in 1980. The largest Metals & Engineering firm, O'Flaherty Holdings (No. 21) could also be described as a sheltered business, since its main manufacturing activity was in the still protected but declining car assembly industry, combined with distribution. The Jones Group (No. 39) was mainly involved in shipping and engineering services, but also does some manufacturing, of radiators under foreign license and steel tube made to order — the latter being essentially a local-oriented, sheltered activity. The Group's exports amounted to only 5% of sales in 1979-80. Other prominent examples of sheltered, virtually non-traded businesses include Cantrell & Cochrane (No. 17) in soft drinks and Independent Newspapers (No. 23).

A number of *long-established* firms, which have not had to overcome barriers to entry for newcomers as most of Irish indigenous industry would have to do, are prominent among the very largest companies. Their early start would explain the fact that they can engage successfully in traded activities with substantial entry barriers for newcomers, whereas newer Irish firms could not easily do so. These include Guinness (No. 3) which is over 200 years old and has long been one of the largest brewing companies in the world.[19] Brewing, as noted in chapter 2, is an industry with substantial entry barriers arising mainly from product differentiation and economies of scale.[20] But it would perhaps be best described as semi-traded rather than fully traded internationally. There are quite substantial exports from Ireland to parts of Britain, for example, but there is generally little large-scale trade over long distances.[21] Carroll's (No. 6) is another old firm, originating in 1824. Its main activity is in tobacco manufacture which is also characterised by substantial entry barriers arising from economies of scale and product differentiation. Carroll's also attempted to diversify into another area of manufacturing for export, in partnership with the US company Fieldcrest in a venture to produce towels. But this project made losses amounting to over £10 million between its establishment in 1977 and its closure in 1982. Irish Distillers (No. 10) has even older roots, being made up of three firms founded between 1779 and 1791 which merged in 1966, followed by a merger with a Northern Irish distillery first licensed in 1608. Its main activity in producing spirits would also be subject to entry barriers for newcomers, arising from economies of scale and product differentiation, as well as finance in view of the investment in stocks required for a long period of maturation before the product can be sold.

Waterford Glass (No. 7) is something of a special case. For its main activity, the manufacture of hand-cut glassware or crystal, is a highly traded activity in which marketing and the 'learning curve' effect must be important entry barriers for newcomers. Yet the present firm is fairly new, having been established in 1947, and it is very successful in its field. In a sense, however, Waterford Glass is not really a newcomer since it is based in a tradition dating back to at least the 1780s, and old Waterford Glass became established as a high-quality product which now has considerable antique value. During the last century the advent of mass-produced glass destroyed the market for the hand-made product and the industry in Waterford closed in 1851. This tradition and the well-established name was a valuable background for the development of the new industry, when the development of high-income mass markets after the Second World War reopened the opportunities for expensive hand-made glass. For marketing is probably the main factor influencing competitive success in this industry, together with design and skill development. So the new Waterford firm had quite an advantage due to the reputation and tradition when it started out, relatively early in fact, in terms of the timing of the new phase of regeneration of the industry (see Brophy, 1985). The company was also sustained through a troublesome teething period of some seven years by financial injections from the established Irish Glass Bottle Co., which was crucial for its survival.

Most of the other top 100 firms in the list in appendix 2, which have not been referred to individually, can be classified as mainly involved in three types of industry: (a) sheltered, non-traded industries such as printing, packaging, building materials, soft drinks or small-scale metal fabrication; (b) basic low value-added processing, such as food (bearing in mind our earlier remarks on the predominance of low value-added activities in food) or leather; or (c) relatively 'easily entered' internationally traded activities with low barriers to entry, such as clothing or textiles. In most cases this is readily seen from the description of the company's activity.

Two quite high-ranking firms, Grassland Fertilisers (No. 26) and Goulding Chemicals (No. 30), might appear to be exceptions since they are in the Chemicals sector. But both of them were involved in low value-added stages of fertiliser production (with very low employment in relation to sales), mainly in blending and packaging. So Chemicals should not be assumed to imply technologically advanced industries in these cases. Smaller companies which do appear to be more genuine exceptions to the generally limited range of activities are Mahon and McPhillips (No. 67), Biocon Biochemicals (No. 73), Memory Computer (No. 85), Hanlon Ireland (No. 92) and Lake Electronics (No. 100). These exceptional cases, however, are rather small and not very significant in the overall context.

Patterns of Expansion in Large Firms

If Irish firms are generally constrained in the type of activity they can enter, it follows that profitable companies, with the means to reinvest in expansion, would probably tend to be similarly constrained in their choice of activities for expansion or diversification. These constraints can in fact be seen in the patterns of expansion of many firms. A successful, growing manufacturing company can expand in various ways: (a) by attaining a more dominant position in the home market in its own sector, whether by internal expansion or acquisition of other companies; (b) by increasing its exports, thereby further expanding operations in its own base country, within its original sector; (c) by diversifying into new manufacturing activities in its own country by means of taking over existing companies; (d) by diversifying into new manufacturing activities in its own country by means of starting up new operations; (e) by acquiring companies in other countries; or (f) by diversifying into non-manufacturing activities, at home or abroad.

A large sheltered, non-traded business like the Smurfit Group (No. 1) or Cement Roadstone (No. 2) has already gone a long way down path (a). It is not in a suitable industry to develop exports, path (b), which would be desirable for national industrial development. Path (d), the establishment of new industries, would also be desirable from the point of view of national industrial development, but here the firm would frequently be deterred by barriers to entry in many sectors arising from the existence of foreign competitors. Consequently, options (c), (e) or (f), i.e. manufacturing takeovers at home, 'going multinational' or moving into non-manufacturing activities, are likely to be chosen. These are the options generally chosen by Smurfit, and a number of other large Irish firms, so that their successful expansion as companies does not result in any very significant further development of indigenous manufacturing.

Apart from its original main activities, Smurfit has invested in natural resource development, distribution of consumer products and financial services, and it has subsidiaries in the UK, USA, Nigeria, Australia, Channel Islands and the Netherlands. By 1980-81, the geographical breakdown of the Group's sales (to third parties, by origin) was reported to be USA 51%, UK 30%, Ireland 17% and other countries 2%. Since that time the Group has made further major purchases of American companies so that most of its activities are now in the USA.

In a similar way, Cement Roadstone (No. 2) first evolved towards greater dominance of the home market, then primarily by going multinational by buying foreign companies in its own sector. It acquired foreign interests in the UK, USA, the Netherlands, Belgium and Cyprus. The company's policy in acquisitions has been stated as 'to seek out in selected countries businesses with good management and good potential, whose products and processes are related to those in which we are already proficient . . .' (Annual Report 1978).

The mode of expansion of Guinness (No. 3) has included all six of the paths mentioned above, to some extent. But the 'multinationalisation' of the company has been much more important and successful than the development of exports and new indigenous manufacturing, though this is not so marked as in a more truly sheltered business like Smurfit or Cement Roadstone. Thus Guinness exports from Dublin, mainly to Britain, accounted for about 40% of the Dublin brewery's output in 1981.[22] But the logistics of the operation of this 'semi-traded' industry have determined that much of the British market is supplied from the London brewery built in 1936. Guinness is also brewed in more than a dozen other countries, either in Guinness subsidiaries or under licence, rather than exported from Ireland. The vast majority of employment in the whole Guinness group is now outside Ireland and the company is now mostly British owned. Various attempts at diversification into new manufactured products in Ireland such as lager, meat processing, pharmaceuticals, plastic processing and 'Guinness Light' have not generally been regarded as the company's greatest successes. Its 'Harp' lager, for example, showed considerable promise at first, but its success induced major British breweries to promote lager in the British and Irish markets and their marketing strength proved strong enough to cut seriously into Harp's market share. Guinness's pharmaceutical venture and 'Guinness Light' were costly failures. Other diversifications have included confectionery in the UK, retail' shops, management services, publishing and leisure activities such as boat hire.

In general then, Guinness's expansion has had a rather greater impact on the development of Irish industry than that of the Smurfit Group, for example. But it has still consisted very largely of multinationalisation and diversification into non-manufacturing activities, with some generally less successful manufacturing diversifications. The poor results of its diversification efforts were the subject of considerable criticism and after 1982 the company sold or closed down many of its subsidiaries to concentrate more on the drinks business.

The expansion of Carroll's (No. 6) has involved diversification within Ireland into pharmaceutical distribution and printing and packaging, by means of takeovers. In these activities, the company has kept within the areas of sheltered manufacturing and services. Its involvement with the American firm, Fieldcrest, in a venture to produce towels proved a commercial failure. It has recently invested in fish farming, however, which is an activity likely to generate exports.

Waterford Glass's (No. 7) further expansion has again been mainly into sheltered manufacturing and services at home, and related manufacturing abroad. It acquired 60% of the Switzer Group of department stores (which accounted for 30% of Waterford's sales in 1979), the Smith Group which used to assemble cars under protection and still distributes them, a printing firm and Aynsley China and Wedgwood of the UK.

The next largest non-Food firm, Irish Distillers (No. 10) has diversified in the home market by adding vodka and white rum to its main product which is whiskey. But whiskey, marketed abroad as a distinctive Irish product, remains the major export, suggesting that marketing barriers to entry abroad present a more severe constraint on the newer products. Another diversification has been the importing of wines and spirits, a service sector activity.[23]

Thus the very largest Irish firms have tended to expand primarily by moving into sheltered manufacturing activities, non-manufacturing activities or by 'going multinational'. The expansion of the largest firms has not, therefore, been a major force in aiding Irish industry to overcome the barriers to entry which prevail in most internationally traded industries. Similar patterns of expansion are evident among quite a number of other companies. For example, all the car assembly firms have run down their manufacturing and concentrated on distribution. James Crean Holdings (No. 18) expanded from soft drinks into distribution in Ireland, the UK and USA. Independent Newspapers (No. 23) acquired provincial newspapers in Ireland, magazines in Britain, outdoor poster companies in France and it has other subsidiaries in Germany, Mexico and Australia. Youghal Carpets (No. 31) has operations in the UK, Holland and North America. The Jones Group (No. 39) has been expanding by acquiring foreign companies in recent years. Sunbeam Wolsey (No. 56) acquired subsidiaries in the UK. The Irish Times (No. 72) has diversified into a variety of services such as mail order and secretarial courses. And the RTD Group (No. 95) originated in Ireland but came to consist mainly of subsidiaries in the UK.

Conclusions

To conclude, this chapter has shown that the greatly improved overall performance of industry in Ireland after the end of the 1950s owed rather little to indigenous industry. Following the removal of protection, indigenous industry suffered declining shares of the home market and little compensating increase in shares of foreign markets. The rate of growth thus achieved was too low to allow any growth in employment since the mid-1960s in indigenous industry. The strongest major sectors were those containing a relatively high proportion of sheltered, non-traded activities or low value-added, basic processing of local primary products. Decline was experienced mostly in internationally traded activities, especially among large-scale plants, and most newly emerging industries remained small in scale and appear to be largely sheltered local-oriented businesses. There was little growth of technology-based activities. Consistent with these findings, the largest firms now are very highly concentrated in virtually non-traded activities or basic processing industries; they also include some long-established firms in sectors which would probably present entry barriers for *newcomers*, and some internationally traded industries with low barriers to entry. The pattern of expansion of large firms shows a marked tendency to remain within sheltered manufacturing or else to diversify into non-manufacturing activities or to 'go multinational'.

Referring back to the concluding section of chapter 2, the experience of Irish indigenous firms seems consistent with the argument that the indigenous industry of latecomers faces special difficulties attributable to barriers to entry. Little or no 'upward' diversification into industries with higher barriers to entry has occurred, and indeed something of a contrary process followed the removal of protection as large-scale traded industries declined markedly. At the same time, the easily entered, sheltered and basic processing industries have proved to be an inadequate basis for growth, so that unemployment and/or emigration have persisted, indicating a failure to mobilise productive resources fully. Some of the 'easily entered' traded industries, within sectors such as Textiles, Clothing & Footwear have also experienced difficulties arising from very low-cost competition (since low-cost NICs can also easily enter the same industries). It was suggested that this could prove to be a factor undermining a process of development which failed to achieve diversification into industries with higher entry barriers.

One could conclude, therefore, that Irish indigenous industry has made little progress, under outward-looking free market policies, in overcoming the constraints on latecomers. Its structural composition is actually little more advanced than that of many LDCs or NICs, and indeed less advanced than some such as South Korea or Taiwan (see chapter 8). Until the 1980s, the weakness of Irish indigenous industry, and the extent of reliance on new foreign firms for industrial growth, was rarely measured or recognised as a matter of concern in official circles. The prevailing attitude, while perhaps implicitly recognising that much of the strength of industry in Ireland was in new foreign industry, appeared to regard this as no great cause for concern. There has, however, been some greater recognition of this problem since the early 1980s, although it is not yet clear that there will be an adequate policy response. The next chapter suggests that there can be no grounds for complacency about future industrial development if foreign firms are to be heavily relied on for growth and the stagnation and decline of indigenous industry continues.

7

Foreign Industries in Ireland

7.i. THE IMPORTANCE OF FOREIGN INDUSTRY

In the last chapter it was concluded that indigenous industry contributed rather little to the improvement in the overall performance of industry in Ireland since the 1950s. Being confined to a limited range of sectors and generally experiencing declining market shares in those which are internationally traded, the growth of indigenous industry was not sufficient to contribute anything to employment growth in the past 20 years or so. And since indigenous firms have remained largely oriented to the domestic market, they also contributed little to the export development which was necessary to ease the balance of payments constraint that had virtually halted growth in the 1950s. It is evident, therefore, that new foreign-owned industries contributed much to industrial expansion and this chapter evaluates the scale and nature of this expansion of foreign industries. It also attempts to draw some conclusions concerning both their likely future contribution to Irish industrial development and the extent of the potential benefits of such foreign direct investment in late-industrialising countries generally.

Section 6.i has already given some indication of the importance of foreign direct investment in the process of Ireland's industrial growth after the 1950s. To briefly repeat the main features, by the mid-1980s foreign firms accounted for more than 35% of manufacturing employment, with over three-quarters of this employment being in firms which had started up since the 1950s. The increase in employment of these foreign New Industries was more than sufficient to account for all of manufacturing employment growth since the mid-1960s when trade liberalisation began; in the 1980s, however, employment in foreign-owned industries has declined. Even more striking has been the contribution of foreign firms to export growth. The foreign New Industries have been highly export oriented with 85% to 90% of their output, on average, going for export. All foreign industries (old and new combined) accounted for as much as 70% of manufactured exports by 1980 (Telesis Report, 1982).

Table 7.1 illustrates the sectoral distribution of employment in foreign industries in Ireland compared with that of indigenous industry, showing a striking difference between the two. It is noticeable that foreign industries are more heavily concentrated in sectors where one would expect to find a relatively high proportion of 'modern' technically advanced activities, with significant entry barriers. Thus over 60% of their employment is in Metals & Engineering and Chemicals alone. By comparison, indigenous industry has a substantially greater proportion of employment in Food, Drink & Tobacco, Paper & Printing, Non-Metallic Mineral Products, and Timber & Furniture. It was already seen, in chapter 6, that these indigenous industries are mostly sheltered from foreign competition or otherwise relatively free from the constraints of entry barriers for newcomers. So this first impression of the composition of foreign industries suggests that they are largely responsible for a shift of the manufacturing sector as a whole into more modern, technically advanced industries.

The scale of foreign direct investment has been such that Ireland, despite its small size, has become quite an important site for transnational manufacturing companies (TNCs), compared with most late-industrialising countries. The most complete data on this concern US-owned manufacturing TNCs. By 1985, the employment of these companies in Ireland was equivalent to 2.3% of their employment in all the 'developing countries' as conventionally defined.[1] Only nine of the developing countries exceeded Ireland's share of these companies' employment, namely Brazil, Mexico, Philippines, India, Malaysia, Argentina, Taiwan, Venezuela and Singapore. With the exception of Singapore, all these countries have much larger populations than Ireland. Other countries besides the United States, of course, are the base of TNCs, but these too have substantial investments in Ireland accounting for over half of Irish employment in foreign-owned industry in the mid-1980s. It is thus unlikely that Ireland's importance as a site for transnational manufacturing investment ranks much lower for all TNCs than for US companies alone.[2]

Furthermore, the fact that TNC subsidiaries in Ireland are very highly export oriented, in contrast to a good deal of such investment worldwide, means that Ireland must rank even higher as a site for export-oriented manufacturing TNCs — probably above India, Argentina and Venezuela. This point is important for the question whether reliance on foreign export-oriented manufacturing companies is likely to prove a useful *general* solution to the problem of late industrialisation worldwide. If this type of investment is so limited in scale that a very small country like Ireland has received an important share of it — without finding this anything like sufficient to resolve its unemployment problem — it must be doubted whether many countries can look to this type of industry for an important contribution to satisfying their development aspirations.

Table 7.1: Sectoral Distribution of Employment in Foreign and Indigenous Manufacturing, 1986 (thousands)

Sector	Foreign	%	Indigenous	%
Metals & Engineering	36.5	48.7	26.0	20.6
Chemicals	9.0	12.0	4.1	3.2
Clothing, Footwear & Leather	6.5	8.7	10.4	8.2
Food	5.9	7.9	34.7	27.5
Textiles	4.3	5.7	6.6	5.2
Drink & Tobacco	2.4	3.2	6.7	5.3
Paper & Printing	2.1	2.8	11.9	9.4
Non-Metallic Mineral Products	2.1	2.8	11.5	9.1
Timber & Furniture	0.8	1.1	9.3	7.4
Miscellaneous	5.4	7.2	5.0	4.0
	75.0	100.0	126.2	100.0

Source: Industrial Development Authority Annual Report 1986, adjusted so that the Guinness brewery is classified as indigenous here.

7.ii FACTORS INFLUENCING FOREIGN DIRECT INVESTMENT

In order to understand the behaviour of foreign industries in Ireland, it is useful to begin with some consideration of the factors which are thought to influence foreign direct manufacturing investment in general. A basic point which should be recognised at the outset is that manufacturing industries do not generally move freely around the world to take advantage, say, of cheap labour or government incentives. Rather, there are factors influencing their choice of location, such that only certain types of industrial activity locate outside advanced industrial areas. This means that late-developers seeking to attract foreign industrial investment are competing for shares of a rather limited amount of it which is sufficiently mobile. Furthermore, most foreign industries aim to produce primarily for the host country's *domestic* market, having been induced to invest by a large market size and/or protection. This means that latecomers seeking export-oriented foreign manufacturing investment are competing for only a segment of those foreign industries which are sufficiently mobile to locate outside an advanced industrial environment.[3]

Local Market-oriented Direct Investment

The strong attraction, for many industries, of an advanced industrial environment and large local markets is reflected in the fact that the bulk of foreign direct manufacturing investment has gone to advanced countries, not the low-income LDCs. The rapid growth, since the Second World War, of such investment flowing between advanced industrial countries has been explained as part of the process of increasingly oligopolistic competition. Hirsch (1976) points out that there is particularly wide scope for interpenetration of high-income foreign markets by advanced country firms in industries characterised by firm-specific assets, such as proprietary technology and marketing strength. These high-technology, product-differentiated industries are generally ones where highly concentrated, oligopolistic structures prevail, e.g. chemicals, pharmaceuticals, instruments, computers, cars, cosmetics, etc. In such industries, as Hymer (1972) argues, there are large overhead costs such as R & D, design, marketing and capital equipment, which must be covered by a high volume of sales. Consequently the successful firms are large and have become intense rivals for market shares since the loss of market shares can lead to cumulative decline, given the advantages of large size. Once such large oligopolistic firms had developed a national (or continental) scale of operations, the dynamics of competition pushed them on to a wider multinational scale, selling their products in other countries.

In many cases direct foreign investment, rather than exporting, was the means chosen to penetrate foreign markets. The decision to produce abroad is apparently often influenced rather little by considerations of transport costs and relative labour costs in the two countries. This may be deduced from the fact that most foreign direct manufacturing investment has gone to advanced countries, which are generally neither the most distant markets from the home base of the firms involved, nor the sites with lowest wage costs. The concentration of foreign investment in advanced countries points to the importance, as factors facilitating direct investment, of a large local market, political 'reliability', and an advanced industrial environment capable of supplying specialised inputs, services and skills. It seems, too, that foreign direct investment in advanced countries is often motivated by the need to compete more effectively with rival firms based in the host country, as well as by the existence or possibility of protectionist measures against imports (Hymer, 1972).

Due to the importance of these considerations in motivating local market-oriented foreign direct manufacturing investment, most less-developed countries have proved less attractive as sites. However, strong protection against imports has proved to be something of a substitute for a large local market, particularly in the more politically 'reliable' LDCs (i.e. reliable from the point of view of the foreign capitalist). However, an industrially undeveloped environment remains a constraint on the types of industry which will go even to protected LDCs.

Vernon's (1966) analysis of the product life-cycle is useful in clarifying the issues raised here. He points out that most product innovations occur in the most advanced industrial countries, and that the inputs, production techniques and final specifications of a new product may vary quite widely for some time. This means that it must be produced in a location which offers flexibility in the choice of inputs and productive equipment, swift and easy communication with the firm's technical development base, and similar ease of communication with customers in a substantial market who will give feedback on the most desirable product specifications. Consequently, such a product will tend to be produced in, or close to, a major advanced industrial centre. Later, as the product matures somewhat and as the existence of a market abroad is established, it will be feasible to produce it in other advanced countries offering similar conditions. But it is only when the product is quite standardised and the production process settled and mature that it will be possible to establish the industry in an industrially undeveloped country.

Export-oriented Direct Investment

The same constraints just referred to are relevant to the type of export-oriented foreign industries which can be set up in industrially undeveloped countries. Thus Vernon's (1966) analysis proceeds to suggest that as products become fully standardised, with mature production processes, their production comes to depend less on the external economies of advanced industrial centres. At the same time, their sales come to depend more on price and less on novelty, product differentiation or strong marketing. At this point, the low cost of labour in less-developed areas would prove to be an attraction for relocation of production (even though the target markets may be in developed countries), especially for relatively labour-intensive products where labour costs substantially affect the price. But Vernon also stresses that only a limited range of industries meet these requirements sufficiently: 'Manufacturing processes which receive significant inputs from the local economy, such as skilled labour, repairmen, reliable power, spare parts, industrial materials processed according to exacting specification, and so on, are less appropriate to the less-developed areas than those that do not have such requirements. Unhappily, most industrial processes require one or another ingredient of this difficult sort.'

Helleiner (1973), writing some years later, adds some other categories of export-oriented foreign investment which would be possible in less-developed countries. In addition to technically mature, unskilled labour-intensive final products which mostly fall within the same category that Vernon discusses,[4] Helleiner includes basic processing of local raw materials and, more importantly, simple labour-intensive activities or processes which are only part of a longer production process. In this last category, which showed rapid growth from the mid-1960s, the *final* product may be relatively new, unstandardised and the product of advanced technology, but one or more *stages* of its production would be technically simple and relatively labour-intensive and hence suitable for less-developed countries. Dunning (1979) describes this type of foreign investment as 'vertical' specialisation by location, as opposed to 'horizontal' specialisation where the whole production process for each product made by the firm is concentrated in a particular place. Examples of 'vertical' specialisation now occur in a wide range of industries including electronics, vehicles and electrical machinery.

In this type of activity, the organisational capability of TNCs enables them to relocate certain parts of the firm's production, or to sub-contract parts to LDC firms, in places far distant from the base of the firm's operations. The organisation of the operation as a whole may still be subject to external economies, so that R & D and often much of the production process remains located in or close to large industrial centres. But certain stages of production no longer are subject to this constraint since the TNC's large size and organisational ability, together with improving communications and transport, enable it to 'internalise' the external economies. In other words, the R & D, design, supply of skill-intensive and technology-intensive inputs, and marketing are arranged by the firm's base in an advanced country, so that the unskilled labour-intensive production unit in the LDC does not need to be in a convenient location where it can perform these functions for itself.

Helleiner (1973) also makes some suggestions about the factors which influence the particular choice of countries as sites for export-manufacturing of this type: 'the important factors in a foreign investor's selection of a country are low labour costs, limited distance, special concessions (which may offset the labour cost and distance factors) and political "reliability" or "stability".' The attraction of Taiwan, South Korea, Hong Kong, and Singapore would be explained by the combination of low labour costs (in the early 1970s) and political reliability, while Mexico's attraction, despite somewhat higher labour costs, Helleiner suggests, showed the influence of distance costs (for exports to the USA). He also mentions that Spain, Portugal, Ireland and Greece have played a similar role in Europe, presumably subject to similar factors influencing the choice of country. Finally, Helleiner warns that local linkage and learning effects and other 'dynamic' benefits for the host countries in this type of export-manufacturing may be small and of rather little help to long-term development.

Nayyar's (1978) analysis confirms Helleiner's on a number of points. He also mentions, as important categories of export-manufacturing by TNCs in less-developed countries, simple labour-intensive final products and specialised, labour-intensive processes in the manufacture of components and in assembly operations which are part of a larger production process. The choice of countries as sites, he argues, is mainly influenced by labour costs, political reliability and labour docility (or repression), though he also recognises that proximity to the target market is an important consideration as well, as in the case of Mexico's proximity to the USA. Nayyar stresses that TNC based, export-led growth could not be feasible for many Third World countries due to the limited amount of it and its special requirements, while he also expresses doubts about its benefits for long-term development.

7.iii.   THE NATURE OF FOREIGN DIRECT INVESTMENT IN IRELAND

The motivation for foreign direct manufacturing investment in Ireland can now be considered in the light of the discussion of the last section. The first significant wave of foreign involvement in manufacturing in Ireland occurred during the protectionist phase of Irish policy which began in the 1930s. As was mentioned in chapter 4, little information is available on the scale or timing of foreign involvement in this period but it did evidently encompass quite an important minority share of manufacturing activity by the early 1960s.[5] The fact that this foreign investment occurred in a period of high protection, and the fact that the overall level of manufactured exports remained very low, indicates that this was essentially local market-oriented foreign investment induced by protection. Probably much of it occurred in the 1930s and 1940s, which was relatively early by most international comparisons. But since most of it was by British firms accustomed to regarding Ireland as a local market and with relatively small logistical difficulties in operating an Irish plant, this was scarcely surprising.

It seems fairly clear that these foreign manufacturing plants were generally engaged in technically mature, standardised industries or in final phase and assembly-type activities. These types of operation are commonly referred to in the literature as characteristic of local market-oriented foreign investment in less-developed countries. Those which would have depended on the high skills, close linkages with related industries and the other external economies of advanced industrial centres were not much in evidence. This conclusion must be deduced largely from general studies of industry in Ireland in the early 1960s, which unfortunately make no special reference to firms with major foreign participation. However, the lack of interest in focussing particularly on them at the time suggests that in many respects the same generalisations were considered to apply to all of industry. So descriptions of Irish industry in the late 1950s or early 1960s (as in reports of the Committee on Industrial Organisation; *Science and Irish Economic Development (1966);* or McAleese, 1971a) probably apply to these 'foreign' plants in many respects. Irish industry at that time was said to be characterised by generally low skills, virtually no R & D, a high import content, low value-added and a virtual absence of capital goods production. It does appear, however, that while these characteristics would have applied to the *Irish plants* of foreign firms, many of them were in industries which, at that time at least, had high skill or R & D requirements at some stage of the firm's operations. They were also often characterised by other barriers to entry such as product differentiation and strong marketing. Consequently many of them were engaged in activities which Irish indigenous firms could not so easily enter, even though the Irish plant's stage of the operation was rather undemanding. Examples would be in car assembly, pharmaceuticals, electrical appliances, highly processed foods and other branded consumer goods.

The Nature of Export-oriented Foreign Industries

From the 1950s onwards, however, there began a large inflow of highly export-oriented foreign manufacturing investment. In due course, these new exporting foreign firms came to employ more people than the older, formerly protected ones.

The new foreign industries, i.e. those which received New or Small Industry grants, have consistently been highly export oriented, as mentioned above. McAleese (1977, table 4.2) found that they exported 87.6% of gross output in 1973. An earlier survey, *Survey of Grant-aided Industry* (1967, table 2.2), found that all New Grant-aided industries (Irish and foreign) exported 85% of gross output in 1966, and this would suggest an even higher percentage for the foreign firms alone. And

O'Farrell and O'Loughlin (1980, p.8) report that new foreign industries exported 89.4% of output in 1976. The IDA (1985) found that exports accounted for 82% of sales of all foreign-owned industries in 1983, but this included the older, formerly protected foreign firms and it would be consistent with a somewhat higher figure for New Grant-aided foreign industries. The question arises whether these new foreign industries fall into the categories of export-oriented industries in less-developed countries suggested by Vernon, Helleiner, Nayyar and others, as discussed in section 7.ii. Much of the evidence, in fact, suggests that many of the exporting foreign firms in Ireland have been engaged in fairly similar types of activities to those found in more conventionally recognised less-developed or newly industrialising countries, although some quite significant differences have emerged, particularly in more recent years.

In the literature on export-oriented foreign manufacturing investment in LDCs discussed above, the main types of activity referred to were: (a) basic processing of local resources, (b) technically mature and standardised labour-intensive final products, and (c) the relatively simple *stages* within a longer process of production of often quite sophisticated goods. The second and third of these categories are generally regarded as the high growth areas in foreign investment in LDCs. It is of interest, therefore, to note Northcott's (1969/70) comments which would place the new foreign plants established in Ireland up to the late 1960s in these two categories. Most of these new plants, he said, tended to be of the kind where dependence on the support of facilities of a major industrial centre were less than average. These were either

> plants making relatively simple products, where all or most of the processes can be done conveniently in a single plant of only moderate size; and plants doing relatively straightforward processes in the construction of a somewhat more complicated product, either assembling a final product, the most difficult components for which have been made elsewhere, or making components for assembly into final products elsewhere. Both kinds of activity tend to depend mainly on semi-skilled labour, and accordingly do not normally pay very high wages.

The *Survey of Grant-aided Industry* (1967) also noted the heavy reliance of new foreign plants on parent organisations and their low backward linkages with the local economy, commenting that many establishments were little more than production units. Heavy reliance on parent companies — for example, for technical development, marketing and supply of inputs — would be consistent with activities fitting into categories (b) and (c) above. Such findings, however, would not be so characteristic of much of the foreign direct investment in advanced industrial countries, where strong marketing functions, some degree of technical development and greater reliance on local suppliers is typical. Concerning innovation, McAleese (1977) found that in 1973 'only one out of every eight overseas firms . . . named the Irish plant as prime source of new products. Most overseas firms leave product innovation to the parent company'. He also found that there seemed to be 'a rather limited degree of autonomous marketing activity on the part of the overseas firms'. In fact 55% of their exports went direct to affiliate companies, and only one-quarter of new foreign firms did not sell any output to an affiliate company.

The picture of new foreign industries sketched above, is filled out by a number of other studies from the early 1970s. On the issues of R & D practices and technical skill requirements of new foreign industries, Cooper and Whelan (1973, p. 31) said

> not only is there a very small demand for R & D, but also the kind of production processes that are involved do not make much call on scientific and technical skills in general.

Buckley (1975) agreed:

> the main gap in the job creation spectrum is in highly trained scientific workers, technologists and research workers.

And Cooper and Whelan drew the conclusion that

> a continuance of present trends would — logically speaking — end up in a situation where a relatively unskilled Irish population at low levels of technical ability and wages provided the labour input to operate the sophisticated technological industries developed in other countries.

Teeling (1975, ch. 1) specifically addressed the question whether the new foreign industries operating in Ireland in the early 1970s were similar to the mature, standardised and labour-intensive activities suggested by Vernon as likely to arise in less-developed countries — suggestions which were borne out in empirical studies of LDCs by Lary (1968) and Mahfuzer Rahman (1973). Teeling finds that in 1954-71, the composition of the new foreign projects coming to Ireland did in fact bear a close resemblance to those found in these two studies of LDCs. This was seen in the common predominance of products such as Textiles, Clothing, Footwear, Plastics, Light Engineering, Electrical and Electronic Goods. He remarks that 'this is in line with the expectation that cheap labour in Ireland was an attraction to offshore investors to undertake labour-intensive mature standardised projects'.

The studies quoted above, however, are based on observations made at various times up to the early 1970s. The composition of new foreign industries in Ireland has been changing since that time, with fine chemicals/pharmaceuticals, instrument engineering and, above all, electronics becoming more important. These are industries which certainly involve advanced technology and high skills. But as noted in the earlier discussion (section 7.ii) of the international literature on foreign direct investment, it is possible that quite simple, relatively low-skilled operations *within* such industries can be located in an LDC while the higher skill functions remain mostly in advanced countries. Consequently, the rapid growth of such industries in Ireland would not *necessarily* mean that the Irish industrial structure was being significantly upgraded.

In practice, it seems that many of the newer 'high technology' industries have tended to lack key higher skill functions, as indicated by a detailed assessment of new foreign firms in Ireland in the 1980s which included the following:

(On electrical and electronic firms)

> Of the 60 companies surveyed, none have a truly stand-alone operation in Ireland, and only three have operations in Ireland which embody the key competitive elements of the company's business. All others are currently manufacturing satellites, performing partial steps in the manufacturing process. Skill development and linkages in Ireland have been limited. The electronics industry is a high-skilled industry worldwide, but the activities in Ireland's electronics industry do not now reflect this.

(On mechanical engineering firms)

> Ireland's foreign-owned mechanical engineering companies consist mainly of sub-assembly and assembly shops of the sort commonly found in newly industrialising countries. . . . Of the 34 shops surveyed, about half had only one or two skilled blue-collar workers and one or two engineers.

(On foreign-owned firms in general)

> Foreign-owned industrial operations in Ireland with few exceptions do not embody the key competitive activities of the businesses in which they participate; do not employ significant numbers of skilled workers; and are not significantly integrated into traded and skilled sub-supply industries in Ireland. (Telesis Report 1982).

Thus, it seems justifiable to conclude that many of the foreign export-oriented industries which came to Ireland had some similarities to those found in countries which are more conventionally classified as NICs or LDCs. This indicates that Ireland was mainly attracting relatively mobile plants which were capable of selecting a location outside the major advanced industrial areas and without a large local market.

An important qualification, however, is that many of the newer foreign firms in the 'high technology' sectors employ significantly greater numbers of technically skilled and professional people than is typical of such firms in the NICs. In the electronics industry, for example, over 90% of employees were unskilled, non-craft production workers in Singapore and Hong Kong in the early 1980s, compared with only 60% in Ireland. At the same time, the figure of 60% for Ireland was a good deal higher than the figures of 34% to 39% for the UK, USA and Denmark (O'Brien, 1985, table 6.10). Thus the proportion of more highly skilled people in this important industry in Ireland is in an intermediate position between the NICs and the advanced industrial countries.

The explanation for this situation seems to be that, as noted in the quotes above from Telesis (1982), key business functions such as R & D which would employ large numbers of skilled people are relatively lacking among foreign firms in Ireland by comparison with the same industries in more advanced economies. O'Brien (1985, table 6.8), for example, finds that R & D expenditure as a percentage of sales in the electronics industry is under 1% in Ireland compared with 6.4% to 10.8%

in Japan, Finland, Denmark, the UK and the USA. But the stages of production conducted in Ireland by many firms in the 'modern' sectors such as electronics do require more skilled technicians and engineers than is typically the case in the NICs, e.g. for testing and quality control associated with final assembly operations. Thus the foreign firms coming to Ireland in such industries have had greater requirements for technically skilled and professional people than they do in the NICs, even though they commonly lack the key technological and business functions of the firm.

Ireland's Advantage as a Location

If many foreign export-oriented industries in Ireland have had noticeable similarities to those in more conventionally defined NICs or LDCs, the question arises why did they choose Ireland rather than somewhere else with much lower labour costs? The factors usually mentioned as important influences on location decisions of mobile TNC production units are low labour costs, a docile or repressed labour force, ease of access to major markets, political 'reliability', an acceptable infrastructure of transport and communications, and government incentives such as grants and tax concessions. In the 1950s and the first half of the 1960s, at least, Ireland would have ranked quite highly on virtually any of these criteria — among countries which would have been seriously considered as potential sites. It should be remembered that few countries made strenuous attempts to attract mobile export-oriented TNC plants until around the mid-1960s, and in fact few in the Third World would have had the basic infrastructure and/or political reliability required to do so. The relatively low-wage countries on the periphery of the developed world, therefore, would have been rated quite highly as feasible sites, so it was possible for Puerto Rico and Ireland to emerge as forerunners in this activity.

By the late 1960s and early 1970s, however, a number of other countries, especially the Far Eastern NICs, were becoming acceptable sites of some importance, with much lower labour costs than Puerto Rico or Ireland. Against such competition, Ireland's continuing ability to attract substantial amounts of TNC investment would have to be put down mainly to advantages of proximity and access to major markets, if one sticks to the conventional influences on plant location mentioned above. Teeling (1975, ch. 2) considers whether tariff-free access to a large market (the UK in this period) and transport cost differentials would account for the attraction of Ireland. He concludes that since Singapore and Hong Kong had similar rights of market access to the UK, and since the cost of transporting the relevant goods was generally small, these factors would not explain Ireland's attraction. There are, however, other advantages of proximity such as ease of communication, short delivery times and ease of travel for salesmen, repairmen and executives. For these reasons, the choice of location even *within* a country such as Britain can be influenced by ease of access to the major markets and service centres.[6]

Teeling recognises that these aspects of proximity do matter but another factor which he stresses is no doubt significant too. He argues that information, uncertainty and risk are all important or perhaps vital variables in offshore investment decisions. Because of such factors as the relatively long and successful history of promoting foreign investment in Ireland, the experience and internationally recognised efficiency of the IDA or SFADCO, Ireland's proximity to advanced countries, and cultural ties with the USA and UK, 'on each of these variables, Ireland was shown to have a comparative advantage over competing locations'. Teeling's main evidence to support this is the fact that most foreign investors in Ireland were quite small and had little international experience, by the standards of most TNCs. This suggests that they would have high information costs and high perceptions of risk and uncertainty — particularly regarding more distant locations — compared with larger, more experienced firms. Over half of the firms he surveyed were undertaking their first foreign investment when they came to Ireland. In 1971, 46% of the Irish subsidiaries had parent companies with sales of less than $10 million, compared with only 6% in Singapore. And whereas 30% of the foreign firms establishing plants in Ireland in 1954-66 had more than six foreign subsidiaries, this proportion fell to 18% in 1967-72; thus in the later period, Ireland's comparative advantage seemed to be shifting more towards small inexperienced TNCs while larger companies were prepared to go to the NICs. Teeling also refers to other studies which found that foreign firms in Puerto Rico and the Mexican border region were also relatively small and inexperienced, suggesting that they too are averse to risk and value the close contact with the USA, which is comparable to Ireland's position in relation to Europe. O'Loughlin and O'Farrell (1980), with data relating to 1976-77, confirm Teeling's earlier finding that most foreign investors in Ireland are relatively small and inexperienced TNCs, probably with high information costs and high perceptions of risk and uncertainty.

Since 1973, Ireland has had the further attraction for export-oriented foreign investors of being a member of the EEC. There is no doubt that this has been very important. According to a survey of foreign firms in Ireland reported in the *Allied Irish Bank Review*, April 1981, two-thirds of them (and presumably an even greater proportion of those established since 1973) regarded a site within the EEC as an important or a necessary attraction, since their main purpose is exporting to Europe. Consistent with this view is the increased proportion of new foreign investment accounted for by firms based in countries outside the EEC, and the increased proportion of manufactured exports from Ireland going to other EEC countries besides the UK. These trends suggest that much foreign manufacturing investment in Ireland in the 1970s and 1980s was by non-EEC firms selecting an attractive site within the EEC to produce for European markets.[7] The attractions for foreign investors of Ireland's membership of the EEC are not confined to the advantages of having a position inside the existing EEC tariff wall. Setting up a plant in an EEC member country also has the advantage of offering insurance against the possible increase of protectionism, which many firms have been concerned about. And in addition, EEC membership appears to be perceived by many as offering some further guarantee of political stability and 'reliability', although Ireland's position in this regard has not been greatly in doubt. Thus the Allied Irish Banks survey referred to above reported that 90% of foreign firms interviewed categorised the Republic of Ireland as politically 'very stable' or 'fairly stable', and 90% also indicated that the political unrest in Northern Ireland did not significantly alter that opinion.

Ireland's membership of the European Community, therefore, has given the country a major advantage over the LDCs and NICs in attracting foreign firms which aim to sell mainly to European markets. In addition, Ireland offers a more highly skilled and educated labour force than most of these countries, with a surplus of some skills which are much in demand internationally, such as those of electronic engineers and technicians. In recent years, therefore, the main sources of direct competition for the sort of foreign projects which would be potential investors in Ireland have been other European countries rather than the LDCs and NICs. As compared with these countries, the main attractions of Ireland have been minimal taxes on company profits, government grants, and labour costs which are among the lowest in Western Europe.

To sum up on the nature of foreign industries which came to Ireland after the 1950s, they were mostly production units, mainly requiring relatively unskilled labour, lacking in key business functions of the firm and having low local linkages. Consequently they were quite mobile or footloose — capable of setting up outside advanced industrial areas in order to take advantage of lower labour costs, tax concessions and grant incentives. In this respect many of them were structurally quite similar to export-oriented foreign plants in the LDCs or NICs. But Ireland was able to sustain higher wage levels than these countries while attracting many such industries, largely because of its favourable location, market access, political 'reliability', and various other factors which reduce risk, uncertainty and information costs for small and inexperienced foreign investors especially. In addition, many of the newer foreign investors in the 'high-technology' sectors in Ireland have had significantly greater skill requirements than is typical of foreign industries in the LDCs or NICs, and the skills required have been a good deal more readily available in Ireland.

The location of foreign New Industries *within* Ireland confirms the view that most of them tended to be highly mobile, at least in the 1960s and 1970s. O'Farrell (1980) finds that 59.1% of those established in 1960-73 were set up in the less-developed Designated Areas in the West, compared with only 42.8% of new Irish-owned projects in the same period.[8] Similarly, four of the most peripheral western regions accounted for 31.1% of employment in foreign firms set up in the period 1973-81 compared with only 19.2% of employment in new indigenous projects established in the same period.[9] This is in line with the view that foreign plants tended to be relatively mobile. Since part of the attraction of Ireland, compared with advanced countries in Europe, lies in Ireland's relatively low labour costs and high grant incentives, it makes sense for highly mobile plants to go to the small towns and rural areas where higher grants are offered and labour costs are somewhat lower.

A few sectors of foreign industry which have grown rapidly

over the past decade, however, are more concentrated in the more industrialised regions, unlike the typical pattern of foreign firms in other more mature industries. Of the nine planning regions in the country, the East, South-West, South-East and Mid-West may be taken as the main industrial areas; these regions have the greatest number of manufacturing establishments and jobs. These four regions together account for 70% of the country's industrial establishments, but they account for as much as 87% of establishments in Office & Data Processing Machinery, 83% in Pharmaceuticals and 77% in Electrical Engineering (*Census of Industrial Production*, 1985). These three sectors are predominantly foreign owned and mostly relatively new.

It appears from this pattern of location that foreign firms in the newer high-technology sectors have tended to concentrate in the more developed regions, while those in other industries tended to disperse to less developed areas. The location pattern of the high-technology industries is probably influenced by the availability of professional and technical skills as well as the attraction of universities and technical colleges. Even though the electronics industry, for example, employs a smaller proportion of professional and technical staff than in more advanced economies, it still has quite a significant requirement for such people. Thus there are indications here that advantages of external economies are developing to some degree in certain sectors which developed mainly as a result of foreign investment.

7.iv.   SECONDARY EFFECTS AND OUTLOOK FOR FOREIGN INDUSTRIES

Some of the issues which arise in considering the secondary effects of foreign New Industries on the domestic economy have already been touched on in the last section. This section looks further into these and other related issues. Under the heading of the secondary effects of foreign industry, the following issues are discussed briefly: their effects on the balance of payments, the question of possible pre-emption of indigenous development, their stimulus to the local economy by purchasing inputs, the extent of their development of skills and knowledge which could assist further development, and the issue of dualism.

The first two issues mentioned — relating to balance of

payments effects and pre-emption of indigenous development — feature prominently in critiques of foreign investment in much of the Dependency literature, which was referred to in section 2.ii. However, such critiques are usually set in a context, as in most Latin American countries, where the bulk of the foreign manufacturing investment is in production for the protected domestic market. When most foreign investment is highly export-oriented these critiques must be reconsidered.

Balance of Payments Effects

The net foreign exchange earnings of foreign-owned plants are determined by capital inflows and export earnings on the one hand, balanced against foreign debt servicing costs, profit outflow, foreign royalty payments and payments for imported inputs on the other. It can be seen, therefore, that if all or nearly all production is for the local market, net foreign exchange earnings on current account will be *negative* so long as some profit outflow, foreign royalty payments or import of inputs occur. The foreign balance on capital account would also be negative eventually so long as debts incurred abroad are fully repaid to the creditor, and the firm's own capital investment gives rise to commercially acceptable profits which are withdrawn from the host country eventually. In addition, loan capital may be raised in the host country to finance at least part of the investment, and any profit outflow arising from this adds to the negative side of the foreign exchange balance.

If all or virtually all of production is for export, however, the net foreign exchange earnings for the host country must generally be *positive*. For the value of total output is made up of the value of material and service inputs and factor payments (wages, rents, the firm's profits, other debt and royalty payments). If all output goes for export, earning foreign exchange, then the value-added domestically to any inputs purchased in the host country and factor payments made there represent net earnings of foreign exchange. And wages, at least, must be paid to host country residents while local purchases of at least some inputs such as electricity, transport and packaging are inevitable. The positive balance of payments effect may, of course, be a good deal smaller than the value of exports if most inputs are imported, value-added is small, and/or wages represent the main local factor payment and receive a relatively small share of value-added.

As regards the net foreign exchange earnings of foreign New Industries in Ireland, McAleese (1977) has made estimates for 1974, shown here in table 7.2. His 'high' estimate is simply the difference between their exports and their imports of raw materials, components and other goods and services. The 'low' estimate, which is probably closer to the reality, is derived by subtracting further from this figure the foreign exchange outflow (i.e. repatriated profits and other payments abroad) arising from their net surplus, which is itself defined as the difference between gross output and current expenditure. The estimates in the table suggest that net foreign exchange earnings of foreign New Industries were probably no more than half the gross value of their exports, though still quite substantial. In a related exercise, McAleese (1978) estimates that the 'net' increase in manufactured exports (i.e. net of import content) in 1961-73 was equal to 48% of their gross increase, whereas the 'net' increase in primary exports equalled 77% of their gross increase.[10] Consequently, although the increase in gross manufactured exports exceeded that of gross primary exports (£348 million versus £306 million), the 'net' increase of primary exports made a greater contribution to foreign exchange earnings (£237 million versus £167 million). These observations would mean, too, that with manufactured exports accounting for an increasing proportion of total exports since the 1950s, foreign exchange earnings would have been a declining proportion of the value of exports.

Table 7.2: Estimated Net Foreign Exchange Earnings of Foreign New Industry, 1974 (£m.)

Exports	Imports	Net Surplus	Import Content of Net Surplus
383.6	161.2	129.9	74.6

Net Earnings		Net Earnings as % of Exports	
Low	High	Low	High
147.8	222.4	38.5%	58%

Source: McAleese (1977), chapter 5.

More recent data from the IDA (1985) show that exports of foreign-owned industries amounted to 82% of their sales in 1983. At the same time, their imported materials and services amounted to 36% of their sales. Their profits were 16% of sales, and it is estimated that between three-quarters and four-fifths of these profits, equivalent to 12-13% of the value of sales, were withdrawn from the country (IDA, 1985, section 5.5). This allows us to estimate that the net foreign exchange earnings of foreign-owned industries in 1983 were about one-third of the value of their total sales, or (assuming a similar cost structure for exports and domestic sales) about half the value of their exports. Thus the net foreign exchange contribution continued to be positive, although substantially less than the value of sales or exports.

Pre-emption of Indigenous Development

The second issue referred to was the question of pre-emption of indigenous development by foreign firms. This is usually argued to occur where foreign firms are selling in competition with existing or potential indigenous producers in the domestic market. In Ireland, however, the vast majority of new foreign investors have received capital grants subject to the condition that they produce primarily for export and are not creating new competition for indigenous firms in the home market. Consequently, new foreign firms have rarely been accused of causing a problem for Irish firms in this regard. Other forms of competition from foreign investors could include competition for skilled labour, capital or local primary products for raw materials. As regards skilled labour, Stewart (1976) reporting on a study of the mid-west region in 1970, mentions that Irish management often remarked on the difficulty of holding skilled workers who tended to move to new foreign firms. Buckley (1975) also mentions that, in some cases, Irish firms suffered from this kind of competition. But, overall, this appears to be a relatively minor problem, going by the relative scarcity of this type of specific complaint about competition from foreign firms. Furthermore, at a time of relatively vocal complaints about shortages of skilled staff in general, in 1979, only about 8% of all manufacturing firms had recruitment difficulties (up from 2-3% in 1975-77).[11]

Again, it must be doubted whether competition from foreign investors in Ireland for capital has represented an important problem for indigenous industry in most of the period under review. Of course, the willingness of the state to grant aid to foreign firms might be seen as reducing the level of *assistance* potentially available for indigenous firms if the state chose to concentrate exclusively on them. However, in the strict sense of capital availability for commercially profitable investments, there appears to have been little question of a capital constraint on indigenous industrial development caused by competition from foreign investors in most of the period under review. From the foundation of the Irish Free State until March 1979, the Irish pound was maintained at one-to-one parity with the pound sterling and Ireland was effectively a part of the same money market as the UK. Credit conditions, interest rates and the availability of capital were thus effectively determined by conditions in the much larger UK economy, and would have been little affected by the activities of foreign firms in Ireland. But since Ireland joined the European Monetary System in 1979, while the United Kingdom did not, exchange controls have been in operation and the availability of capital and rates of interest are now much more affected by conditions in Ireland. With foreign investors apparently raising an appreciable proportion of their capital in Ireland, they could have affected capital availability for others at times.

Competition from foreign firms for inputs of local primary products has caused problems for some indigenous manufacturing firms but this would be important in only a relatively small number of cases. To put this issue in perspective, most of foreign New Industry purchases a small proportion of its materials and components in Ireland while importing a far great proportion. Outside the Food sector, they purchased only 11.2% of such inputs in Ireland in 1974, but in Food the figure was 96.3% (McAleese, 1977, table 5.4). Clearly, then, this problem would be unlikely to arise to any great degree outside the Food industry since that appears to be the only manufacturing sector where access to raw materials may have been an important motivation for foreign investment in Ireland. The foreign-owned portion of the Food industry is relatively small, however, employing just 6,000 in 1986 compared with 35,000 in Irish-owned firms. Thus the overall scale of any problems for indigenous industry caused by competition for primary inputs would be relatively small, although there have been some cases of this.[12]

It is fairly clear, then, that the potentially adverse economic effects of foreign investment on the domestic economy have been quite limited in Ireland since the 1950s. For the most part the relative unimportance of these issues, as compared with some other countries, arises from the fact that highly export-oriented branch plants have different, less adverse effects than local market-oriented foreign investment. The discussion which follows, however, suggests that the type of foreign investment which has occurred in Ireland has also been of limited positive benefit in improving the country's potential for long-term development.

Linkages

Foreign New Industry has had rather limited stimulating effect on local industry through purchasing of inputs. The *Survey of Grant-aided Industry* (1967, p. 104) reported that: 'It is roughly estimated that no more than 1 per cent of the domestic sales in 1966 of the transportable goods industries, excluding the grant-aided industries, went to the latter firms.' Later studies relating to 1974, by McAleese (1977) and McAleese and McDonald (1978), find that the Irish content of materials and components purchases by new foreign firms was 33.7% overall — broken down into 96.3% for Food and 11.2% for other sectors. They find too that the proportion of purchases from Irish sources by these firms had been increasing, but at quite a slow rate of about 2-3 percentage points per decade. O'Loughlin and O'Farrell (1980), using regression analysis on cross-sectional data for 1976, however, did not find evidence of backward linkages continuing to increase. The IDA (1985, table 1) found that in 1983 foreign-owned industries purchased 35.8% of their materials requirements from Irish sources, which was just 2% higher than McAleese's figure for 1974.

These aggregate figures, however, understate to some degree the extent of progress made in developing purchasing linkages, because of changes in the sectoral composition of foreign industry. It seems that most sectors of foreign industry, taken individually, have been increasing the proportion of their materials purchased from Irish sources. But sectors which initially had relatively low purchasing linkages have tended to have the fastest growth in production, so that the proportion of materials purchased from Irish sources by foreign industry as a whole changed little even though the proportion for individual sectors was growing. In particular, foreign firms in the food industry always had the highest purchasing linkages with the local economy, but this sector grew relatively slowly, while other sectors with much lower linkages grew faster. But there has been a noticeable increase in the linkages of non-food industries, starting from a very low level. The proportion of materials purchased in Ireland by foreign firms in industries other than food rose from 11.2% in 1974, as reported by McAleese (1977), to 25% by 1983 (IDA, 1985).

It may be assumed that the very high backward linkages of foreign firms in the food sector are mainly due to purchases of agricultural produce, so that the materials purchases of firms in other sectors would give a better indication of the level of purchases in Ireland of manufactured output. It can be estimated that the purchases of materials inputs in Ireland by foreign non-food industries amounted to £439.8 million in 1983. If all of these purchases were from indigenous manufacturing firms, they amounted to about 6% of the sales of indigenous industry.[13] Thus the backward linkage stimulus to indigenous industry, although not exactly trivial, has not really made a major contribution to indigenous development.

As well as purchases of materials, however, foreign industries have broader linkages with the domestic economy. Wealth generated by industry can be retained in Ireland in the form of wages and salaries, purchases of Irish goods and services as inputs, and reinvestment of profits. In this way, too, further employment and incomes are generated indirectly within the country. On the other hand, part of the value of industrial output leaves the country, in the form of payments for imported materials and services, and profit outflows from foreign-owned companies. Table 7.3 gives a breakdown of the cost structures of a number of categories of industry in terms of percentages of sales, distinguishing items which clearly involve expenditures retained in the Irish economy from other items which involve expenditures abroad or a potential outflow of factor payments.

The table shows that expenditures in the Irish economy are a much higher proportion of the sales of Irish indigenous industry (at 79%) than of foreign-owned industry (at 44%). All the individual items of Irish economy expenditure are a higher proportion of sales among Irish firms, but the main difference from foreign firms is the higher proportion spent on Irish material inputs. This is balanced mainly by the higher propor- tion of the value of foreign industry's output accounted for by imported materials and profits. Their profits do not all necessarily leave the country but the evidence suggests that most of them do eventually; we return to this issue below.

Part of the reason for the relatively high Irish economy expenditures of indigenous industry is because most of the food industry is Irish owned, and Irish materials account for a very high proportion of the value of its sales, as is also shown in table 7.3. But even leaving out the food sector, Irish economy expenditures accounted for 69% of sales of indigenous non-food industries compared with 38% in foreign non-food industries (IDA, 1985, chart 6). Thus, on average, a pound's worth of output from Irish non-food companies means about 80% more spent on Irish inputs than the same output from foreign non-food companies. It may be concluded that growth of foreign industries generally contributes proportionally less to the economy than growth of indigenous industries.

Table 7.3: Industry Cost Structure 1983 (Per Cent of Sales)

	Irish	Foreign	Non-Food	Food
Wages & Salaries	18.85	16.22	21.84	11.28
Irish Materials	45.84	16.38	11.43	64.95
Irish Services	14.10	11.56	15.80	8.58
Irish Expenditures	78.79	44.16	49.07	84.81
Imported Materials	13.45	29.43	27.68	9.87
Imported Services	1.04	6.87	5.60	.71
Profit	1.07	16.07	11.72	1.85
Depreciation	3.02	2.45	3.42	1.78
Interest	2.63	1.02	2.51	0.98
	21.21	55.84	50.93	15.19

Source: Industrial Development Authority (1985), table 1.

To take this point a step further, the composition of the foreign-owned manufacturing sector itself has been changing, so that the fastest growing industries, which have become increasingly important, tend to be those with the lowest Irish economy expenditure. To illustrate this point, table 7.4 shows

Irish economy expenditures as a percentage of sales in those sectors of industry which are predominantly foreign owned. It can be seen that the fast-growing sectors generally have levels of Irish economy expenditures which are significantly below the average for foreign-owned industry. Largely as a result of these trends, it was possible for Ireland to have the highest rate of growth in industrial output in the OECD in the first half of the 1980s while industrial employment slumped and the economy grew a good deal more slowly than in many other countries (see OECD, 1985, table 18).

Table 7.4: Growth Rates and Irish Economy Expenditures in Predominantly Foreign Sectors, 1980-87

Sector	Output annual average growth %		Irish Expenditure as % of Sales 1983
Office & Data Processing Machinery	31.9		24.3
Instrument Engineering	11.9	Instrument Engineering	31.6
		Healthcare Products	38.5
Electrical Engineering	11.4		42.9
Chemicals & Artificial Fibres	8.2	Pharmaceuticals	24.0
		Artificial Fibres	38.8
Mechanical Engineering	2.6	Mechanical Engineering	42.8
		Precision Toolmaking	69.3
Rubber Products	1.6		54.5
'Other' Manufacturing	—5.6		41.6
Total Foreign Manufacturing	n.a		44.2

Sources: Central Statistics Office, Industrial Production Indices for column 1, and unpublished data from the survey reported in IDA (1985) for column 2.

It is worth focussing on the question of profits of foreign companies and profit outflows from Ireland, since this has become an important issue recently. The outflow of profits of foreign companies has grown very quickly in the 1980s and has increased from 2.8% of GDP in 1980 to 7.6% in 1985 and 6.6% in 1987. This outflow includes profits of non-manufacturing companies but estimates of the amount arising from manufacturing suggest it accounts for between 78% and 92% of the total (OECD, 1985, pp. 47, 48, and IDA, 1985, section 5.5). The IDA (1985, section 5.5) estimates that between 75% and 80% of profits of foreign manufacturing firms left the country in 1983.

The main reason for the rapid growth in profit outflows in the 1980s was because the profits themselves increased very quickly, rather than because of a greater propensity to withdraw a higher proportion of profits. The fact is that most of the fastest-growing foreign-owned industries, such as those listed in the top half of table 7.4, are exceptionally profitable (see O'Leary, 1984, for a discussion of factors underlying their high profitability). Profits as a percentage of sales for foreign-owned firms in 1983 were 46% in Pharmaceuticals, 32% in Healthcare Products, 23% in Instrument Engineering, 22% in Office & Data Processing Machinery and 10% in Electrical Engineering — as compared with an overall average for manufacturing of 8% (unpublished data from the survey reported in IDA, 1985). A good deal of these industries are relatively new, established in the second half of the 1970s and early 1980s, with the peak in new foreign investment occurring around 1979-81. As the new industries came on stream, continuing to build up their output for some years after the initial investment, profits increased rapidly as well. O'Malley and Scott (1987) have shown that the trend in profit outflows has been very closely related to trends in the combined sales of the highly profitable, foreign-dominated sectors mentioned above.

It is worth remembering, however, that despite the large profit outflow from foreign companies and their high levels of expenditure on imported inputs, they are still significant net contributors of foreign exchange to the Irish economy because they export a very high proportion of their output.

Development of Skills and Technology
Apart from the linkages with the domestic economy discussed above, foreign firms could, in principle, also provide an

important stimulus to indigenous industrial development by employing and training highly skilled technical, scientific and managerial staff. In this way they would serve to expand the skilled and professional labour force, preparing the way for development of other advanced industries which would be enabled to start up in such a high-skill economy. They could also generate 'spin-offs', in the sense of staff leaving to set up new firms with the benefit of the experience, knowledge and ideas gained while employed in foreign firms. They could, in other words, help to overcome latecomer disadvantages arising from a lack of external economies in skills, from an absence of 'learning by doing', and from a small indigenous R & D base. In practice, however, due to the nature of employment in foreign firms in Ireland, they do not seem to have made a decisive contribution in this regard although their impact has no doubt been positive, perhaps particularly in enhancing managerial skills.

Evidence of the relatively low level of skills in most sectors and the scarcity of R & D activities in foreign firms in Ireland has already been given in section 7.iii, which referred to the conclusions of Cooper and Whelan (1973), Buckley (1975) and the Telesis report to the NESC. A broad reflection of the limited scale of the secondary effects of this type of employment in foreign industry is seen in the continuing relatively low technical skills and scarcity of R & D activities in indigenous industry in general. Another more precise reflection is seen in the small scale of 'spin-offs' from foreign firms. In the electronics sector, Cogan and Onyenadum (1981) found that only five out of the 35 Irish-owned firms had spun off from the 74 foreign firms. All of the five were very small, with average employment of only 24 people by 1981 (a total employment of only 120, or 1% of the industry's total). The foreign 'incubator' firms were all among the minority which undertake some R & D in Ireland. This suggests that the general scarcity of R & D activities in foreign plants in the country is an important constraint on the development of 'spin-offs'.

Dualism

The rapid growth of foreign direct investment in Ireland, with foreign firms behaving differently from Irish ones in some important respects, has led many observers to speak of a 'dualistic' industrial structure. The flavour of these observations is exemplified by Cooper and Whelan's (1973) view that the policy of sustained protection coupled with export promotion through new firms has created a dualistic structure in most industrial sectors. In each sector the protected small firms which characterised the industrial economy in the 1950s co-exist with competitive export-oriented firms which are very frequently foreign owned; and there are some new subsectors where foreign-owned export-oriented firms account for virtually all the production.

Similarly, the OECD (1978, p. 95) said that industrial policies

helped to shape an economy consisting on the one hand of foreign firms which accounted for a large share of the country's output, and moved into the most modern, dynamic sectors, and on the other hand of Irish firms which remained very small and were active in the more traditional industries or in the primary sector.

When such a dualistic structure is apparent, it frequently gives rise to questions such as Kindleberger (1980) asks — whether foreign enterprise

is responsible for dualism and enclaves as the dependencia school seems to think, or is it merely the vehicle for starting the transition from traditional forms of production to modernisation, so that enclaves are the result of resistance on the part of traditional sectors to change, and duality the outcome when the economy and society are only half modernised?

The discussion of this section has suggested that the branches of multinationals set up in Ireland under outward-looking policies have not been responsible for dualism, in the sense of damaging or holding back indigenous development, although at the same time they have not been a major force in promoting indigenous development. It does not necessarily follow, however, that multinationals in Ireland are simply trail-blazers of modernisation, with resistance to change in indigenous industry being the main cause of continuing dualism. The main argument of this book, which is not allowed for in Kindleberger's two alternative explanations, suggests that the established competitive strength of large advanced firms — as represented to a great extent by multinational firms *worldwide* — greatly limits the possibilities of latecomers' indigenous development. This constraint applies no matter how 'modernised' or dynamic are the attitudes and culture of the latecomer.

The Outlook for Expansion of Foreign Industry

Since it has been shown that foreign firms were largely responsible for the improved industrial performance in Ireland after the 1950s, it is important to consider to what extent can they be relied on to make a similar contribution to growth in the future.

First, a few remarks on the older, formerly protected foreign firms, as represented by those which have *not* received New or Small Industry grants. The IDA's employment survey showed a decline in employment in these firms from 20,000 in 1973 to 17,000 in 1980, a fall of about 15% which was worse than the record of Irish-owned industry during the same period. These figures suggest that old foreign firms, as a group, have been in secular decline and probably cannot be relied on to make much contribution to future expansion. Many of the older foreign firms probably simply went into decline following the removal of the protectionist barriers which originally motivated their establishment. But there are some which adapted to more specialised production for export — reacting in much the same way as foreign New Industry to Ireland's outward-looking policies, except that in their case they already had a plant in the country. Some of these firms, in fact, received New Industry grants for expansion and hence they are not included in the figures just quoted.

Even among the newer grant-aided foreign firms, however, there are some worrying signs for the future. It appears that new foreign plants commonly experience rapid employment growth in the early years as they build up to the initial target size, followed by periods of slower growth, stagnation and eventually decline or closure. This life-cycle pattern was in evidence even before the general decline in industrial employment in the 1980s, as is seen in table 7.5 which shows employment change from 1973 to 1980 in foreign-owned New and Small Industry grant-aided plants which were already established before 1973.

Employment in the whole group of firms established prior to 1973, and in most sectors within the group, declined over the following seven years at a time when Ireland had the fastest growing manufacturing sector in the EEC. Thus the rapid overall growth of employment in foreign industry at that time was sustained only by the continuing and growing inflow of *new* first-time foreign investors. This is consistent with the suggestion that foreign firms tend not to grow much after reaching their initial target size but rather tend to decline after some time.

Table 7.5: Employment in Foreign New and Small Industries Established Prior to 1973

	1973	1980	% Change
Food	2,246	2,514	11.9
Drink & Tobacco	376	548	45.7
Textiles	3,829	3,419	—10.7
Clothing & Footwear	3,095	2,168	—30.0
Wood & Furniture	562	448	—20.3
Paper & Printing	1,402	1,209	—13.8
Chemicals	3,490	5,493	57.4
Clay, Glass & Cement	938	941	0
Metals & Engineering	15,017	14,063	—6.4
Other Manufacturing	7,223	6,486	—10.2
TOTAL	38,178	37,289	—2.3

Source: Derived from *IDA Employment Survey.*

In fact, the most recently established firms included in table 7.5 were generally still in the phase of expansion to initial target size during the 1970s. Thus, if we leave out those established in the period 1969-72, employment in firms established before 1969 fell by as much as 12% in 1973-80. (Incidentally, the exceptional growth in Chemicals in table 7.5 is almost entirely due to relatively new firms established in 1969-72.)

These trends would not have been evident in the earlier stages of the inflow of foreign New Industry, since the overall picture would at first have been dominated by the expansion phase of relatively new plants. Thus McAleese and McDonald (1978) found that foreign New Industries established prior to 1966 actually increased their employment up to 1974 by over 40%. However, as time passed, with the average age of plants increasing and the proportion of new expanding plants declining, the situation changed to that shown above.

Furthermore the *overall* trend of employment in foreign-owned firms has been increasingly influenced by the large stock of relatively old declining plants, so that an ever greater inflow of new first-time investors would be needed to maintain any specified growth rate. If there is a lower rate of new first-time investment, the overall trend can eventually turn to decline. The deterioration in the employment record of foreign industries in Ireland in the 1980s was quite largely caused by the combination of the growing influence of this life-cycle pattern and (as will be shown below) a decline in new first-time investment.

In order to judge whether eventual decline of each generation of new firms is likely to be a persistent pattern, one must consider why it has occurred in the past. But in the absence of more detailed research, answers to this question must be rather tentative. First, the technologically mature, labour-intensive foreign industries, which were typical of those established in the 1960s, arrived in Ireland at a relatively late stage of the industry life-cycle. Consequently they would have tended to face weak growth in demand, as is typical with mature industries. In addition, because they were technically mature, companies in the same industries could locate in less-developed countries. Thus at about the same time or soon after the time when such industries were set up in Ireland, they could also be established in low-wage less-developed countries. As Teeling (1975) suggested, this meant that each generation of these industries could tend eventually to come under competitive pressure from lower-cost producers and this too could have created difficulties for some of the plants in Ireland. In essence, therefore, the life-cycle of such foreign industries in Ireland would have been a shortened version of the life-cycle of the industry internationally, consisting only of the late growth or mature phase before stagnation or decline set in.

The newer, more technologically advanced generation of products, such as chemicals, instruments and electronics is a somewhat different matter, however, since many of these industries were established in Ireland much earlier in the life-cycle of fairly new industries with rapidly growing sales. But usually only certain relatively technologically undemanding stages of production are carried out (i.e. as compared with the activities carried out in their home countries). Thus in some cases, at least, further dispersal of such activities to lower-cost countries may again tend to occur. Such industries also tend to undergo a process of concentration, as the smaller and weaker firms which prospered in the initial upsurge of new products succumb to stronger competition. This 'shake-out' process may tend to be damaging eventually for many of the companies which established plants in Ireland, since these companies have tended to be relatively small by the standards of multinational corporations. Perhaps most important, the life of individual products in new high-technology industries tends to be relatively short since developments in product technology lead to rapid obsolescence. Thus Irish plants without a strong product development capability may be vulnerable unless new products are continually introduced by the parent company.

All things considered, one might expect the newer, high-technology industries to have a somewhat longer period of growth in Ireland than the mature labour-intensive industries, but they would still have a shortened life-cycle compared with the same industries internationally.

Since the strongest growth among foreign-owned industries in recent years has been in electronics (which includes most of Office & Data Processing Machinery and part of Electrical Engineering), it is worth examining the electronics industry in some detail to see whether companies in it tend to follow the life-cycle pattern outlined above.

Table 7.6 shows employment changes in foreign electronics firms, by date of establishment in Ireland. There is consistent evidence of the expected life-cycle effect. Employment in the two oldest cohorts, of firms established up to 1968, was already

Table 7.6: Employment Change in Foreign-owned Electronics Firms by Date of Establishment in Ireland

Date of Establishment	Employment (Numbers)			Average Annual Percentage Change	
	1973	1980	1985	1973-80	1980-85
Up to 1964	1,810	1,347	807	—4.1	—9.7
1965-68	1,560	1,064	773	—5.3	—6.2
1969-72	381	1,589	1,744	22.6	1.9
1973-76	0	2,231	3,309	—	8.2
1977-79	0	1,203	3,705	—	25.2

Source: Derived from *IDA Employment Survey.*

Note: Only companies still in existence in 1985 are included. If companies which closed before then were included, the rates of growth would be somewhat lower, or the rates of decline would be greater.

declining in the 1970s, and the next cohort, of firms established between 1969 and 1972, grew rapidly at first but this growth flattened out in the 1980s. And the two following cohorts grew a good deal faster in the 1980s, but the more recent of the two had a far higher rate of growth. The rapid overall growth of electronics in recent years masks this underlying trend only because most of the industry is so new, but the logical outcome of persistence of the trends illustrated in table 7.6 is a slower rate of growth before very long.

If this type of pattern persists in foreign-owned industries future trends will increasingly be influenced by the growing proportion of relatively old declining plants, so that an ever greater inflow of new first-time investors will be needed to attain employment increases of any given amount. It is rather doubtful, however, if this will occur.

Prospects for New Inflows of Foreign Investment

It has been suggested above that export-oriented foreign plants established in Ireland are fairly mobile production units, capable of operating in some degree of isolation from major industrial centres. The attraction of Ireland for such plants, as compared with lower-wage LDCs, would lie in ease of access to large European markets, a relatively well-educated English-speaking workforce, political 'reliability', the effective promotion efforts of the IDA and other factors which reduce uncertainty and information costs, as well as attractive tax concessions and grants. And the attraction of Ireland, as compared with most other European countries, would lie mainly in tax and grant incentives and relatively low labour costs. Most foreign investment in Ireland in the 1970s and 1980s could be characterised as mobile production units seeking a low-cost, tax-free and politically 'reliable' site in which to produce for sale in European markets.

The special attractions of Ireland for such investors have probably been eroded recently since there has been growing competition from many other European countries to attract mobile foreign investment because they have experienced persistent unemployment problems. In the United Kingdom, in particular, there are now quite intensive efforts to attract foreign firms. A further source of increased competition is the recent accession of Greece, Spain and Portugal to the EEC. These developments have probably produced new sources of close competition for the same type of mobile, European-oriented, foreign investment which Ireland attracts. Parts of the UK may well be the strongest of these competitors. A survey in the *Allied Irish Bank Review* (April 1981) found that 80% of foreign firms in Ireland had seriously considered setting up elsewhere before deciding to locate in Ireland, with Britain being the most favourably considered alternative site some way ahead of Belgium and Spain. This preference was most clearly marked among companies established in Ireland within the previous five years.

It is not possible, however, to quantify exactly the effect of increased competition on Ireland's 'market share' of mobile foreign industry. One indicator of the amount of new foreign investment coming to Ireland each year is IDA data on fixed asset investment planned (but not necessarily all actually undertaken) by new projects from overseas which are approved for grants. Table 7.7 shows recent trends in this planned investment. New overseas investment had been growing in the 1970s and it reached a high level by the years 1979-81, but the table shows that it was lower over the next five years, particularly when measured in constant prices.

Table 7.7: Planned Fixed Asset Investment in New Overseas Projects, £ million

	Average 1979-81	1982	1983	1984	1985	1986
In Current Prices	271.7	196.3	86.5	284.1*	102.4	231.0
In Constant (1980) Prices	270.5	161.4	67.2	204.8*	71.0	160.0

Source: IDA Annual Reports for data in current values, deflated by the price index for fixed capital investment in manufacturing, from *National Income and Expenditure*, to obtain constant price data.
Note: These figures include £180 million (current values) in one very large project which did not go ahead.

Another indicator which is available is the United States Department of Commerce data on capital expenditure (i.e. actual expenditure, unlike the IDA data in table 7.7). Table 7.8 shows the amount of such investment going to Ireland, as well as Ireland's share of such investment in Europe, as an indicator of 'market share'. American manufacturing investment in Ireland stopped growing at the end of the 1970s and it has been fairly stable since then, and Ireland's share of US investment in Europe followed a similar trend. Table 7.8 presents a rather more favourable impression of trends in foreign investment in Ireland than Table 7.7, but whichever one is accepted as more meaningful, there is little sign of growth in the inflow of new investment, which would probably be needed to regain the momentum of growth experienced in the foreign-owned sector up to the early 1980s.

Table 7.8: Capital Expenditures by US Manufacturing Firms in Ireland

	1977	Average 1979-81	1982	1983	1984	1985	1986	1987	1988*
Amount ($ million)	99	216	190	186	244	193	201	205	216
As percentage of Europe	1.7	2.1	2.1	2.4	3.3	2.4	2.3	2.2	1.9

Source: US Department of Commerce, *Survey of Current Business*, various issues up to March 1988.
* Forecast.

The relatively weak inflow of new foreign investment in the 1980s has partly been a reflection of stronger competition from other European countries, which causes difficulties in increasing Ireland's share of the available foreign investment. But it is also due to the fact that new US investment in Europe was declining or stagnating for much of the 1980s. This was partly due to recession and probably also to the fact that the marked surge of US investment in the European Community, which followed the integration of substantial markets since the 1960s, was coming to an end. Given that competition from other European countries trying to attract mobile investment is likely to continue to be strong, the inflow of new investment to Ireland seems unlikely to increase very significantly in the years ahead, unless perhaps there is another upsurge of investment coming into the European Community as a result of measures to 'complete the internal market' by 1992.

Conclusions

To conclude, the prospects for future manufacturing employment growth in Ireland seem to depend heavily on a continuing inflow of new foreign firms. And in fact the employment generated by new firms probably has to *increase* continuously in order to attain net employment growth of any given amount, due to the growing proportion of ageing and declining foreign firms. But conditions for attracting new foreign investment appear to have become more difficult. Thus it is possible that the period of quite strong industrial growth depending mainly on foreign firms was a phase of the 1960s and 1970s which is effectively finished. The same strategy may no longer be capable of producing the results experienced in the 1960s and 1970s. Consequently, and no doubt correctly, the emphasis in industrial policy is now shifting more to developing Irish indigenous industries in internationally traded activities, without by any means ruling out new foreign investment. For as the White Paper on *Industrial Policy* (1984) recognised: 'The policies which had clearly served us well in the 1960s and 1970s are now having less success. Competition for a declining volume of mobile investment is constantly intensifying from both industrialised and developing countries.'

This position, which Ireland now faces in the relatively favourable circumstances of political 'reliability', a European location, membership of the European Community, a developed infrastructure etc., suggests a more gloomy prospect for other less-favoured countries which attempt to follow a similar strategy. In view of the limited amount of mobile foreign investment worldwide, and the much lower wage levels at which many countries would price themselves out of the market for attracting it, few if any of the LDCs could expect to get close to full employment or to raise their incomes close to those of Ireland by relying on this strategy.

8

The Experience of Other Latecomers with 'Outward-looking' Policies

It has been shown in chapters 6 and 7 that the experience of industry in the Republic of Ireland since the 1950s could scarcely be regarded as a process of evolution into an advanced industrial country. Indigenous industry has shown little sign of such a transformation, and the main feature of industrial growth has been the successful development of the country as a site for a large concentration of mobile, export-oriented foreign industries. A strategy based on continuing reliance on this process, however, looks likely to be frustrated.

These conclusions are obviously of some relevance to Ireland itself. But, as mentioned in chapter 1, this book is intended not only to clarify issues of relevance to Ireland's own industrial development, but also to draw from Ireland's experience in order to shed some light on certain more general issues. These general issues are whether special difficulties exist for late-industrialising countries, and whether the conventionally recommended strategy of 'outward-looking' free market policies is appropriate for latecomers. Ireland's experience indicates that there are indeed important constraints on latecomers and that the conventional strategy is not adequate to overcome them. This conclusion arises from the fact that Irish indigenous industry has shown little sign of any fundamental transformation, being largely confined to a limited range of easily entered and/or sheltered industries. This is the most important consideration in assessing the general viability of the conventional strategy, since most countries could not expect foreign industries to make an impact comparable to that observed in Ireland.

There are, however, a number of other relative latecomers to industrialisation which have often been regarded as examples of the success of the conventional strategy. The most notable of these are Japan, South Korea, Taiwan, Singapore and Hong Kong. The existence of these other cases, which are often considered to justify the conventional view, might be thought to cast doubt on the general conclusion suggested above which is drawn from the single case of Ireland. For this reason it seems necessary to make some mention here of these other countries. It is not intended to consider these other countries in great detail, so this chapter has only *very limited objectives*. First, it questions whether these countries really are examples which support the conventional view, and second, it draws on the experience of some of them for ideas on what type of policies can help to overcome the constraints on latecomers. It will be suggested that some of these countries have adopted policies which actually depart significantly from the conventional strategy, and these are the ones whose policies for late development are of particular interest. And the others have, as yet, progressed little further than Ireland.

Substantial departures from the conventional strategy — including strong protection, state controls on foreign investment and imports of foreign technology, and active and selective intervention in the private sector to achieve long-term aims — have been features of policy in Japan, South Korea and Taiwan. Such measures, it appears, have been consciously used in an effort to overcome the constraints on latecomers. These countries' degree of success in developing indigenous industries in sectors with substantial entry barriers could therefore be largely attributable to such special measures, which are *departures* from the conventional strategy. This suggestion seems consistent with Ireland's failure to develop indigenous industries in sectors with substantial entry barriers while using a much purer form of the conventional strategy. It is also consistent with what seem to be similar limitations in the development of both Singapore and Hong Kong while using a fairly pure form of this strategy. The city-state of Singapore has been similar to Ireland in so far as it has proved to be exceptionally attractive to mobile export-oriented foreign industries, which largely accounted for its particularly rapid industrial growth. And although Hong Kong has owed less to such foreign investment, its indigenous development has mainly involved rapid growth of easily entered, labour-intensive industries, so that it too has not progressed beyond the barriers that seem to constrain Ireland.

In this chapter Japan is discussed first, with most attention being devoted to that country since it is the only one which could be considered an advanced industrial country today after being relatively backward or underdeveloped earlier in this century. It is, in other words, the only fully successful latecomer among these countries. Next South Korea and Taiwan are discussed, and finally Singapore and Hong Kong.

8.i. JAPAN

In referring to Japan as a latecomer to industrialisation in the twentieth century, it should be borne in mind that this country had actually attained a certain degree of industrial development during the last century, well in advance of the others mentioned here. As a reflection of this, Japan built up armaments and shipbuilding industries quite early, and was able to play an important independent role in both world wars. Japan also became a regional imperial power dominating more economically backward neighbours, including Korea and Taiwan. Nevertheless, until its period of rapid development after the Second World War, Japanese industry was undoubtedly relatively backward compared with the USA or much of Europe.

As compared with the other, even more economically backward countries mentioned in this chapter, however, Japan had certain advantages arising from its longer history of development when undertaking its post-war industrial drive. These included a relatively educated population, an existing capitalist class, a well-organised bureaucracy and quite extensive technical skills, even if the technology in use was somewhat backward. There was also a structure of large industrial and trading companies which, although disrupted by the war, could later serve as a basis for successful international competition in large-scale industries. Japan, like South Korea and Taiwan, had the further advantage of being in a strategically important position after the war. Consequently the USA in particular was keen to encourage her development, both by means of aid and toleration of import barriers in Japan while relatively free access for Japanese exports to developed country markets was allowed. Japan also felt a stronger need to develop internationally competitive exporting industries after the war, since her natural resources are poor and the loss of her colonies meant that imports of food and materials would have to be paid for by manufactured exports.

Industrial development policy in Japan in the period since the war involved both the use of protection and a system of controls, regulations and incentives to direct investment into selected sectors which were intended to become internationally competitive eventually. By various means such as preferential cheap loans, subsidies, administrative directions and industry cartelisation, the government distorted profit criteria with the intention of channelling resources into chosen industries and assisting their development. Patrick and Rosovsky (1976) point out that the economic ethos behind these policies 'contrasts with the traditional Anglo-American economic ideology of the "invisible hand" of perfect competition, whereby individualistic maximisation of one's own benefits results in the greatest social welfare, with government interference limited to maintaining the condition of perfect competition'.

This type of policy has been pursued in Japan mainly through influencing the private sector. The public sector accounts for a smaller share of GNP than in most advanced countries, and commercial state enterprises are mainly limited to the conventional public utility fields such as railways and telecommunications. Tobacco manufacture, a traditional government monopoly for revenue purposes, is the only significant state manufacturing venture (Patrick and Rosovsky, 1976).[1]

Protection

Protection against imports in the 1950s and 1960s was justified on the grounds of Japan's relatively backward condition — the 'infant industry' argument for latecomers, in fact, which has, as Patrick and Rosovsky point out, been used at some time in all of today's advanced countries which industrialised after Britain. The protectionist policy was applied strongly, against a background of a high degree of natural protection due to the country's distance from the advanced industrial areas of Europe and North America, and a further degree of protection arising from Japan's complex distribution system. The protectionist measures used included tariffs — often at fairly moderate levels — but these were combined with foreign exchange quotas for imports, import licensing, discriminatory excise taxes and preferential state purchasing (Adams and Ichimura, 1983).[2] Until 1960 approximately 60% of Japan's imports were subject to quotas (Yamamura, 1986). A well-known example of preferential state purchasing has been the Nippon Telegraph and Telephone Co., the state monopoly telecommunications company, which only began to consider foreign suppliers as recently as 1981.[3]

Many latecomers have used protection to foster industrial development, of course, but in the twentieth century most, like Ireland in the 1930s-1950s, have had very limited success in bringing protected infant industries to a mature capability to compete in international markets. Japan differed from some of these countries in that it was always the *intention* to use protection for a limited period, during which industries would be developed as quickly as possible to a competitive position. So in this sense the policy was *ultimately* 'export-oriented' or 'outward-looking'. A Japanese policymaker quoted by Allen (1981) says: 'The policy was: carefully select industries, prevent ruinous competition at the infancy stage, nurse them to competitive stature and then expose them to outside competition.'

This careful selection of industries, the methods of ensuring that they were undertaken, and the methods of intervening in the market to nurse them to fully competitive maturity distinguish Japan's approach from simple indiscriminate protection. At the same time, the strength of Japan's protection, the capital-intensive and/or technically demanding nature of the industries chosen, and the accompanying selective intervention in the economy distinguish its strategy from the 'outward-looking' free market strategy advocated by neo-classical economists.

Whereas the conventional free market strategy would leave the selection of industries to private enterprise, the state played an important part in Japan, in close consultation with business interests. Being concerned about long-term development, the Ministry of International Trade and Industry (MITI) was not content to take a static view of Japan's comparative advantage, which would have meant concentrating on technically simple, labour-intensive industries. Instead, MITI selected industries on the basis of 'dynamized comparative-cost', meaning that selection took account of the potential to create a *new* comparative advantage over time, by developing large-scale firms and improving skills and technology during a period of temporary protection and concerted investment (Adams and Ichimura, 1983). Selection of industries also took account of the prospects for growth in demand and the likely spin-off benefits through linkages with other industries. On this basis, MITI selected some technologically advanced and/or capital-intensive industries such as steel, petroleum refining, petrochemicals, cars, general machinery and consumer electronics. Some of the choices, which turned out to be major successes, were resisted at the time by academic economists who took a more traditional and static view of Japan's comparative advantage.

Foreign Direct Investment

In developing the target industries, a highly selective approach was adopted to foreign direct investment in Japan. Foreign investment was restricted in order to supplement protectionist measures, by preventing foreign competition in the form of direct investment from hindering the development of indigenous industries. Indigenous industrial development was always considered to be essential, and multinational companies were not regarded as an acceptable substitute. The criterion for approval of foreign direct investment was whether it would 'expedite the industrial development and self reliance of Japan'. Consequently foreign direct investment was very largely confined to joint ventures with at least 50% Japanese participation. It was also subject to rules which ensured that the local participation was not merely decorative and that the local partner would be capable of extracting long-term benefits from the venture.[4] As a result of these measures, Japan was host to by far the lowest amount of US-controlled assets among the six major capitalist market economies (other than the USA) in 1970. Furthermore the sectoral distribution of foreign investment reflects the policy of aiming to use joint ventures with foreign firms as a means of technology transfer in advanced industries, rather than accepting what would have been a more natural flow of foreign investment into simple labour-intensive industries. Petroleum (32.7%), Chemicals (24.9%), Machines (22.6%) and Metals (6.1%) together accounted for 86.3% of foreign investment in 1950-65. Textiles, Clothing, Footwear and the like were very much less important (Rosser, 1980).

Methods and Aims of Intervention

One of the most important methods by which the state influenced the pattern of industrial development was through the supply of credit. Industrial companies tended to rely heavily on loan rather than equity capital, and lending by the commercial banks, in turn, could be guided by the central monetary authorities. Thus the authorities had considerable leverage on industrial investment and used it to direct capital to approved destinations (Yamamura, 1986). The various official banks, such as Japan Development Bank and the Export-Import Bank, have also supported selected projects more directly, especially those related to exports, by granting very low-interest loans (Allen, 1981; Adams and Ichimura, 1983).

A major concern of Japanese industrial policy was to promote the formation and growth of very large firms. As Caves and Uekusa (1976) explain:

> [the] goal has been to enlarge the scales of plant and firm in certain industries — larger plants from an abiding faith in economies of scale, larger firms from a belief that, as controls on foreign trade and investment were lifted, Japanese firms must be as large as their American competitors in order to compete with them effectively. This goal has led at times to a considerable enthusiasm for mergers and the restriction of new entry into industries of interest to the MITI (Ministry of International Trade and Industry).

Selective credit policies, tax measures and subsidies were used to encourage the formation of large oligopolistic firms capable of competing internationally, and legislation was also used to bring about mergers or the formation of cartels. New entrants to certain industries were also restricted by MITI's control of licences to import inputs and technology, and this device was used to allow a limited number of relatively strong firms to grow large without excessive domestic competition. Any stultifying effect of this limitation of competition would have been mitigated by the experience of having to compete in export markets. For the granting of licences to import technology was frequently made conditional on the firm's guaranteeing the attainment of export targets.

Exports were further encouraged by tax and credit instruments and by policies designed to promote the formation of export cartels. By 1962, 40% of Japan's export trade was cartelised, and this arrangement allowed the country to gain export markets by initially dumping goods at prices below cost while profits were made up through agreed higher pricing on the home market (Allen, 1981; Rosser, 1980). A further important aid to developing exports was Japan's unusual structure of very large general trading companies. In the 1960s, the ten largest of these handled about half the country's exports and almost two-thirds of imports, so that each of these — handling up to 20,000 different items — would have detailed knowledge of foreign trading conditions and considerable market power. One result of the opportunities generated by such powerful marketing companies is the unusually large number of small Japanese manufacturing firms which specialise in exporting (Krause and Sekiguchi, 1976).

Japanese industrial policy has also been greatly concerned with technological issues. It is well known now that the guiding principle was mainly to capitalise on the one big advantage a latecomer *can* have, by importing technology so as to catch up rapidly with the more advanced countries. It was recognised that this process might not happen automatically, but rather that an active interventionist policy was needed to realise this potential advantage. As Rosser (1980) remarks: 'The striking feature about Japan is the extent to which their borrowing of technology was an overwhelmingly conscious and directed process.'

The strategy, which has been termed 'innovative imitation', involved importing licensed technology to indigenous firms which were protected from foreign competition. These firms would then spend substantial sums on R & D aimed primarily at absorbing, adapting and making minor improvements to the technology, so that in due course they would become internationally competitive (see Peck and Tamura, 1976; Rosser, 1980). This strategy was co-ordinated with the policy of developing larger firms since large firms can best afford to pay large initial licensing costs, to spend heavily on R & D and to absorb losses in new activities while techniques are being perfected. They also have the greatest bargaining strength with foreign licensors since they have attractive prospects of large sales (in a big protected market), leading to substantial royalties.

The need for conscious direction of the technology strategy arose from a number of considerations. First, it was necessary to ensure that importation of technology would in fact be linked with R & D work to achieve the catch-up effect. It was also necessary to ensure that technology imports went to the firms most capable of utilising and improving on them, and to ensure that the most desirable technology was being purchased from the point of view of long-term aims. Finally, it was desired to guide the selection of sectors for concentrated development, so as both to maximise long-term gains and to ensure that the industrial structure would be 'upgraded' continuously. It was believed that, in order to maximise long-term gains, certain key sectors must be developed and raised to a high standard so as to encourage many other industries and raise standards throughout the economy. This would occur either by backward linkage effects on suppliers (as with the car industry) or forward linkage effects on user industries (as with steel and machine tools). And the strategy of 'upgrading' the industrial structure was based on the idea that industrial development is essentially a process of structural transformation. From initial concentration on technically simple, labour-intensive industries, the emphasis should change to more technically demanding and more capital-intensive industries, and finally to the 'knowledge-intensive', advanced technology sectors.

Peck and Tamura's (1976) analysis of the changing pattern of Japan's exports shows that the goals of this policy were successfully achieved. They stress, too, that the success of the policy of concentrating on importing technology did not mean that R & D expenditure in Japan has been low. Rather the commitment to adapting and improving on imported technology involved R & D expenditures which, as a proportion of GNP, have been comparable to the levels of non-military R & D in the advanced western countries. This would scarcely have occurred in a relatively backward country without an active government policy. The pursuit of this policy has also required a highly sophisticated and concentrated effort to develop a business and technology intelligence-gathering capability in other countries. Initiated with state participation and encouragement, Japan's effectiveness in this area is widely regarded as second to none.[5]

Causes and Effects of Industrial Policy

This brief outline has focussed on the nature and aims of the industrial policy adopted by the Japanese state. But there is some controversy about whether the state really directed industry or whether, on the other hand, industry set its own goals so that industrial policy was no more than a formal expression of the aims of industry and a means of co-ordinating efforts to achieve them. No attempt can be made here to resolve this question, though Patrick and Rosovsky (1976) plausibly suggest that a strong measure of consensus exists between business and government on broad issues. Adams and Ichimura (1983) reach a similar conclusion: 'Business and enterprises accept administrative guidance just as MITI emphasizes that its decisions are made on the basis of consultation with business. . . . The whole-hearted determination of business circles, civil servants, and politicians alike to reconstruct the devastated nation bred the spirit of co-operation. The success of collaboration established trust and constant consultation.' Whether the Japanese industrial strategy originated with businessmen, politicians, civil servants or a consensus among these, however, the fact remains that it was a conscious industry-specific strategy, well designed to overcome the constraints on latecomers which are posed by barriers to entry.

During the 1980s, it has often been said that Japan's former cohesive strategy of protection and selective guidance and intervention was being abandoned. This change was a theme running through many of the articles in *International Business Week's* (14/12/81) special issue on 'Japan's Strategy for the 80s'. It is noticeable, however, that Japanese spokesmen, responding to complaints from foreign competitors, were most insistent that the change was occurring while US businessmen generally remained more sceptical. Thus a typical response to questions about the selection of 'targeted industries', and access for foreign competitors to the Japanese market in those industries, was this statement from Mr Kikuchi, former official spokesman on trade policy:

> There are no targeted industries. I have heard those words very often from people in the [US] State Department and in the EC Commission. I object very much to that kind of industry-government co-operation, the idea of Japan Inc. — government, MITI and businessmen — using the tax-payers' money. . . .[6]

Significantly, however, he freely admitted that past policy was strongly interventionist and protectionist:

> What they are saying was true in the 1960s, when we had this form of protection. That is over. In the 1980s we have stopped picking winners and targeting industries. Curiously, now European and the American governments are trying to learn how we did that in the '60s.

Thus there is no dispute here about the fact that Japan used protection and selective interventionist policies for a considerable period of time, rather than relying on the 'invisible hand' of market forces and only generalised incentives as conventional economists recommend. To the extent that there has been some change recently (and it scarcely amounts to a complete abandoning of earlier policies), this could be seen as a reflection of the fact that Japan has essentially succeeded in becoming an advanced industrial country. The 'latecomer' phase is over and consequently the need for policies designed to overcome the disadvantages of that status is diminished. (Yamamura, 1986, refers to the 1970s as the end of the 'catching-up' period and outlines policy changes since then.)

Finally, some would suggest that the Japanese government's industrial strategy was not really a significant cause of her success. Rather, success might be attributable to special cultural factors, such as a compliant and hard-working labour force, a patriotic spirit leading to co-operation among enterprises in the national interest, or a culture and entrepreneurial spirit which are exceptionally conducive to capitalist development. But such general explanations seem inadequate, although there is probably some truth in them, when one considers that some Japanese industries are very successful while others are not, despite the fact that all operate in the same environment with these suggested special advantages. For example, Magaziner and Hout (1980, p. 1) point out that by the late 1970s Japan had become the world leader in steel, motor cycles and consumer electronics but remained a marginal producer in marine engines and industrial electronics. These differences between the success of different industries could scarcely be explained by general cultural factors, but they could reasonably be put down to variations in the priority given to targeted and non-targeted industries. To some extent, they could also be due to variations in the success of strategic planning and policy implementation. For a detailed, selective industrial policy is necessarily prone to variations in results due to the complexities of understanding and judgement involved, which mean that some mistakes will be made and some only moderate results will be achieved. Thus the variations of success rates would be quite consistent with the view that Japan's industrial strategy was a major factor in explaining her experience, and the excellent overall results argue strongly for trying to learn from the principles behind that strategy.

This is not to say, however, that *all* the success stories in Japanese industry were due to selective government policies, with no role being played by unaided private initiatives. As Adams and Ichimura (1983) conclude:

On the one hand, it is certainly not correct to attribute all of the spectacular development of Japanese industry in domestic and foreign markets to IPs [industrial policies]. Indeed, private enterprises, many operating with little or no government aid, are responsible for some of the greatest successes of Japanese industry. On the other hand, there is evidence in many directions that the policies achieved many of their objectives. For example, an analysis of changes in Japanese industrial structure shows clearly that the shift toward heavy industries and the chemical industries, which had been planned in the earliest visions of MITI, occurred by 1970 . . . . With regard to allocation of funds, the evidence supports the notion that funds went more heavily into the industries selected for development.

They also suggest that the role of selective state policies was more important in the 1950s and 1960s, with unaided private initiative playing an increasingly important role more recently. This would be consistent with the view that active and selective state policies are necessary for relatively weak late-developers, whereas private initiative can be more successful in a stronger, more developed economy. It should also be remembered that industries developed in Japan by private initiative without selective government aid generally had the benefit of protection, at least, so that this type of government intervention was probably a factor in their success.

Boltho (1985) and Yamamura (1986) reach somewhat similar conclusions on the importance of industrial policies in accounting for Japan's industrial growth, up to the early 1970s at least. In particular, Boltho remarks: 'No doubt the role and influence of industrial policies changed through time. They worked most smoothly and successfully in the 1950s and 1960s when it was easiest to "pick winners", since these had already been recognised in more advanced countries. From now on Japan must, on the other hand, choose strategic sectors and technologies at the frontier. . . .' The point here is essentially that 'picking winners' is a more uncertain and risky process for an advanced economy, which must assess the technologies and markets of the unknown future; a less-developed latecomer on the other hand, can make progress by selecting target industries on the firmer basis of what is already known about markets and the requirements for competing in industries actually existing in advanced countries.

To sum up, Japan adopted protection and selective interventionist measures to an extent which departed substantially from the conventionally recommended strategy of the neo-classical school. These measures were consciously used to overcome entry barriers in many industries, in a way which seems logically consistent with the nature of those entry barriers. Thus the generally successful experience of Japanese industrial growth can be regarded as consistent with the view that constraints on latecomers do exist due to the prevalence of entry barriers, and that substantial departures from the conventional strategy are required to overcome them.

8.ii. SOUTH KOREA AND TAIWAN

South Korea and Taiwan both began the post-war period as very much more economically backward countries than Japan. Both were, in fact, among the poorest countries in the world and of course they remain *relatively* poor and underdeveloped compared with Japan, generally being classed as Newly Industrialising Countries rather than advanced industrial countries. They have, however, a record of quite spectacular economic growth, especially industrial growth, which has made them a focus of much attention in development studies.[7] Although South Korea and Taiwan have often been regarded as examples of the success of outward-looking free market policies, there is sufficient evidence to suggest that they actually departed substantially from that strategy. In practice, they appear to have adopted a strong protectionist and selective interventionist approach not unlike Japan's, and they have succeeded in developing some internationally competitive indigenous industries in sectors with substantial entry barriers. Their degree of success in this matter, like Japan's success, and in contrast with Ireland's experience with the conventional strategy, could therefore plausibly be linked to their significant departures from the orthodox strategy rather than adherence to it.

External Support
Like Japan, both South Korea and Taiwan have been strategically important for United States foreign policy in the Far East. For this reason both were recipients of large amounts of aid from the USA and also benefited from liberal US trade policies to encourage their exports. Foreign aid was most

important in the 1950s and early 1960s. During this time fully half of Korean government revenue came from the USA; foreign investment accounted for 42% of total investment in 1953, 65% in 1961 and a declining proportion since then. In Taiwan, US aid contributed about 34% of total gross investment in 1951-65, going mainly to infrastructural and agricultural development. Jacoby (1966) estimated that this aid to Taiwan doubled what would have been the annual rate of growth of GNP in the period mentioned. The main benefits for *industrial* development arising from the aid inflow would have been not only in developing a good infrastructure, but also in virtually removing the foreign exchange constraint on imports of capital goods, fuel and materials.

Evidently, flows of aid on such a scale must have contributed significantly to the growth of these two economies, but its importance should not be over-rated. In both countries, aid petered out after the mid-1960s whereas the 1970s and 1980s have seen some exceptional developments and continued rapid growth. Until the late 1960s or early 1970s it could perhaps have been argued that the record of Korea and Taiwan did not really suggest that they had found a way to overcome the general constraints on latecomers, or at least not a way that others could readily follow. Rather, it could have been suggested, the exceptional amount of aid which they received enabled them to expand domestically oriented production without a foreign exchange constraint, and to move rapidly into labour-intensive, technically mature export industries. At the same time, they offered exceptional political 'reliability', due to the supervision of a superpower and strong domestic right-wing governments, which helped to attract export-oriented foreign investment. Indeed their very success in developing the limited range of easily entered, indigenous export industries, and in attracting a large share of a globally limited amount of mobile export-oriented foreign industries, could be seen as a pre-emption of these limited opportunities, leaving less scope for others to repeat the process.

Such a Dependency-type explanation of their growth, however, could not be valid as regards their record in the 1970s and 1980s. For foreign aid has diminished, their indigenous industry has diversified and has developed exports in industries with significant entry barriers, and it has become clear that foreign industries are not by any means the main contributors to their export growth. For this reason it seems worth considering how these more recent results were achieved, and it is reasonably clear that it was not done by reliance on the conventional strategy.

State Policies

Both South Korea and Taiwan have adopted protection and active, selective industrial policies. State enterprises have also been important in both countries, though less so in Korea where the state nevertheless intervened by other means. Thus Luedde-Neurath (1980) says:

> The State, it appears, has been far more active as an initiating, implementing and controlling factor in the Korean economy than is commonly recognised.

It is worth quoting Luedde-Neurath at some length to give an indication of the methods of Korean state intervention:

> These included the government's right directly to initiate industrial projects and to designate specific firms to take them up; strict financial control which is likely to have been the single most important directive tool . . .; the power to interfere directly with prices, profit margins, taxes and even the organisation of enterprises by way of selective measures directed at specific firms; and finally, trade controls, which in Korea did not merely comprise the commonly reported tariffs and selective quantitative restrictions, but were supplemented by certain highly effective direct measures. (Individuals or firms required a licence and registration to engage in foreign trade, in addition to which they often also required a specific licence for every transaction; the 'export-import link' system in turn could make permission to import conditional on a satisfactory export performance . . . .)
>
> All this was apart from the incentive measures and fiscal and monetary policies often misleadingly presented as the only tools operating in Korea to promote the strategy.

Luedde-Neurath (1980 and 1984) also points out that Korea's controls on foreign direct investment have been much more rigorous than is generally recognised. Prior screening and the frequent imposition of export conditions and ownership share ratios were practised even before 1974, when a more explicit and formal system of selecting 'eligible' types of direct investment was introduced. It was only in the free trade zones (employing about 1% of the country's labour force in 1975) that government interference was indeed of the minimal nature that is often thought to typify Korea's approach. The vast majority of foreign investments in South Korea have in fact been in the form of loans rather than direct investment, which seems to have been desired as a means of retaining indigenous control while benefiting from a capital inflow.

Government policy also involves an approach to technological development like the earlier policy of Japan. A major expansion of local R & D was encouraged, while the import of foreign technology through licensing was preferred to joint ventures, let alone foreign direct investment. At the same time foreign firms operating in Korea have been increasingly required to train Koreans in specific skills, and skilled foreigners have been engaged with a view to diffusing technological knowledge and skills among indigenous enterprises. The aim, as in Japan, has been to push ahead in developing capital-intensive and technologically advanced industries, by indigenous firms, rather than accepting what would be Korea's natural role, according to the orthodox principle of comparative advantage, in the technically undemanding, labour-intensive industries (Luedde-Neurath, 1980).

The overall extent of South Korea's departure from the conventional free market strategy is strongly indicated by the *Financial Times'* description of the country as '. . . one of the free world's most tightly supervised economies, with the Government initiating almost every major investment by the private sector and wielding enough power to ensure that companies which make such investments also make a profit'.[8]

In the case of Taiwan, too, there are good grounds for suggesting that strong protection and an active, selective interventionist role for the state have been important features of policy. Wade (1984) describes how the published list of relatively low, non-discretionary tariffs on imports was actually supplemented by much higher discretionary tariffs and quantitative controls on selected items in order to protect targeted indigenous industries. If this conflicts with the popular image of Taiwan as an open, free-trading economy, Wade explains: 'For the most understandable of reasons the government is anxious not to be seen to be doing anything which might provide a pretext for other countries (notably the United States) to put up barriers to its exports; and takes great care to keep the mechanisms of quantitative import control out of sight.'

Taiwan has also used tax concessions in a highly selective manner to develop targeted industries. Wade (1984) gives examples of just how selective these measures are. In heavy electrical machinery, six types of product were eligible including transformers — but not all transformers, only those of 154 kv class or above. And in electronics, not all semi-conductor devices were eligible, but only those equipped with diffusion facilities or ion implantation facilities. Such detailed selectivity gives a distinct impression that the planners have a clear idea of exactly what industries they intend to develop.

Taiwan has made less use of discretionary control over credit and less use of direct influence over private firms than Japan or South Korea. Instead there is a very large state enterprise sector. State enterprises have accounted for about one-third of fixed capital formation in recent years. And by 1980 the six biggest industrial state enterprises had sales equal to the fifty largest private industrial concerns. The state enterprises

> are concentrated on the commanding heights to which European socialists wistfully aspire: petroleum and petrochemicals, fertiliser, steel and other basic metals, shipbuilding and heavy machinery (in addition to the standard electricity, gas, water, railway and telephone utilities). If there is less pushing and prodding of private firms in Taiwan than in the other dirigiste NICs, it is partly because the state has this large public enterprise sector as an instrument of selective and discretionary intervention. (Wade, 1984).

Foreign investment in Taiwan is also subject to selective controls, although perhaps to a lesser extent than in South Korea. Of course, part of foreign investment in Taiwan was attracted to free trade export zones where government involvement or intervention is minimal — the situation sometimes exclusively represented as the approach of Taiwan both to foreign capital and state intervention.

The Nature of Industrial Growth
In considering the nature of industrial growth in South Korea and Taiwan, the main issue of interest here is whether these countries have overcome to any extent the suggested constraints on latecomers, which seem to be apparent in Ireland's case. This reduces largely to the question whether they have developed indigenous industries capable of competing

internationally in activities with substantial entry barriers; or whether, on the other hand they have only developed sheltered and easily entered indigenous industries and attracted a great deal of foreign industry.

In both countries, it is clear that foreign direct investment has been fairly important, but it is far from being the major contributor to industrial growth. Nayyar (1978) estimates that foreign-controlled companies accounted for at least 15% of manufactured exports from South Korea and at least 20% from Taiwan in the early 1970s. And Luedde-Neurath (1984) reports that *wholly* Korean-owned firms accounted for over three-quarters of Korean exports throughout most of the 1970s. Thus although foreign involvement is important, it is clearly much less significant than indigenous growth, in sharp contrast to Ireland's experience.[9]

As regards the nature of indigenous industry, the role of the easily entered labour-intensive sectors, such as clothing and textiles, in the expansion of exports was initially of major importance in both countries. But they have also successfully developed other industries that would be substantially more difficult to enter. These industries include some where the major barriers to entry would arise from economies of scale and capital requirements, such as steel, shipbuilding and fertilisers. They also include some where technology and specialised skills would be entry barriers, as in machine tools and branches of electronics. An indication of these developments is the substantial and growing share of industries such as chemicals, steel, machinery, ships and electronic goods in Korea's exports, as shown in table 8.1.

Table 8.1: Percentage Shares of South Korean Manufactured Exports, by Product

	1978	1983
Ships	7.1	16.3
Iron & Steel	4.8	10.8
Machinery	2.3	4.7
Chemicals	3.6	6.6
Electronic Products	9.8	13.2
	27.6	51.6

Source: Financial Times survey on South Korea, 2/7/84.

Leudde-Neurath (1980) suggests that it is symptomatic of Korea's emerging strength in technologically advanced industries that Japanese companies are increasingly reluctant to supply advanced technology to Korea, for fear of creating strong new competitors. As a further indication of the emergence of large-scale industries, he also refers to the fact that nine Korean firms were included in *Fortune's* list of the top 500 non-US corporations by 1977. This was an increase from only three the previous year. These developments would indicate that South Korea and Taiwan have progressed significantly further than Ireland in the matter of overcoming entry barriers inhibiting latecomers. It seems likely that, as in the case of Japan, this may be linked to interventionist policies which are designed to overcome entry barriers and which depart significantly from the conventional strategy, which has been much more closely adhered to in Ireland.

8.iii. SINGAPORE AND HONG KONG

Singapore and Hong Kong are rather dissimilar places in some respects, but for the limited purposes of this chapter they are sufficiently similar to be discussed together here. This is because both of them are small and neither has shown clear signs of overcoming the constraints on late industrialisation which are apparent in Ireland's case. Rather they have found it possible partially to evade these constraints by exploiting exceptional and limited opportunities which exist in the world economy. They have done this to an extent which had a substantial impact on their very small economies but would not appear to hold out great prospects for larger countries or the underdeveloped world in general.

These exceptional and limited opportunities were, for Singapore as in the case of Ireland, primarily the possibility of attracting a particularly large share of a globally limited amount of mobile export-oriented foreign industry. And Hong Kong has succeeded in capturing a large share of export markets for the limited range of products of labour-intensive, small-scale and technically mature indigenous industries. The experience of rapid industrial growth of these two, therefore, could still be regarded as consistent with the view that serious constraints on late industrialisation exist as the *general* case, and that the conventional strategy would not generally be adequate to overcome them.[10]

Singapore

Singapore's adoption of outward-looking policies began after its break from Malaysia in 1965. It experienced very rapid growth in the period since then, particularly in the manufacturing sector and — within manufacturing — particularly in export industries. In the case of Singapore, it is evident that foreign industries have been very largely responsible for this growth. *Wholly* foreign-owned firms were responsible for 71% of manufactured exports in 1978, compared with only 8% for wholly local-owned firms. And in the same year, *foreign-dominated* firms accounted for 52% of employment, 71% of output and 84% of exports in the manufacturing sector (Cheah, 1980). Private indigenous manufacturing firms mostly tend to be rather small and mainly engaged in processing and repairing activities oriented to the local market. Thus they would not appear to have had noticeably greater success in overcoming the constraints on latecomers than Irish indigenous firms. The relative importance of foreign firms, in fact, is significantly greater than in Ireland. The largest indigenous companies are state enterprises under the umbrella of the Singapore Technology Corporation. Some of these are involved in advanced large-scale industries such as armaments, again underlining the role of the state in developing such activities in latecomers.[11]

Singapore has proved to be an extremely attractive location for mobile foreign industries, capable of attracting a greatly disproportionate share of such firms, in relation to its size. The reasons for this include its geographical location, a modern infrastructure, a high degree of political 'reliability', tight controls on the labour movement, fiscal incentives and (until the end of the 1970s) a firm policy of wage restraint. In the late 1960s, wages were very low and industrial exports were concentrated mainly in standardised, labour-intensive, light consumer products. But the development of such industries proved, before long, to be limited by import restrictions in the advanced countries and the difficulties of competing with Hong Kong and Taiwan, which were already entrenched in this limited range of sectors (Cheah, 1980). There later began a boom, however, in other sectors for which Singapore probably had particular attractions arising from its location and role as an *entrepot* trading centre — especially ship-building and repairing, oil rig construction, and petroleum refining.

Singapore has proved so attractive to foreign industries to

date that virtual full employment has been achieved despite substantial immigration and a rapidly growing labour force. It is probably the only state in the world where such a result has occurred with a strategy which relies heavily on attracting mobile foreign industry. Indeed there was such confidence in the continuation of a surplus of prospective foreign investment that the government aimed, after 1979, to push wages up, in order to discourage the more labour-intensive projects and to favour the 'higher-grade' projects. In view of the limited amount of mobile foreign industries worldwide and the fact that Singapore has attracted a large proportion of them, however, this experience could not be seen as an indication that a similar strategy would lead to the same results for LDCs in general.

For some time, too, Singapore seems to have taken a more interventionist approach in several respects, such as the encouragement of joint indigenous/foreign ventures with a view to promoting the transfer of technology and skills, and the selective allocation of more resources to indigenous technological development (Cheah, 1980). But it is early yet to judge the effectiveness of these measures and until the early 1980s, at least, indigenous private industry remained relatively insignificant.

Hong Kong

Unlike Singapore, Hong Kong's industrial growth was not based so heavily on foreign-owned industries. Nayyar (1978) finds that in the early 1970s only about 10% of Hong Kong's manufactured exports were accounted for by foreign firms. But large foreign firms have played important roles in other respects, particularly as buyers and distributors who sub-contract simple manufacturing operations to indigenous firms in Hong Kong, thus perhaps playing a key role at times in overcoming marketing and technological barriers to entry.

The dominance of indigenous manufacturers raises the question whether Hong Kong's rapid export-led growth under the conventionally recommended strategy provides an example of success in overcoming barriers to entry for the indigenous industry of latecomers. The answer appears to be no, since this growth has been heavily concentrated in the limited range of 'easily entered' labour-intensive industries. Furthermore, much of Hong Kong's 'indigenous' growth was initially attributable to a large inflow of capital and businessmen from China, including a large segment of the Shanghai business community involved in textiles. Thus one commentator observes that a 'significant component of Hong Kong's "growth" was simply a transfer of economic activity from one industrial centre to another, and as such it should not be compared with the more indigenous growth found in other countries'.[12]

Manufacturing establishments in Hong Kong tend to be small in scale, reflecting the fact that they are mainly engaged in industries with low entry barriers. In 1985, their average employment was just 18, compared with 40 in Ireland or 56 in South Korea. Clothing and textiles are the major industries in Hong Kong, accounting for 44% of manufacturing employment in 1985. Other easily entered sectors, including plastic products, printing and publishing, footwear, leather products, wood products, furniture and radios, accounted for a further 28% of manufacturing employment in the same year (United Nations *Industrial Statistics Yearbook 1985*). Foreign firms have been important in bringing about some diversification beyond such easily entered industries, since they are engaged in electronics, metals and chemicals, as well as textiles.

There is little sign, therefore, that Hong Kong has been successful in overcoming barriers to entry for the indigenous industry of latecomers. Its quite rapid growth, while remaining largely confined to easily entered sectors, does not indicate that many other LDCs could repeat the process with the same results, since such opportunities are rather limited. Indeed the fact that Hong Kong and a few other countries captured these opportunities relatively early has tended to have the effect of shutting others out. For in order to attain its present position, Hong Kong had to win a very large share of available world markets in the limited range of industries concerned. Thus, despite its small size, it was among the top three exporting countries in the world in all categories of clothing in 1986 (at the 3 digit SITC classification level), with 12-22% of total world exports in most categories. Its world ranking as an exporter was similar in several categories of textiles, travel goods and handbags, watches and clocks, toys, sporting goods and radios (United Nations *International Trade Statistics Yearbook 1986*).

There is some indication that Hong Kong may be approaching the limits of its particular type of industrial development, since its manufacturing employment peaked in 1980 and then fell by 7% in the period 1980-85 (United Nations *Industrial Statistics Yearbook 1985*).

Conclusion

To conclude, the experience of rapid industrial growth of the countries referred to in this chapter does not offer much support for the general validity of the conventional view on industrial strategy for latecomers. The policies adopted by some of these countries (Japan, South Korea and Taiwan) have actually departed significantly from the conventionally recommended policies. These countries have used protection combined with systematic detailed intervention in a way which seems well designed to tackle directly the problem of overcoming barriers to entry for newcomers in many industries. Consequently some useful lessons can be learned from their approach, and these will be drawn on in making suggestions, in chapter 9, on an alternative approach to industrial development strategy for Ireland.

In contrast, Hong Kong and (to a lesser extent) Singapore seem to have kept more closely to the conventionally recommended strategy, but they have not really made much progress in overcoming the constraints on latecomers which are apparent in Ireland's case. Rather their growth has been due to an ability to take advantage of exceptional and limited opportunities which were sufficient to have a major impact on these small economies. These opportunities were the attraction of large shares of a globally limited amount of mobile export-oriented foreign investment and/or the capturing by indigenous industry of a large share of export markets for the limited range of 'easily entered' industries. Because such opportunities are of limited scope, the experience of these countries with the conventionally recommended strategy could still be seen as consistent with the view that serious constraints on latecomers exist as the *general* case, and that the conventional strategy would not generally be adequate to overcome them.

9

Constraints on Irish Industry and Future Prospects

Chapters 6 and 7 have pointed out that the apparently strong performance of industry in the Republic of Ireland from the 1950s to the end of the 1970s in fact concealed certain features which must cause serious concern for the future. Indigenous industry has shown little sign of a real transformation and in fact has been in relative decline. The main feature of industrial growth was the successful development of the country as a site for an exceptionally large concentration of mobile foreign investment, but a strategy based on continuing reliance on this process looks likely to be frustrated. The symptoms of this underlying weakness have become more apparent in the 1980s.

This chapter reviews a number of conceivable causes of the failure of native industry, in order to identify the principal constraints on development. It is argued, first, that the factors generally regarded in the conventional view as the main constraints on development do not apply to any great extent to Ireland, so focussing on them will not offer satisfactory solutions. It is concluded, as suggested throughout this book, that the main constraint on the country's industrial development is the prevalence of barriers to entry for latecomers. Then the possibilities of overcoming this constraint, and the strategy required to do so, are discussed.

9.i. THE CONVENTIONAL EXPLANATIONS OF UNDERDEVELOPMENT

In what was called the 'conventional view' in chapter 2, under-development is seen as an absence of development — an original state existing before a country follows a path similar to that already travelled by the developed countries. And this failure is explained very largely by the presence of characteristics in the underdeveloped country which inhibit development, not by external factors which prevent it from following a similar path. This view focusses on factors such as a lack of entrepreneurship in a 'traditional' society, a lack of capital, insufficient education, an inadequate physical infrastructure or a low-quality labour force. The implication is that if these internal problems can be overcome, the way is open for the underdeveloped country to evolve into an advanced country, in much the same way as the developed countries are said to have done, by relying on free market forces.

While it may be agreed that some or all of these concerns with internal problems do refer to conditions that are *necessary* for successful industrial development, the Irish experience suggests that they are not *sufficient* conditions. For they are generally reasonably satisfactory in Ireland and yet fundamental development problems remain. The satisfactory state of a number of these conditions is indicated by the inflow of numerous foreign firms, which have found it possible to operate effectively in many parts of Ireland. This indicates the existence of suitable conditions in the physical infrastructure, the political and bureaucratic environment, financial and professional services, and in the attitudes and productivity of the labour force. Such conditions could, no doubt, be even more suitable for capitalist development than they are, but the performance of foreign industry suggests that they do not represent important constraints which would explain the markedly poorer performance of indigenous industry in the same environment. It is clear, too, that the large inflow of foreign firms was not simply based on prior misapprehension about these conditions, since they have indicated in a number of surveys that their experience in Ireland in these matters has generally been satisfactory; (table 9.1 is one example).

The only subject of substantial criticism in table 9.1 is Transport and Communications. A report for the National Economic and Social Council (1981) examined this issue in detail and found that the main problems concern telecommunications, but concluded (p. 84): 'In spite of these shortcomings most of our interviews suggested that their impact in the great majority of cases is a nuisance rather than having a serious effect on the profitability of the concern. Often they were anticipated and . . . most firms had found ways of alleviating their effect satisfactorily.' This assessment seems consistent with the very high overall approval of Ireland as a location expressed in the last two answers in table 9.1 despite the criticism of telecommunications facilities.[1]

Table 9.1: Survey Conducted Among 114 Foreign Companies in Ireland

How Do You Rate:-	Good	Fair	Poor	N.A.
Labour Relations?	55%	38%	6%	1%
Productivity?	65%	31%	3%	1%
Professional Services?	59%	33%	8%	—
Government Assistance?	78%	20%	2%	—
Transport and Communications?	2%	46%	48%	4%
Return on Investment?	76%	21%	3%	—

	Yes	No
Would you recommend Ireland to a company seeking relocation?	89%	11%
If you had to make a locational decision would you again choose Ireland?	91%	9%

Source: Survey published in *The Business Location File*, November 1978, and reprinted in *Business and Finance*, 15/2/79.

Another endorsement, from an 'international' source, of Irish labour relations and productivity came from Tony O'Reilly, an Irish businessman who still has wide-ranging interests in Ireland as well as having become president and chief executive of Heinz, a major US multinational company with 60,000 employees worldwide: 'Irish hourly earnings are not yet a deterrent, he says. Neither, for the most part, is trade union activity. "Irish workers properly led are as good as any".'[2]

Newspaper interviews with foreign businessmen operating plants in Ireland quite often elicit similar remarks. For example:

. . . Milton L. Glass, treasurer of the giant Gillette Corporation . . . says the Irish worker is just as good as the legendary German worker . . .

Other US perceptions of the Irish industrial economy are that wage levels are not a major factor affecting the position of firms . . . political instability or a low credit rating are not seen as important potential problems and the Irish worker is well educated. Most surprising is the American view of the country's bureaucracy — they rate it highly.[3]

Taken together with table 9.1, and similar findings in a survey of foreign firms in Ireland in early 1981,[4] such remarks suggest that the tendency of some Irish businessmen to blame the work-force and other conditions in the economy for the problems of Irish industry is misplaced.

It has been argued, however, that the success of foreign firms in Ireland does not necessarily mean that conditions are good for indigenous industry, because foreign multinational companies can benefit from artificial transfer-pricing. Transfer-pricing is the practice of buying inputs from other branches of the same multinational company, or selling products to other branches of the company, at prices which are artificially rigged to suit the company's overall interests. It is widely believed that this practice is used to boost the profitability of multinational branch plants in Ireland, in order to benefit from Irish tax concessions. Thus it is sometimes argued that foreign firms find Ireland attractive because they can benefit from transfer-pricing, whereas most indigenous firms cannot do so and are held back by an unconducive economic environment.

This argument is not convincing, however, partly because it is implicitly based on a recognition that Irish taxes on industry are exceptionally lenient by international standards. This should be *good* for Irish industry, even if it is a much greater advantage for foreign companies. If this argument is to explain the simul-taneous failure of indigenous industry and success of foreign companies, it must be claimed that the benefits which foreign firms gain from transfer-pricing are so great that they substantially outweigh other disadvantages in the environment which are sufficient to cripple native firms — despite the fact that they too face negligible profit taxes. This suggestion seems quite implausible, especially in view of the attitudes of foreign firms to various aspects of the Irish environment reported above.

To turn to the question of 'entrepreneurship', could the contrast between Irish and foreign industry be a reflection of serious deficiencies in this regard in Ireland? By entrepreneurship in this context is meant the effect of the attitudes and social structure prevailing in Ireland in producing people of enterprise and initiative, who are willing to start up and run businesses. Although this is sometimes put forward as a problem in Ireland, there is evidence to the contrary. For example, it can be calculated from the *IDA Employment Survey* that as many as 1,486 new Irish indigenous manufacturing firms were set up between January 1973 and January 1980.[5] This represents a large number of entrepreneurs emerging in a period of only seven years, in the manufacturing sector alone. These new firms accounted for as much as 37% of the total of 3,996 Irish manufacturing companies operating by 1980. The *rate* of establishment of new native industrial firms in the 1970s, in relation to the size of indigenous industry, was similar to the USA and Canada in the 1950s and 1960s, and about 40% greater than in the UK in the late 1960s/early 1970s (O'Farrell and Crouchley, 1984). Thus there are many active industrial entrepreneurs, despite the evidence of declining indigenous industrial employment. Many more new firms would also have been initiated in services and building.

New firms, however, have generally remained small and, along with longer-established firms, they tend to remain confined to a limited range of activities, many of which are not traded internationally. So could it be argued that Irish entrepreneurs are generally unwilling to become involved in activities where they would meet foreign competition? Again this seems an untenable view. It was seen in section 6.iii, for example, that the largest Irish manufacturing companies, including those in non-traded activities, move readily into multinational operations, presumably when the scale and logistics of their business make this appropriate.[6]

Apart from manufacturing, some of the larger building firms, such as Abbey, McInerney, Sisk and Rohan, also conduct substantial multinational operations. Several of the state enterprises also operate internationally, such as Aer Lingus, the Electricity Supply Board and Bord na Mona (the Peat Board), in transport, management consultancy, engineering and other services abroad. And finally, not only do Irish financial institutions dominate their sector in Ireland but several of them, such as Allied Irish Banks and the Bank of Ireland, have numerous branches in Britain and other offices and subsidiaries further afield. These two Irish banks, in fact, both ranked among the 200 largest in the world and earned about 20% of their revenue abroad in 1982. This ability of the major companies to expand internationally, as well as the record of start-ups of many new companies, reflects not only on the question of entrepreneurship but also suggests that the availability of capital for investment has not been a general problem holding back expansion.

The extent of active entrepreneurship which is evident in

Irish business — outside manufacturing activities with high barriers to entry — appears to rule out any presumption of a general lack of enterprise. Instead it points towards the more specific difficulties associated with breaking into advanced manufacturing industries as a latecomer. It could reasonably be argued, of course, that Irish entrepreneurship is deficient in the sense of lacking the *specialised skills and experience* required in specific advanced industries. Such 'entrepreneurial' deficiencies are really a form of entry barrier, rather than a social-psychological deficiency, since specialised business knowledge and competence based on experience is not easily acquired in an economy where the industries concerned do not already exist. Thus the fact that Irish entrepreneurs have not attempted to develop many traded industries in sectors with substantial entry barriers could reasonably be interpreted as rational and realistic behaviour for profit-seeking private individuals. For they may be conscious both of conventional entry barriers and the need for some familiarity with a complex area of business before setting up a new enterprise in it.

9.ii. MARKET DISTORTIONS

If it is accepted that the general business environment and the spirit of enterprise are not greatly deficient, orthodox analyses of the causes of slow growth and persistent unemployment tend to focus on market 'distortions'. The distortions which are considered by them, however, are not those caused by 'imperfect competition' and barriers to entry. Rather it is simply assumed that 'perfect competition' prevails, which means that it is taken for granted that markets will work smoothly — unless some agent intervenes to distort the market. Starting from this assumption, persistent unemployment and slow growth is inevitably seen as evidence that somebody *is* causing distortions, since other possible explanations are ruled out by the basic assumptions. The two possible sources of such distortions which are generally identified are high labour costs, due for example to the activities of strong trade unions, and the actions of the government, which imposes taxes and controls a good deal of expenditure in ways which may reduce the efficiency of free markets. Both of these factors have commonly been put forward as causes of the difficulties of Irish industry, so this section considers whether focussing on them can really provide solutions.

The Role of Labour Costs

In the orthodox view, it is thought that in an economy at any particular level of development — the level of development being indicated primarily by the size of the capital stock — there is a wage level at which full employment is attainable. Consequently persistent unemployment may be attributable to an excessive wage level. The attainment of full employment, therefore, would depend largely on reducing wages, or freezing them while the capital stock expands, so as to attain the wage level consistent with full employment at the stage of development achieved. Excessive wage levels, causing unemployment, would be put down to some distortion of the labour market. Ruane (1980) is more specific than most of such analyses in the Irish literature in suggesting why such distortions would arise. Endemically excessive wages, she suggests, would arise in Ireland as a result of factors such as government pay policies, strong unions, and the fact that mobility of labour between Ireland and Britain makes the two countries virtually a common labour market.

According to this view, lower labour costs would benefit employment through several mechanisms. Most generally, lower labour costs mean higher profits, other things being equal, and hence a greater ability and incentive to invest in expansion. In the particular context of a small open economy, a decline in labour costs relative to major trading partner countries may also allow relative prices to be reduced and larger market shares to be gained. Alternatively, lower labour costs may allow profits to expand, with prices unchanged, thus providing the ability and incentive to expand production for an international market which is seen as infinitely large in relation to the small domestic productive capacity. And in addition, a reduction in the price of labour relative to that of capital provides an incentive for the use of more labour-intensive techniques in any particular industry and/or for investment in those industries which are naturally more labour intensive.

Some variant of these basic principles has characterised a number of analyses of the major constraints on Irish development and the steps required to attain full employment.[7] It may be readily agreed that pay restraint enhances the prospects for increasing employment directly in public services so long as the exchequer has limited resources. The analysis in chapters 6 and 7 of this book, however, would suggest that the identification of pay restraint as the crucial requirement for influencing the expansion of *industrial* employment exaggerates the importance of this factor, since other factors are more important.

Doubts about the relevance of the conventional analysis to the present circumstances of industry in Ireland arise at several points, particularly in relation to the following assumptions: (a) that increased profits, resulting from pay restraint, which increase firms' *ability* to invest, would in fact generally lead to a corresponding increase in manufacturing investment in Ireland; (b) that labour costs have a major influence on prices and that prices in turn have a decisive influence on competitive ability; and (c) that labour-capital ratios are quite flexible and influenced by the relative prices of these factors (in any particular industry), and/or that there is significant scope for selectivity of investment among industries according to their labour-intensity.

Profits and Investment

As regards the first of the above assumptions, there is little evidence of a relationship between profitability and subsequent job-creating investment in Ireland. Vaughan (1978) looked for such a relationship but concluded that 'in the period under study, up until 1973, no simple relationship between profits, output and employment would have been immediately apparent'.

This absence of such relationship can be explained in the light of the industrial structure and behaviour already outlined in chapters 6 and 7. To show this, it is useful to consider separately four different types of industry: the non-traded sector, the basic processing sector, the indigenous traded sector (other than basic processing), and the foreign-owned traded sector.

A good deal of indigenous industry is in the sheltered or non-traded sector, and its expansion is limited primarily by the level of domestic demand. Any profits surplus to the amount required to maintain capacity at this level could go simply to increase shareholders' consumption. If they go to investment, entry barriers would deter investment in traded industries and direct it to services, property, takeovers of existing firms or foreign acquisitions.[8] Such a pattern of investment was, in fact, seen in the behaviour of the large firms in this category, in chapter 6. In the basic processing sector too (which is mainly Food), increased profits cannot be invested indefinitely in expansion since output is limited primarily by the supply of material inputs.[9] Investment in other sectors by basic processing firms would be constrained by barriers to entry, in much the same way as it would for non-traded industries. And this, as was seen in chapter 6, appears to include serious constraints on substantial investment in downstream, higher value-added processing where entry barriers tend to be high and oligopoly prevails.

In the mainly export-oriented foreign sector, plants in Ireland are only one part of a larger corporation. They are often not even wholly responsible for one product but conduct only one stage in the longer process of research, development, production, assembly and marketing of a product. Although some minimally acceptable level of profits from the Irish plant would be a precondition for its expansion, its cost-effectiveness would very often not be the major influence on final cost or on investment decisions. Rather, expansion would depend largely on foreign demand and the competitiveness and profitability of the enterprise as a whole, which is influenced largely by its operations elsewhere.[10]

Another consideration concerning the foreign-owned sector, however, is the fact that wage costs have an influence on the location decisions of potential new first-time foreign investors. Here one is dealing not with the effects of *changes* in wage costs on an existing industrial structure, but rather with a comparison between absolute cost levels in Ireland relative to alternative sites. Since Ireland seems to be selected mainly by new foreign investors whose first requirement is a site with access to EC markets, the most relevant comparison is between costs in Ireland and other EC countries. On this criterion, Irish labour costs are reasonably competitive, although they are close to British (or Spanish) labour costs and higher than in Greece and Portugal. Consequently wage restraint might do little to increase new investment, although it could help to defend Ireland's attraction for new foreign firms to some extent. At present, however, Ireland tends to attract relatively 'mobile' foreign firms, which do not need to be located in an advanced industrial environment. Lower labour costs would do little to attract the more technically advanced industries which do need such an environment, so that wage restraint would not overcome the main barrier to increasing the amount and quality of foreign investment.

Finally, the indigenous traded sector, unlike the other three, is one area where greater profitability resulting from pay restraint or reduction might lead to significant reinvestment, beyond what would otherwise occur. This might not result in much actual expansion of manufacturing output and employment, although it could help to delay the prevailing decline.[11] But pay restraint would also have some adverse effects on these largely domestically oriented industries, through its effect on domestic demand. Further implications of concentrating concern on these industries (as constituted at present) are discussed below.

Labour Costs, Prices and Competitiveness

To move on to the question of the influence of labour costs on prices, and of prices on competitive ability, first it should be noted that labour costs have for long been a relatively small part of total costs. In the 1973 *Census of Industrial Production*, wages and salaries accounted for only 16.6% of manufacturing gross output and this fell to 12.7% in 1985. For many goods, there must be added to these figures the labour cost component of inputs purchased in Ireland (such as electricity, packaging, some materials, etc.), in order to measure the full effect of Irish labour costs on total costs. Nevertheless, with much of materials, fuel and capital goods being imported, it is probably only rarely that the Irish labour cost component exceeds one-third of total costs. Wages and salaries, of course, amount to a greater proportion of *net* output, at 32.6% in 1985, so that sharp relative wage *rises* could undermine the profitability of firms with given cost structures. But the fact that labour costs are a relatively minor influence on total costs and hence on price means that it would take very large, and probably unrealistic, wage reductions to achieve significant price reductions, with a view to enhancing firms' competitive ability.

Irish labour costs, in any case, are already quite competitive with the country's principal trading partners, whether one looks at hourly labour costs or labour costs per unit of output (see table 9.2).[12]

Of course, it could be said that the aggregate figures in the second column of the table conceal sectoral variations. Ireland's high productivity in relation to labour costs may be largely due to new foreign firms in advanced industries, while traditional indigenous industries have much lower productivity and may be less competitive in terms of output in relation to labour costs. This may well be true but it still means that labour costs are not Ireland's main problem, for it implies that native industries

Table 9.2: Manufacturing Labour Costs

	Hourly Labour Costs (Deutschmarks)	Index of Output per Unit of Labour Costs
USA	29	96
West Germany	26	100
Italy	20	90
France	19	112
Japan	16	116
U.K.	16	102
Ireland	14	136

Source: Draft Irish government White Paper on Industrial Policy, 1983.

cannot compete *despite* having relatively low hourly labour costs, which have appeared to suit foreign firms. So the main problem of indigenous industries must lie in the *other* influences on competitiveness and productivity — such as economies of scale, technology, design, marketing and after-sales service. It would make little sense to seek to redress these deficiencies by emphasising the need for further restraint of labour costs, which appears to be the one influence on competitiveness where Ireland already scores relatively well.

As regards the role of prices in determining competitive ability (in traded industries), prices are most important in standardised and commodity-type goods which vary little in quality, and in the lower quality range of more differentiated consumer products such as clothing. Such cases are, in effect, taken to be the general case in the conventional analysis. There are, however, a great many industrial products unlike these — including most capital goods, consumer durables and other branded consumer goods — in which factors such as quality, reliability, after-sales service, innovation and marketing exert a strong influence on competitive ability. Activities which have low barriers to entry and highly competitive market structures generally fit into the first group, where price is important. But the second group, where price matters less, has high barriers to entry with oligopolistic structures as a general rule.[13] Consequently the first-mentioned group, where price is an important influence on competitiveness, would include most of Irish indigenous traded industry, whereas a large and growing proportion of the foreign-owned firms in Ireland would fall into the second group. Thus the concentration of concern on the influence of prices on competitiveness would seem to be broadly justified as regards indigenous traded industries, but prices are less important for the foreign-owned traded sector.

In the long term, however, concentration on improving price competitiveness could, at best, serve primarily to strengthen the easily entered industries where prices matter most. It would not stimulate a general shift by indigenous firms out of these industries and into more oligopolistic activities with higher barriers to entry. This is a crucial point because the easily entered price-elastic industries are limited in number, and experience strongly suggests that they are unlikely to provide an adequate basis for expanding or possibly even maintaining employment. Indeed this problem may be accentuated with demand shifting more to other products as incomes grow and many NICs with much lower costs successfully entering the same fields. Furthermore, if Irish industry is to consist largely of such activities, relatively low or declining wages seem inevitable for the foreseeable future, in view of growing competition from NICs in the same limited range of industries.

In conclusion, sharp and sustained increases in unit labour costs relative to competitors could undermine the viability of many existing traded industries as structured at present. But on the other hand, wage restraint or reduction of an order that could plausibly be aimed for seems unlikely to do much to enhance overall competitive ability. To concentrate on the issue of labour costs is to overlook the more important necessity to gain entry for Irish industry into sectors with significant barriers to entry, in order to open up wider areas for employment and to generate higher incomes. The predominance of such industries in the traded sectors of advanced industrial countries is the main reason why they can maintain much higher labour costs than Ireland without having such high unemployment rates (though greater efficiency in other traded industries probably also plays a part).

A paper from the OECD (1981) has reviewed the evidence from a wide range of sources on the relationship between unit labour costs and competitive ability in advanced industrial countries. It concludes that the conventional theory can no longer be justified. This paper remarks:

When facts act as 'perversely' as countries' world market shares have in relation to their domestic wage costs, one is forced to conclude that a dangerous gap has developed between reality and theory. This is obviously the case with the theory lying behind price and cost indicators as measures of international competitiveness. They must be abandoned, and have been so to a very large extent.[14]

Thus the evidence from the advanced industrial countries suggests that, for them at least, there is no very important link between relative unit labour costs and competitive ability. This implies that if Ireland is to seek to 'upgrade' its industrial structure, improvements in relative labour costs are most unlikely to be the key to developing more advanced industries. For the competitive performance of the developed industrial countries, which have established many of such industries, does not appear to be related to relative unit labour costs.

Labour-Capital Ratios

As regards the possibility of increasing employment by increasing the labour-intensity of Irish industry, this may be broken down into two separate issues. First, there is the question of selectively promoting industries which are naturally more labour-intensive; and second, there is the question of encouraging greater labour-intensity within particular industries or firms, by means of wage restraint (or labour subsidies) so as to reduce the price of labour relative to that of capital. On the first question, the view of the IDA has been that in their experience the major issue is how to generate sufficient projects, not how to select the most desirable, such as the most labour-intensive, from an excess of project proposals. They have said that they assist industries of widely varying labour-intensities because job needs are such that all sources of employment must be welcomed and they cannot afford to be selective to the extent of turning away viable industries (Killeen, 1975). McKeon (1980) made it clear that few viable project proposals are refused IDA grant approvals, and indeed in the case of Irish indigenous projects some have been grant-aided which would not be considered viable without assistance.[15] It is significant too that, while being prepared to grant-aid virtually all such viable projects, and some non-viable Irish ones, the IDA has practically never stated (as Ross, 1981, points out) that a lack of funds has prevented it from supporting any industrial project. It may be concluded, therefore, that there is little or no excess of viable project proposals beyond what are undertaken. Consequently there is little or no scope for increasing employment creation by selectively favouring the more labour-intensive projects. Rather, such selectivity would tend to reduce job creation since it means rejecting some proposals.[16]

Turning to the question of increasing the labour-intensity of individual firms or industries, the IDA (according to Ruane, 1976, ch. 4) apparently sees little scope for this in new projects. They believe that it is unwise to encourage firms to depart from the technologies which they consider to be suitable, and that many firms appear to have quite rigid capital-labour ratios. As the main practitioners in this field, the IDA's views must merit some consideration. Furthermore, evidence from other countries offers some support for their view. Lall's (1978) survey of literature on the behaviour of multinationals in less-developed countries concludes that their choice of technology is generally fairly rigid. This is because the very source of their competitive strength is often in their production technology and marketing, which would require goods to be produced to pre-determined specifications. This would be relevant to the foreign firms in Ireland. Another survey article by Baer (1976) refers to other findings that choice of technique is often determined by quality considerations, especially for export industries, rather than by relative factor prices. Baer also refers to examples of basic processing industries in which material inputs represent the major cost, so that the choice of technology is determined largely by the need to make the most efficient use of materials. Again these considerations are relevant to a large portion of industry in Ireland. Some of this literature suggests that ancillary activities, such as handling of materials and products, can be fairly flexible as regards capital-labour ratios even if core production processes are not, although Baer's article includes some warnings against such a general assumption. It might be concluded that some scope for flexibility of capital-labour ratios exists but it is unlikely to be very great. The effect of such flexibility on employment, as a result of wage restraint of a realistic degree, would scarcely be dramatic.

To sum up this discussion of the role of labour costs in orthodox economic language, the conventional analysis focusses on this issue because it is thought likely that 'imperfections' exist in the labour market, causing market distortions. However, little consideration is given to the possibility that serious imperfections may also be common in other respects — such as oligopoly, product differentiation and non-price competition, the non-availability of common production technology, and imperfect substitutability of capital and labour. The conventional analysis rarely attempts to refute such suggestions which would imply that entry barriers are common. Rather, it assumes away such imperfections, while (selectively) recognising that imperfections can exist in the labour market. An analysis based on these assumptions can be misleading and is not capable of identifying important problems. This is not to say that labour costs are irrelevant to the issue of generating employment and development, but rather that an emphasis on the role of labour costs exaggerates their importance and tends to ignore other factors which are more fundamental to the issue. One could agree that sustained rapid increases in relative unit labour costs could undermine profitability and employment in many firms with given cost structures. But it should not be assumed that reductions in unit labour costs relative to competitors would serve to increase industrial employment substantially. That would require strong policies designed to overcome what appears to be the main constraint on Irish industrial development — namely, the prevalence of barriers to entry for latecomers in many manufacturing industries.

Distortions by Government
As well as focussing on labour costs, the conventional view also blames the government for distorting market forces, causing unemployment and inhibiting industrial development. Part of this argument, as put forward in Ireland, is an extension to the argument on labour costs, since it is said that high government expenditure leads to high taxes which pushes up labour costs and thereby undermines employment. Taxes are said to push up labour costs mainly because workers demand higher wages to compensate for higher taxes, while expansion of the public sector and increases in public sector pay are also said to 'bid up' wage rates. A second strand of the argument is that public sector borrowing to pay for high expenditure channels investment away from private industry. This is because the tax system is said to be biased to encourage lending to the government. And a third strand of the argument is that a high level of personal taxation discourages entrepreneurs and investors, because the

government claims much of the reward for their efforts.

The first part of the argument, concerning labour costs, has largely been dealt with already. It has been shown that Irish labour costs are not uncompetitive, whether due to the effect of taxation or for any other reason. And, as has also been argued, labour costs are not crucial to the question of industrial employment and development in any case.

The second strand of the argument, which says that tax incentives to lend to the government sucks investment away from private industry, is also unconvincing. For there was no lack of native investment in *non-traded* types of industry, which (as seen in chapter 6) grew quickly while domestic demand was strong up to the early 1980s. Thus it is hard to sustain the view that there has been a general tax disincentive for industrial investment. The difference between the rapid growth of non-traded indigenous industries and the relative decline of traded activities cannot be linked to differences in tax incentives — quite the contrary in fact. Until 1981, there was no tax on profits arising from manufactured exports while profits arising from domestic sales were subject to the normal corporation profit tax. The lack of investment in native traded industries, therefore, cannot be due to the tax system. Rather it must be due to inherent deficiencies in competing internationally — not, as already argued, because of labour costs or the effect of taxes on labour costs — but more likely because of the prevalence of entry barriers for late-developers.

The third strand of the argument about the debilitating effect of taxation on development says that high personal taxation discourages entrepreneurs and investors. But, again, the rapid growth of non-traded industries indicates that they were not discouraged when market opportunities existed. In addition, as was pointed out in section 9.i when discussing entrepreneurship, there has been a high rate of start-ups of new indigenous manufacturing firms by international standards. Personal taxation has not prevented many active entrepreneurs from emerging. Of course, most new firms have remained very small, but high personal taxation could not account for this since it should positively encourage re-investment, if anything.

Finally, the whole argument that government taxation is responsible for the current weakness of indigenous industry also lacks a sense of historical perspective. The growth of taxation which has provoked this critique is primarily a phenomenon of the 1970s and 1980s. But indigenous industry has shown signs of great weakness at all times since at least the 1840s, apart from the period of protection from the early 1930s to mid-1960s. As seen in chapter 6, the present phase of relative decline of native industry began with the removal of protection in the mid-1960s.

Since the various constraints on industrial development which are considered in the conventional analysis do not seem to explain the weakness of Irish traded industries, it may be concluded that the major problem is the prevalence of barriers to entry for latecomers.

9.iii. FUTURE STRATEGY FOR IRISH INDUSTRIAL DEVELOPMENT

It has been argued in the last two sections that the main concerns of the 'conventional' analysis of underdevelopment and persistent unemployment do not deal adequately with the problems of Irish industry, either in uncovering the major constraints on development or in identifying the type of solutions that are called for. Before going on to outline an alternative type of solution, it will be useful to clarify the role of the industrial sector in the development of the economy as a whole. The general importance of industrial development arises primarily from the fact that as incomes grow from very low levels, an increasing proportion of additional income is spent on industrial products rather than primary products. With further growth in incomes, too, an increasing proportion is spent on the products of technologically advanced industries rather than the basic or staple industries such as food, clothing, housing and furniture. Even when, at high levels, incomes come to be spent increasingly on services, these services often use large inputs of industrial goods so that their growth still requires industrial expansion.

An individual country, however, could import many of its requirements of industrial products and pay for them with exports of primary products or services. Some countries have been able to do this, thus attaining high income levels with normal expenditure patterns, without a strong industrial sector.[17] For many countries, however, such a process is not feasible beyond a certain point. 'Exportable' or traded services such as tourism, insurance, shipping and banking tend to be only a minority of all services and not all countries can develop them to a high degree.[18] And primary products, as export earners, suffer from the defect that rather few countries have very large mineral or hydrocarbon resources in relation to the size of their population, while land resources are also limited and demand for agricultural products tends to grow relatively slowly.

Many countries, therefore, must aim to develop their manufacturing industry. It is not necessary to produce the whole range of industrial products which they require, since that would be impractical for most countries. Rather they must aim to satisfy home demand for at least some industrial products, while also exporting increasing quantities of manufactured goods to pay for the growing imports of others. Growing imports are both a prerequisite for economic growth, in the case of capital and intermediate goods, and a result of growth, in the case of consumer goods. The necessity to increase output and exports follows not only from the aim of increasing *incomes*, but also, in the case of an unprotected economy operating in a competitive world, follows from the aim of increasing or maintaining *employment*. To maintain or improve their competitive position, companies in modern competitive sectors usually have to keep increasing their investment and improving their production techniques, which results in increasing output per worker. This means that output must grow at least as fast as output per worker in order even to maintain employment. The process of competition, in other words, leads either to economic growth, if successful, or to unemployment if unsuccessful; there is no option of low or zero growth without unemployment in a capitalist market economy.[19] And the growth of output which occurs in the case of success generally leads to growth of imports, and hence a necessity to develop exports.

The Foreign Exchange Constraint in Ireland
In Ireland, it was the failure to develop exports adequately that cut short the process of protected industrialisation and led to prolonged recession in the 1950s, since the rising import bills could not be paid. In a small economy which spends more than half of its income on imports, it is still the case that the ability to sustain growth and to increase employment ultimately depends on the country's ability to obtain foreign exchange to pay for imports. Thus, as an extreme example, if limitless supplies of foreign exchange could somehow be obtained, all traded manufactured goods could simply be imported and the entire labour force could be employed in agriculture and expanded services and non-traded industries, at higher levels of income. But if, on the other hand, there are chronic balance of payments

deficits and a shortage of foreign exchange, there are constraints on imports of the capital goods, materials and fuel required for growth, and deflation becomes necessary to curb consumer spending on imports as well.

After the early 1970s, agricultural exports (or slightly processed food) and foreign borrowing played a major part in pushing back Ireland's foreign exchange constraint. Agricultural and food exports benefited greatly from accession to the EEC in 1973, since the EEC market, under the Common Agricultural Policy (CAP), is highly subsidised and protected. This guaranteed market remains in existence for Ireland's main agricultural and food exports. But there will be no further substantial rise in prices such as occurred when the country first gained access to the high-price market of the EEC, and indeed financial constraints on the CAP mean that price increases may not keep pace with inflation. Thus there has been a once-and-for-all shift to a new price 'plateau', and agricultural exports cannot be depended on for comparable major increases in foreign exchange earnings in the future.

Foreign borrowing by the public sector began to expand at around the same time. The accumulated foreign debt rose from £567 million in 1975 to £2,207 million in 1980. It then rose very quickly to £7,621 million by 1984. Although this represented a higher level of debt per capita than many developing countries with a serious debt crisis, Ireland would not have had similar difficulties in borrowing more since international bankers still evidently regarded the country as a reasonably good credit risk. *Euromoney* magazine ranked Ireland 22nd out of 112 countries as a low risk debtor in 1984. The reason was because Ireland has higher incomes per capita than debt-ridden developing countries and also exports a very high proportion of its output. Thus interest payments on the Irish debt as a percentage of export earnings were less than 8%, compared with about 40% in Argentina or Brazil in 1983. Since this indicator is most widely used to assess ability to repay foreign debt, Ireland had probably not reached the limits of its ability to borrow more abroad.

Nevertheless, by the mid-1980s there was quite a widespread consensus in Ireland that the foreign debt had become a very serious problem, even though it was probably possible to borrow more. For interest payments abroad had become very substantial, at almost 5% of GNP in 1984, which represented a serious drain on the country's income. It has now been recognised that borrowing further, unless it is for clearly *productive investment,* would only be buying consumption in the short-term at the expense of still further losses of income some years later. Since this is now widely understood and accepted, further significant growth in foreign borrowing is unlikely to occur. So foreign borrowing, like agricultural exports, is unlikely to be as great a source of growth in the availability of foreign exchange in the future as it has been in the past.

In the industrial sector, the high level of foreign direct investment in export industries was a further source of growth in foreign exchange earnings in the 1970s. As was shown in section 7.iv, however, such investment has shown little or no growth since 1981. Furthermore, the growth in profit repatriation by foreign companies reduces the *net* foreign exchange earnings associated with their exports.

For all these reasons, the foreign exchange constraint must be regarded as a serious medium- to long-term issue for the country. At the time of writing (late 1988) this may not seem immediately apparent since the balance of payments has moved into surplus recently. This has occurred, however, in the context of prolonged recession, with unemployment rising to 18% of the labour force and tens of thousands of people emigrating each year. The depression of the economy, with relatively low import growth, has contributed substantially to improving the balance of payments. But there seem to be limited prospects of an upsurge in (net) export earnings, which would be needed to keep the balance of payments deficits low in a context of sustained growth with falling unemployment. There is also little prospect of a major increase in foreign borrowing, which would be needed if deficits were to emerge again. Thus there is ultimately a foreign exchange constraint on sustained economic recovery.

Even more than in the past, the solution to this problem will have to be sought quite largely through the development of export-oriented industries. Development of import-substituting industries would also be of value, so long as they are genuinely substituting for goods now imported and are not simply non-traded industries catering for expansion of domestic demand (which are sometimes mistaken for import-substitutes).[20] While expansion of internationally traded manufacturing industry would directly contribute to increasing employment and output, this sector must also play a part in pushing back the foreign exchange constraint, so as to allow employment and incomes to expand in non-traded industries, services and building as well. This means that, even if expanding employment is seen as the main goal of economic policy, industrial development policy must take account of the foreign exchange effects of industrial expansion, as well as immediate employment effects.

From the analysis of foreign industries in Ireland contained in chapter 7, it seems likely that they will have definite limitations as a source of expansion of foreign exchange earnings. This is because they generally have a very high import content and they withdraw a good deal of their profits from the country. There should be some value in aiming to attract more higher-level functions of foreign companies to Ireland, in order to anchor them more firmly to the local economy and to raise the 'retained value' in the country. But past experience suggests that companies have a strong attachment to their home countries for high-level functions, so that it would be unrealistic to expect major success in this endeavour.

In recent years the IDA has stressed that opportunities also exist in the development of 'service industries' — such as computer software, architectural and industrial design, testing laboratories and research centres. Such services can be 'exportable' as well as substituting for imports. The IDA's managing director has said that it is intended 'to make Ireland in the services sector what Switzerland is in the financial field'.[21] Such service industries are indeed a growth area in Ireland but they remain very small compared with manufacturing. By the end of 1987, internationally traded service industries aided by the IDA employed only 5,700 people, about half in indigenous companies. While they probably will grow in importance, it is obvious that an extremely dramatic development would be required before they could fill a role comparable to manufacturing, and there is no firm reason for believing that this will occur.[22] There has probably been a certain amount of euphoric overstatement of the prospects of such services, although they are likely to make a contribution to development. There is also likely to be scope for further development of export services in more traditional fields such as education and healthcare (see Kennedy, 1985).

One is drawn, nevertheless, to the conclusion that it will be crucially important for Ireland to aim to develop a stronger indigenous manufacturing sector, more capable of competing internationally and earning substantially larger amounts of foreign exchange than at present. This will require, most importantly, breaking into some activities with substantial barriers to entry. This is necessary both in order to widen the range of areas for employment and to gain the increased foreign exchange returns which would be available in such activities, which generally have high value-added and can sustain higher incomes due to higher productivity.

An Alternative Approach to Industrial Policy

It is not intended to propose a detailed plan here for pursuing this general aim, since this is a matter that could only be properly worked out by teams of well-informed and experienced specialists in fields such as corporate strategy, finance, marketing, engineering and various areas of industrial economics. Detailed consultations with business people would also be necessary. The most that can be attempted here is a broad outline of the type of approach that seems to be called for. The suggestions which follow are broadly in line with the proposals of the Telesis Report (1982). To some extent, too, Irish industrial policy has been moving in the direction of such recommendations very recently, and examples of relevant new departures are mentioned below.

The first essential feature of a new approach is that it must involve active and selective government policies; an attempt must be made to choose target industries which are to be developed by indigenous firms, and resources must be quite highly concentrated on their development. Furthermore, rather than simply offering incentives for private firms to undertake investments and waiting for such firms to come forward with proposals, the state agencies must be prepared to take initiatives much more strongly than in the past. This is necessary to ensure that the required investments are made, even if they do not appear immediately attractive to private firms.

It is worth stressing that there is no suggestion here that the state is somehow *more competent* or better able to select investment projects than private firms. Rather, the need for state initiatives arises because the state can mobilise greater resources and can have a different motivation to private firms. It has been shown in chapter 2 that many manufacturing industries are characterised by entry barriers, which make them unattractive to relatively small private investors who seek a reasonably quick and secure profit. Indeed, from the private point of view, an enterprising Irish entrepreneur or firm with money to invest would be well advised to steer clear of trying to start up this type of industry. And indeed, few of them do attempt this difficult task. Instead, they have tended to invest in property, services, non-traded industries and government bonds; and they have also sent money abroad to buy foreign companies and bonds. It makes sense for them, but it is not good enough for the development of the Irish economy. The state, however, can take a broader, longer-term view. What the state can do is to identify *relatively* suitable internationally traded industries, in which barriers to entry are not too high, so that a competitive capability could be developed over some years, even though the prospect of initial losses would deter private investment. Then it can mobilise substantial sums of capital and make a concerted and sustained effort to develop the selected industries to a competitive standard.

There is an Irish proverb 'An té nach bhfuil láidir ní foláir dó bheith glic' — meaning the person who is not strong had better be clever. That could be applied to countries too. Since Ireland is not strong in the matter of competing internationally in industry, it is essential to be clever. Being clever, in this instance, is basically a matter of picking out industries which would not be too difficult to succeed in, and then concentrating resources in them. Because the country has limited resources, it is necessary to marshal what strength it has in a concerted effort to make breakthroughs in areas where the resistance is not too great. Such an approach necessarily calls for serious state planning, guidance and initiative.

Government initiative of this type must be quite highly selective because the creation of indigenous industries in areas with barriers to entry would generally involve the development of firms and industries which would be fairly large by the standards of existing Irish industry. Consequently only a limited number of activities can be chosen, although ideally they should not be so few as to gamble excessively on a very few successes. The general necessity for an active and selective approach for latecomers is underlined by the fact that the more successful latecomers discussed in chapter 8 have used such methods.

A strategy of this type requires a strategic planning capability, to select suitable new high value-added traded industries for development. Selections would have to be made at quite a detailed level of the sub-sector, or industrial segment, rather than the broad industrial sector, though the final precise choice of products and markets should be based largely on the judgement of enterprises themselves. This selection would have to be based on exhaustive analysis of the requirements for international competitive success in specific industries and markets, as compared with the competitive capabilities that could be developed most readily in Ireland. It must be recognised that such strategic planning expertise may be in short supply in Ireland at present, largely because there has been little attempt to operate a selective directed industrial policy, at least until very recently. Thus it may be necessary to tap foreign sources for advice initially. Meanwhile considerable effort should be devoted to education and training to develop the necessary expertise, in corporate strategy and the analysis of international competition, in public agencies concerned with planning and development.

In choosing target industries for development, account should be taken of the specific nature of the barriers to entry concerned. Then the difficulty of overcoming these and the rewards for doing so successfully would have to be weighed against the capabilities existing in Ireland and the costs and risks involved. Some of the most desirable industries to enter would be characterised by impossibly high barriers to entry for Ireland, while others with high entry barriers for Ireland might not be particularly desirable to enter at all. The aim would be to seek out relatively desirable industries with relatively low entry barriers for Ireland.

Assessment of potential target industries would need to take account of whether the entry barriers arise primarily from economies of scale, capital requirements, marketing and distribution, technology, external economies, specialised skills, advantages in input purchasing, or some combination of these. It would generally be necessary to reject activities characterised by large economies of scale and/or high capital-intensity. Large established firms in advanced countries would have strong advantages over Irish newcomers in such industries. Furthermore, if the technology is relatively mature in large-scale industries, some larger NICs, with the aid of protection, can move relatively easily into them. Having attained the necessary scale and efficiency, they can then turn to exporting relatively cheaply in these activities where price competition is often important. Consequently Ireland would find the capital costs large, the necessary scale excessive (even if initial protection of the small home market were possible), the competition strong and the returns very poor or negative if she attempted to develop such industries.

Similarly industries based on an advantage in direct development of new basic technologies (e.g. laser technology, fibreoptics) would have to be ruled out. For the largest advanced countries dominate such industries, often backed by massive military or space research programmes. A more suitable type of involvement by Ireland in high-technology industries would be in specialised 'niche' industries — aiming at relatively narrow markets which may be specialised by product, by customer, by geographical area or by a combination of these. Skilled, high value-added 'niche' industries can be developed by importing new basic technologies and developing further specialised *applications* for them — thus avoiding direct competition with the major technological leaders and the very large high-volume producers. Perhaps a suitable long-term goal for Ireland would be to develop, say, 50-100 sizeable indigenous firms in new traded industries. Each of them would be relatively large by Irish standards, but sufficiently focussed on small-to-medium scale or specialised industries to avoid competing directly with the very largest firms abroad. These firms could each be employing between a few hundred and a few thousand people.

Although Ireland can learn something about the basic principles of selectivity and intervention from relatively successful latecomers such as Japan or South Korea, there would clearly have to be important differences in the type of industries selected, due to Ireland's much smaller size and more open economy. The main barriers to entry which Japan and Korea had to overcome were in the area of technology and skills. Scale was much less of a problem for them, since they could develop firms of a competitive size in large-scale industries with the help of protection of their large domestic markets.

Thus Japan in the early post-war period, and South Korea more recently, generally concentrated on entering quite large-scale industries which were technically quite mature (motor cycles, cars, televisions, steel, ships etc.). This strategy was based on a recognition that they were initially too weak technologically to engage in introducing many new products or to compete in industries based on new advanced technologies. But by using imported technology under licence or embodied in capital goods, at the stage when such technological transfers are most readily available — i.e. in relatively mature industries — they could develop large-scale production for large protected home markets. Their R & D efforts were concentrated on relatively minor improvements, particularly with respect to reliability and product performance. Having developed high-volume production and high-quality products, they were then able to penetrate export markets rapidly, thus achieving high growth even in industries growing more slowly worldwide. A further stage of the strategy, which is well under way in Japan, is to enter more technology-intensive industries, drawing on increasing domestic technological strength.[23]

Ireland, too, has weaknesses in the area of technology and skills, so that the Japanese type of approach to technological development is of some relevance. But, as mentioned above, economies of scale present a further entry barrier of major importance for Ireland. Perhaps the first and most obvious step in selecting suitable industries for Ireland is to identify those in which a very large scale of operation is not necessary for competitive success.

An impression of the importance of economies of scale in different industries can be gained from United States data on concentration ratios, firm size and industrial location, in the US *Census of Manufactures*. These data can be quite highly disaggregated, with 449 distinct categories of industry. In the analysis which follows, it is assumed that the degree of concentration and size of firms in each industry in the USA is a reflection of the underlying importance of economies of scale in some form — whether it be economies of scale in production, research and development, marketing, after-sales service or whatever. The justification for this assumption is that the USA is a very large integrated economy, with free trade and open competition within its own boundaries at least, so that the industrial structure which has emerged there has been shaped largely by competitive forces. The size structure of firms there should therefore be a reasonable reflection of the scale which is actually necessary for competitive success in any particular industry.

The 449 US industries can be ranked according to various measures of industrial concentration. The particular measure used here is the Eight-Firm Concentration Ratio, which is the percentage of sales in an industry accounted for by the eight largest companies. It is presumed that a high concentration ratio in an industry indicates the existence of significant economies of scale in that industry. A high concentration ratio and significant economies of scale, however, can have different implications for the level of barriers to entry for new or small firms, depending on the overall size of the industry concerned and the consequent size of the dominant companies. For example, other things being equal, a small industry which is 80% concentrated in eight firms employing only 500 people each should be easier to break into than a large industry which is 80% concentrated in eight very large firms employing 10,000 people each. So as well as concentration ratios, one needs to look at the absolute size of the companies concerned to gain an appreciation of the likely entry barriers due to scale.

Table 9.3 indicates the distribution of the 449 US industries according to their eight-firm concentration ratios and the average employment in the top eight firms. The table indicates, for example, that there are seventeen industries in which the top eight firms account for over 80% of shipments and employ an average of over 3,000 people. It may appear at first sight that a rather small proportion of US manufacturing is highly concentrated in large firms, as indicated by the number of industries in cells towards the top right-hand corner of the table. But this is something of an illusion since the industries in this part of the table tend to be the largest and most important ones. For example, there are seventeen industries, or 3.8% of the total, in the top right-hand cell, but they account for as

Table 9.3: Distribution of US Industries, by Degree of Concentration and Size of Top Companies

Average Employment in Top 8 Firms	Eight-Firm Concentration Ratio				
	0-20	20-40	40-60	60-80	80-100
Over 3,000	0	12	24	19	17
2,001-3,000	1	18	12	14	5
1,001-2,000	7	35	27	26	22
501-1,000	11	40	34	33	14
Under 500	10	32	16	12	8
	29	137	113	104	66

Source: Derived from US *Census of Manufactures, 1977, Concentration Ratios in Manufacturing.*

much as 11.7% of manufacturing output (value-added). In contrast, the ten small-scale fragmented industries in the bottom left-hand cell account for 2.2% of the number of industries but only 0.9% of manufacturing output.

Since barriers to entry due to economies of scale would generally be very significant in industries found towards the top right-hand part of the table, these would generally not be suitable targets for Irish indigenous development. The most extreme examples include motor vehicles, primary aluminium, refrigerators and freezers, aircraft, photographic equipment and sanitary paper products.[24] Admittedly the method used here is too crude to justify completely ruling out whole industries, since industrial structures are too complex to analyse satisfactorily by such simple means. It is possible for much smaller firms to find some limited niches in highly concentrated large-scale industries, for example by focussing on specialised segments of the market or on selling in limited geographical areas. It should probably be accepted, however, that highly concentrated large-scale industries offer strictly limited prospects for small firms and newcomers.

In order to find suitable target industries for indigenous Irish firms, it should be more fruitful to examine first the industries found towards the bottom left-hand corner or the middle of table 9.3. Those at the extreme bottom left-hand corner, however, include many which are virtually non-traded, e.g., concrete products, typesetting, wood partitions and fixtures, fabricated metal products and sheet metalwork. Because such industries tend to serve only limited local markets, they are relatively small in scale and exceptionally fragmented, particularly in relation to the size of a very large economy such as the United States. Being naturally sheltered and non-traded and therefore easily entered, it is no accident that they are already well established in Ireland. They have little prospects of significant export growth and so they are not of much interest as targets for selective development. Ireland's need at present is to progress *beyond* this stage of development.

Some of the other small-scale fragmented industries may be subject to significant entry barriers due to external economies. For they are sub-supply industries which flourish mainly in concentrated industrial centres where they are in close contact with their major purchasers, e.g. special dies, tools and jigs, metal plating and polishing and industrial patterns.[25] Hence, these may not be easy to develop even though they are small in scale, unless it is done as part of a broader plan to develop an integrated structure of related industries.

Since there are scarcely sufficient interesting prospects among the very small-scale and most fragmented industries alone, it would be necessary for Ireland to take on some rather more difficult industries — located more towards the middle of table 9.3. Table 9.4 below lists a number of examples which might be worth considering. These industries are *not* being put forward here as definite proposals but rather as illustrations of the type of activity which might be worth examining further as possible targets for establishment or further development by Irish enterprises.

As was already mentioned, however, there are other entry barriers besides economies of scale which have to be considered in selecting target industries. No doubt the learning curve effect and the need to develop specialised technological competence are widespread barriers in many industries but these types of barriers can eventually be overcome with a sustained and concentrated commitment backed by the state, although they would initially tend to deter new entrepreneurial investment. As well as the whole question of entry barriers, other factors

Table 9.4: Selected Medium-Size US Industries

	Eight-Firm Concentration Ratio	Average Employment in Top 8 Firms
Food Processing Machinery	24	1,100
Pumps & Pumping Equipment	29	2,000
Measuring & Controlling Devices	35	1,800
Mobile Homes	37	2,100
Process Control Instruments	46	2,800
Natural & Processed Cheese	48	1,300
Surgical & Medical Instruments	48	2,300
Lawnmowers & Garden Equipment	50	1,000
Dehydrated Fruit & Vegetables	53	900
Pickles, Sauces, Salad Dressings	62	1,200

Source: Derived from US *Census of Manufactures, 1977, Concentration Ratios in Manufacturing.*

must also be considered before concluding that any industry would be a good prospect, e.g., the prospects for demand growth, whether excess capacity exists abroad, whether low-wage newly industrialising countries can compete effectively and, of course, whether Ireland's existing capabilities go some way to meeting the capabilities required in the industry concerned.

The main considerations and suggested procedures for assessing potential target industries are outlined in the literature on corporate strategy, such as Porter (1980). This literature takes in considerations such as those outlined above and develops them in greater detail. However, such studies generally focus on strategies for growth and diversification for large corporations rather than for countries. For a country there is the further issue of developing external economies — or the pool of knowledge and skills, and inter-related specialist services and suppliers, which create advantages external to individual firms but are important for strengthening an industry as a whole. A national development strategy for a late-industrialising country would therefore have to take this additional consideration into account (particularly in various branches of engineering, for example) and would need, where necessary, to have the intention of developing an integrated industrial structure.

It is difficult to make firm suggestions as to which industries would emerge from this type of detailed assessment as most suitable for Ireland to develop. This is primarily because the essence of the problem is that the advanced countries have established competitive advantages over latecomers such as Ireland in *most* internationally traded industries. So, apart from those already operating in Ireland, there are not many which stand out as obviously good prospects. Thus the purpose of the type of assessment suggested above would be to identify — among the many industries which could be developed only with some difficulty — those which may be *relatively* easily developed, with *least* difficulty, by Ireland. It is likely too, that specialised 'niche' type activities would tend to prove most feasible, and these are by nature not very well known or easily identified.

Higher value-added, processed foods, however, does seem to be one area which should offer some possibilities due to access to inputs and an existing structure of fairly large firms which could be developed further. And among the many specialised niches in mechanical, instrument, electrical and electronic engineering there also appear to be some relatively good prospects (as well as many areas which are clearly out of the question). The existence in the advanced countries of many successful specialised firms in these sectors suggests both that there may be a relatively wide selection of licensing opportunities and that the demands of size may not be excessive in some activities. Engineering industries also have the advantage that they would involve the development of certain skills and knowledge which can be utilised for many related purposes. Thus they offer good prospects for continuing diversification into new activities which would be related in skills and technology to those initially selected.[26]

Following from the selection of target development industries, the next question is the means of implementing the strategy. First, and most generally, its implementation would evidently require a significant degree of state initiative and guidance. Initiatives by the state to develop target industries could take several forms. One way would be direct state investment in new enterprises, for example, through the National Development Corporation or existing state enterprises. Another possible way would be to build on selected enterprises by drawing up detailed company development plans in consultation with the business concerned. Payment of loans, grants and other incentives could then be linked to progress in the planned development of new traded activities. A third possible method, as suggested in the Telesis Report (pp. 232-234) would be to establish entirely new 'corporate shells' to undertake selected projects by assembling a consortium of interests (state or private, with or without some foreign participation) with the required capital and managerial skills.

Each of these options would involve quite substantial new departures from the industrial policy practised up to the early 1980s, although there have been some examples of such initiatives more recently, as outlined below. Consequently, it may be prudent to proceed initially with a relatively small number of major initiatives, followed by a phased introduction of an increasing number of new projects as improved skills and techniques are acquired with experience.

Having chosen and initiated such projects, a battery of co-ordinated aids and incentives would be required to ensure the best possible prospects for them to attain an internationally competitive stature. Strong general protection against imports to shelter such 'infant industries' could not be readily acceptable in the context of membership of the European Community, and withdrawal from the EC is scarcely a realistic option now since most of the country's foreign exchange earnings come from agricultural or food exports and the exports of foreign companies, both of which depend heavily on EC membership. But substitutes for protection could be found in specific grants to encourage other firms to purchase the new products and investment in the new industries by state enterprises which would be permitted to absorb initial losses. To maintain the incentive to become competitive, schedules could be drawn up for phasing out such special supports.

Much greater use could be made of low-interest loans or interest-free loans to selected industries as a form of support, particularly if the government was to control the supply of credit, or at least to exercise substantial influence on it. Indeed, in such circumstances the government could not only give preferential financial support to target industries but could also put pressure on private firms to co-operate in development plans by restricting credit or raising interest rates for companies which do not attempt to develop internationally traded industries. Grants to industry would also need to be made more selective, focussing primarily on target traded industries. They would need to be selective too in the sense of focussing on overcoming specific entry barriers, such as marketing or skill-training, rather than being mostly capital grants. As further aids to overcoming marketing barriers to entry, one or more large state trading companies could be established, and it could be aimed to gain control of distribution companies, in Ireland and abroad.

Technological entry barriers could be tackled by assisting firms with the costs of seeking out and importing best-practice technology, whether under licence or embodied in capital goods or materials. Aids for technology import could also be linked to commitments by the firms to avail of grants for further R & D work to improve on or develop new applications for the imported technology. In addition, technology could be acquired by employing foreign engineers, by arranging joint ventures with foreign firms, and by gaining control of (necessarily relatively small) technically advanced foreign firms with a view to training Irish staff, making licensing arrangements or even diverting much of the firms' future expansion to Ireland.

It would be important, too, for new investment initiatives and development incentives to be carefully co-ordinated in the case of target industries which are related in skills, technology or purchasing linkages, in order to develop the advantages of 'external economies'. For example, an engineering skill-training programme in a selected area, coupled with initiatives to establish a number of inter-related engineering projects located in the same area, could serve to provide additional support for each individual project.

In addition, an incomes policy designed to keep labour costs competitive would also be of some importance, though not so crucial as is often thought in Ireland (see section 9.ii). If it is to be successful, however, considerable trade union involvement in planning, and greater industrial democracy, are necessary to secure their full commitment to the strategy. Already, in fact, the trade unions have accepted 'that genuine national economic planning must involve some planning of incomes', and it is clear, too, that what they mean by 'genuine' economic planning, with which they would want to co-operate, includes an industrial strategy along the same lines as that outlined above (Irish Congress of Trade Unions, 1984.)

Financial and Political Constraints
While a shortage of planning skills and political will could be constraints on the implementation of this strategy, certain of the suggestions also raise the question of finance for the state's role, particularly in the context of the existing substantial public debt. The financial constraint, however, is by no means insuperable. First, it should be remembered that the suggested strategy involves selectivity, i.e. concentrating resources quite largely on selected areas and refusing to subsidise activities of less strategic importance. In other words, it involves diverting financial aid which has been given rather indiscriminately to a vast range of companies into more concerted expenditure on selected industries and companies.[27] Thus, it could be partially implemented at least, without extra expenditure. But realistically, however, increased spending on industrial policy would also be needed to make a significant break-through. One source of funds for this increased spending could be borrowing.

Undoubtedly the suggestion of further public sector borrowing would meet objections in Ireland, since the present level of public debt and borrowing is perceived to be already excessive. Nevertheless, as was outlined earlier in this section, the government could still borrow more because the country's credit rating is fairly good and its foreign interest payments are not very high in relation to export earnings. Furthermore, the main legitimate cause for concern about the present level of debt is because much of it was incurred to finance *non-productive* expenditure which yielded no return to repay the debt. Continuous increases in *that type* of borrowing and expenditure would indeed become unsustainable and would lead to a serious financial crisis. But further borrowing by the government would not necessarily be wrong or risky in itself.

The only necessary condition for healthy borrowing is that the borrower should be able to repay the debt. If borrowed money is invested productively so that it increases the country's income and also yields a sufficient return to the government, public debt and interest payments present no real problem. In the short term, debt service costs might rise faster than GNP because the borrowed money would be invested in a way which takes time to generate income. But so long as the selected investment projects are ultimately successful, the addition to GNP would be at least sufficient to cover the extra debt servicing. To pay off the debt, the state would then have to claim some of this extra income — but no larger a proportion of GNP than at the start. The necessary financial return to the government could arise directly, as in the case of returns to investment in state enterprises, or indirectly, as in the case of higher tax receipts and lower unemployment payments as a result of support for successful private enterprises. Thus so long as borrowed money is invested in successful productive projects, extra borrowing should give no cause for concern.

As the National Planning Board (1984) concluded, the limit to borrowing for public investment 'will not be set in the immediate future by difficulties in borrowing abroad but rather by the supply of productive investments within the public sector or financed in part by it. The basic problem is to increase the supply of productive projects.' The strategy outlined above is basically a way of increasing the 'supply' of productive projects, recognising that this cannot happen automatically without an active and systematic approach to identifying and initiating relatively suitable target industries. There should be no objection in principle to borrowing to finance such projects.

Even if new industrial projects financed by state borrowing fail to break even commercially they can still generate a sufficient return to the government to cover debt servicing. For the government's return on investment in industrial projects is not only gained through the commercial revenue and profits of state enterprises, but also through higher tax receipts and lower social welfare payments. These effects occur both as a result of extra employment and income generated by the project itself, and through indirect or induced employment and incomes which are generated outside the project due to its additional stimulus to demand. For these reasons even a loss-making enterprise can generate a positive return to government investment. It would not be satisfactory, of course, to have many new investment projects operating at a commercial loss indefinitely since they should be generating profits for future re-investment. But, nevertheless, the fact remains that even in the case of commercial failure, the state has this cushion against the risk of failing to cover the cost of its investment. This is a further reason why the state can countenance investment in industries which would not attract unaided private entrepreneurs.

Apart from borrowing as a source of finance, however, the planned expansion of EC structural funds for Ireland could provide an important additional source of investment funds for industry.

The objections to increased state initiative and investment in industry would also refer to examples of bad investment decisions and a poor commercial record in existing state enterprises. For these reasons, it is argued, direct state involvement in industry has proved to be a costly failure already. There are some serious points here which underline the need to proceed with great care, but this is not ultimately a conclusive argument. For it must be recognised that most of the existing state enterprises originated under quite a different type of policy to that proposed here. Some companies became state enterprises when loss-making private firms were taken over in order to preserve employment or services — a form of social policy more than industrial policy. These had already failed as private companies, so that state involvement can scarcely be seen as the main cause of their subsequent commercial losses.

The establishment of most of the other large state enterprises was based on principles quite different to those outlined above. For the most part, they were set up during the 1930s-1950s, when the guiding policy principle was to attain greater national self-sufficiency, not to build internationally competitive companies.

Most of these enterprises had a reasonable commercial record in the period of protection, and if some failed to meet the subsequent test of international competition this is scarcely surprising and it had many parallels among large private companies. The commercial difficulties of such companies do not necessarily indicate that the state cannot build competitive industries since the issue of international competition was not really a major consideration in deciding to establish these earlier companies.

There have been, however, at least two important examples of more recent investments in state industrial enterprises which made substantial losses in the 1980s — in NET (a producer of fertilisers) and in the re-equipment of Irish Steel. Both of these were undertaken at a time when policy was generally oriented towards free trade and the need to compete internationally. There is some excuse for these investments perhaps, since there were similar experiences in both state and private companies in this type of industry in many other countries. In large-scale capital-intensive industries such as steel and fertilisers, each new addition to productive capacity is substantial and plants take a long time to become operational after the initial decision is made to build them. Consequently the decision to invest is partly based on long-run projections of demand. If demand grows more slowly than expected over a long period, as occurred in Europe for more than a decade after 1973, quite a number of large new plants may still be coming on stream for some time after demand has slowed, resulting in a general excess of productive capacity in relation to demand. Consequently cut-throat competition and persistent widespread losses may occur throughout a whole industry, as in much of the European steel industry after the early 1970s.

Similarly, mistaken long-run projections of domestic demand would have been partly responsible for the development of excess capacity in a non-traded state enterprise, the Electricity Supply Board. This situation was paralleled by the development of excess capacity in the privately owned cement industry — a similar virtually non-traded large-scale industry where investment decisions depend on long-run projections of domestic demand. Again these situations have occurred in other countries too, in private companies as well as state enterprises.

There is, therefore, no very convincing proof that Irish state investment and enterprise *per se* must be inherently more subject to major blunders and commercial losses than comparable private companies. The past record of Irish state enterprise can actually tell us rather little about the viability of the strategy outlined above, since previous state involvement in industry was not usually based on the principles of selectivity put forward here. Nevertheless the record is sufficiently disturbing at least to serve as a strong warning of the need to select target industries with great care, and to attract the best quality management available to handle major enterprises. It should be clear that investment decisions cannot be made on the basis of a hunch or a rule of thumb, such as 'we should have a domestic supply of basic materials' or 'we should process our own natural resources'. Although such ideas are not necessarily wrong, they are also not necessarily right since there are many more aspects to the selection of target industries, as outlined above. In fact, it seems rather unlikely that steel or fertilisers would emerge from a full strategic analysis as particularly suitable target industries for Ireland.

A further argument against active state involvement in industry has been that it is politically very difficult for the government to close down state companies when they fail, so that resources are continually wasted in propping up lame ducks. There may be some truth in this argument, but there is little convincing evidence to back it, so that it is far from convincing as an argument for ruling out state investment altogether. For one thing, it is not clear that there have been many cases where it would actually have made economic sense to stop subsidising loss-making state enterprises. As pointed out above, even subsidised loss-making companies may be costing the government less than the alternative of closing them down, due to the tax revenue they generate and the welfare and redundancy payments which would have to be made if they closed. Furthermore, in some cases a major component of state companies' losses has been due to interest on debt, while they have been making or almost making a profit on current operations. To close down such a company would be of no financial benefit to the government since the debt would still have to be repaid.

In addition, it has become clear in recent years that the government is in fact prepared both to close down state companies which lose a good deal and to prop up large lame-duck private companies whose closure would have widespread repercussions. The state enterprise, Irish Shipping, has been closed down and the government has ceased to absorb losses in

Verolme Cork Dockyard in which it had a 49% holding, leading to the loss of over 1,000 jobs in Verolme alone. And the government also committed itself to heavy costs in order to rescue the privately owned Insurance Corporation of Ireland to avert serious instability in the insurance and finance sector. Thus there does not appear to be a convincing argument that state investment is a certain or unique road to heavy costs in propping up lame-duck companies.

It is also evident, however, that the possibility of adoption of the type of strategy suggested here depends not only on acceptance of the economic argument but also on political acceptability. Policies such as promoting state enterprises, intervening selectively in the private sector, and state influence over the supply of credit are all issues which might be regarded as fundamental to the political division between Left and Right. Nevertheless, important elements of this type of strategy *have* been adopted in some late-industrialising countries which do not have left-wing governments. Japan, South Korea and Taiwan are prominent examples which were mentioned in chapter 8.

Thus, it is possible to have such a strategy which is technocratically controlled under the guidance of a non-socialist political leadership. Such a strategy acts in the broad interest of private capital by assuring profitability to those who co-operate and by providing the best long-term prospects for growth at the expense of short-term restrictions on the uses of capital. Alternatively, a socialist version of a functionally similar economic strategy would presumably aim for more democratic control and social forms of ownership, with the distribution of the benefits being more in the interests of the wider population. In other words, an economic strategy along the lines suggested above could, in principle, be adopted by either a capitalist or a socialist latecomer, with the political difference being reflected in the issues of who controls the strategy, who controls or owns enterprises and who benefits the most.

What is possible as a general principle, however, is not always likely in a particular case, so it is worth considering the political background in the Irish situation. The development of the Irish party system up to the 1950s was outlined in chapters 4 and 5 and changes since that time have not been very great. Fianna Fail and Fine Gael remain the two largest parties, with four-fifths of the seats in the current Dail between them. Fine Gael has become more like Fianna Fail, in the sense of becoming a more broadly based 'centrist' party. For both of these parties, therefore, a major consideration is to avoid alienating any substantial section of society, since they both rely on some support from virtually every social group. Consequently they tend to be quite similar on matters of policy, and averse to the risks involved in major changes, favouring a cautious or 'moderate' adherence to the status quo. In so far as their differences are consistently discernible, Fine Gael tends to be somewhat more conservative on economic policy and somewhat more liberal on 'social' issues, while Fianna Fail takes a more traditional nationalist line on Northern Ireland. But even these generalisations are not always self-evidently true. Both are essentially in favour of reliance on private enterprise rather than state enterprise, but neither of them is strongly opposed to considerable state support for industry in some form. The new Progressive Democrats Party, with 8% of Dail seats at present, is somewhat further to the right on economic policy issues.

The type of industrial strategy suggested here is officially supported by the trade union movement, and at least some of the major elements of it are supported by the Labour Party and the smaller socialist parties. Labour's Dail representation is just 7% of the seats, while the Workers Party and the Democratic Socialist Party have succeeded in gaining parliamentary representation through a handful of deputies in recent years. Clearly, then, the political forces pushing for a more interventionist industrial policy are not very strong at present. But since an interventionist selective type of industrial strategy need not be inherently anti-capitalist in principle, it could conceivably be accepted for pragmatic reasons, at least partially or in modified form, by one of the major parties under pressure from the Left and the trade unions. Such a situation may be arising due to continued high unemployment. The politicians cannot fail to have noticed that outgoing governments have lost all of the six elections held in the 1970s and 1980s to date, mainly due to discontent over economic issues.

As outlined in chapter 5, a similar series of election results during the long recession of the 1950s eventually created a political mood for fundamental change in economic policies, so that Fianna Fail practically reversed its basic economic philosophy. The actual implementation of policy changes was drawn out over more than a decade but Fianna Fail was rewarded by 16 continuous years in power from 1957 to 1973 when it was seen to preside over the recovery from the 1950s recession.

It also appears that there is by now a social basis for some greater support for the political Left, which could be tapped more effectively, even if a Labour/Socialist government remains a rather long-term prospect. Naturally, the social and distributional impact of a more active and selective strategy would be rather different if implemented by Fianna Fail or Fine Gael to that of a functionally similar strategy under socialist leadership. So basic differences on issues of control and distribution would continue to separate socialists from conservatives, although some working agreement between them on the technical requirements of late industrial growth may not be always out of the question.

The type of active selective industrial strategy proposed here is fairly similar to both the recommendations of Telesis (1982) and the National Economic and Social Council (1982), so that the official and governmental reaction to their proposals gives some indication of the reluctance, initially at least, to implement such recommendations. There were long delays and repeated drafting before the publication of a government White Paper, which was due to follow from the NESC proposals, and there were indications that, within the Fine Gael/Labour government elected in November 1982, resistance to the more interventionist proposals was quite strong in Fine Gael. The final White Paper on *Industrial Policy* (1984) subscribed in principle to the Telesis/NESC strategy. But its practical proposals fell short of what Telesis had in mind, so that it looked like an uneasy compromise between differing points of view with the more conservative view dominant. In fact, the White Paper was generally received with disappointment by advocates of a more active and selective strategy, and with relief by critics of such an approach, so that there appeared to be agreement that the White Paper did not represent a fundamental new departure in that direction.

For example, Telesis recommended a major shift in allocation of funds to traded indigenous industries, from 40% of the total to 75% by 1990, but the White Paper contained no such target. A National Development Corporation was proposed in the White Paper, as the major vehicle for active state initiatives, but it was to be allocated only £7 million and was to be required to sell off successful ventures once they were profitable. Although the establishment of a National Development Corporation had been agreed between Fine Gael and Labour some years before, disagreements on the matter still continued within the government after the publication of the White Paper in July 1984. Furthermore, the White Paper took the view that 'the state of government finances does not allow for any real expansion of expenditure on job creation' and that at firm level 'the overall amount of money which firms will receive in grants will be at the same average level'. Since Telesis had argued plausibly that the development of traded indigenous firms would be initially more expensive, there could scarcely be a major drive to develop such firms within these constraints set on funding (see Kennedy 1985).

Thus, there appeared to be fairly strong resistance to important elements of a more active, selective strategy, focussing on indigenous traded industries. On the other hand, the White Paper did include a statement that the future direction of industrial policy would 'entail the concentration of resources on internationally traded manufacturing and services, particularly Irish-owned firms'.

Thus there was an indication that the emphasis would shift towards promoting indigenous industry more, even though there was no specific target for a decisive change in the allocation of funds. The change in emphasis was later reflected in a reorganisation of the Industrial Development Authority along lines which give formal recognition to the distinction between Irish-owned and foreign-owned firms. A recent (April, 1988) policy statement from the IDA said that the proportion of its resources devoted to domestic industry was expected to increase from 40% to 50% or more over the next few years.

Giving some substance to this expressed concern to focus more on developing indigenous industry, a number of new policy measures have been introduced in the 1980s to cope with specific weaknesses which would be most typical of Irish indigenous firms, particularly with respect to management, export marketing and technology acquisition. These are areas in which indigenous firms frequently have weaknesses which are not so commonly found among the multinationals. The 1984 White Paper announced that assistance would be made available to companies to help pay for costs associated with acquiring foreign technology, market research, and development of export marketing. Grants are now available for these purposes, as well as general management development.

In addition, industrial policy towards indigenous industry has become somewhat more active and selective in certain respects, rather than just passively offering grants and tax concessions to any company and waiting for them to take advantage of the incentives. One example of this is the 'Company Development Programme', in which a number of state development agencies with a variety of expertise work with selected mainly Irish-owned companies to identify and implement strategic development initiatives. The role of the state agencies in this is to act as catalysts, sharing opinions, acting as information brokers and making suggestions about how they can assist in a company's development through their range of grants and services.

Another example of a more active and selective approach is the 'National Linkage Programme' which aims primarily to develop selected indigenous firms as suppliers to the multinational companies. This, too, is an inter-agency programme which aims to make available to the target companies a range of business and technical expertise from the state agencies, with a view to developing them as acceptable suppliers to multinationals in Ireland and ultimately abroad.

Both of the programmes mentioned above involve selectivity since the agencies select the companies which are invited to participate. They are 'active', too, in the sense that the agencies take the initiative in approaching promising companies and in making proposals for their further development, although the companies do not have to co-operate.

There are also signs of greater selectivity as regards the types of industrial sector which can get state support. Non-traded or sheltered activities, some of which used to be given significant grant aid, are not supposed to be eligible any longer. And the IDA has prepared a plan for the Food and Drink sector, *A Future in Food* (1987), which contains some quite specific details about what types of products are eligible or not eligible for assistance.

At a more informal and experimental level, another relevant inter-agency initiative was a recent in-depth review of the problems and potential of a selected indigenous sector, namely, mould-making for the plastics industry. The aim here was mainly to identify what the industry requires in order to develop, and to consider what precisely the state development agencies should do to maximise the potential. This is a departure from the more passive approach to the extent that it involved selecting a sector with apparently good prospects for indigenous development, and aiming to tailor policy initiatives to its specific requirements.

To sum up, since the early 1980s a distinctly greater commitment to promoting indigenous industry has developed, and the new policy measures to achieve this include some which are both more selective and more active than formerly. These new initiatives involve a learning process by the state agencies responsible for assisting industrial development, so that they are discovering more about the specific problems and opportunities of indigenous industries. But it certainly could not be claimed, as yet, that the active and selective element constitutes the major feature of overall industrial policy.

Comparing present industrial policy with the type of approach outlined earlier in this chapter, it appears that there is now a willingness to focus to some degree on indigenous industry, to select target industries and companies (although this process could still be taken a good deal further), and to encourage and assist selected firms to move in the desired direction. The major element of the recommended strategy which is not much in evidence is a willingness to take the lead in committing direct state investment to starting up or developing selected major projects, whether alone or in co-operation with private companies. Thus the potential of present industrial policies is still largely limited to what Ireland's relatively small private indigenous firms can be encouraged or persuaded to do, with grant assistance from the state which is generally limited to some proportion of investment costs incurred by such firms. Compared with what should be possible with a greater degree of state initiative and participation, this must impose limits on the type of projects which can be seriously considered, in terms of the scale of investment or the time horizon required for attaining profitability.

10

Summary and Conclusions

In the Introduction it was stated that this book has two related aims. First, it is intended to make a contribution to understanding the general implications of making a late start to industrialisation, and second, it offers an interpretation of the experience of Irish industry in terms of the problems of late development, and aims to clarify the type of industrial strategy which Ireland requires. By considering the experience of industry in Ireland with the problem of late development in mind, it has been sought both to draw general lessons on the issue from this case study, and to develop a better understanding of Ireland's own problems.

The Republic of Ireland is a particularly useful case to consider for the general purpose of this book because, since the beginning of the Industrial Revolution, it has been in the position of a relatively late-industrialiser in close competition with more advanced economies. Furthermore, in the twentieth century it has adopted both a protectionist inward-looking strategy and an outward-looking free market strategy for a considerable period of time. Most attention has been devoted in this book to the period of outward-looking free market policies since the 1950s, because that strategy is now conventionally recommended for developing economies and Ireland is one of only a small number of late-developing countries to have adopted it in full. From the 1950s until the end of the 1970s, at least, Ireland would have appeared to be quite a 'success story', suggesting that relatively late industrialisation is not particularly difficult and that it can be achieved successfully with the conventional strategy. Consequently, it has been necessary to consider whether Ireland's experience could really be generally applicable to other latecomers, or whether it was attributable to quite exceptional circumstances. And particularly in the light of events in the 1980s, it was also necessary to question whether Ireland has found a strategy that can continue to produce favourable results for the country itself in the future.

In contrast to the conventional or orthodox theory, an alternative theory was also outlined in chapter 2 which suggests that there are major difficulties inhibiting late industrialisation. These difficulties would not generally be overcome by reliance on the orthodox strategy, although there could be a few *exceptional* cases of countries achieving quite rapid industrial expansion, for some time at least, while adopting this strategy. According to this alternative view, the indigenous firms of latecomers which are open to international competition and which trust mainly in market forces would generally be unable to develop many important internationally traded industries. This is because established firms, largely based in advanced countries, have overwhelming competitive advantages which create barriers to entry for newcomers. Such barriers to entry exist in the wide range of industries which are characterised by factors such as economies of scale, large capital requirements, product differentiation, advanced technology, specialised skills or dependence on the external economies inherent in large advanced industrial centres. For this reason, it was suggested, the indigenous industry of latecomers adopting the conventional strategy would be confined to a limited range of activities — such as non-traded industries, basic processing of primary resources and other sectors which are relatively easily entered. Some diversification into other sectors could continue to occur as the nature of barriers to entry changes over time, but such progress would be difficult and too slow to allow the attainment of near full employment. This is so particularly because the growing involvement of many low-cost NICs in the same limited range of easily entered industries would simultaneously be creating tough competitive conditions for these sectors.

These considerations, which apply to the indigenous or native industry of latecomers, were regarded as being of central importance, in the 'alternative' view. For foreign direct manufacturing investment in latecomers occurs on quite a small scale relative to the size of these countries. Only in the case of export-oriented industries could foreign investment be regarded as of significant benefit, and this type of foreign investment occurs on an even more limited scale. Nevertheless, a small number of relatively small latecomers, which are particularly desirable sites for foreign investors, might achieve quite rapid industrial growth by attracting a disproportionate share of export-oriented foreign investment, even though their indigenous development is constrained as suggested above.

It was suggested that Ireland's experience could be shown to be just such an exceptional case and, being exceptional for this reason, offers no general support for the conventional view. Rather, the performance of Irish indigenous industry would be particularly important for drawing general conclusions. And it was suggested that the performance of indigenous industry would bear out the alternative view of the constraints on latecomers and the inadequacy of the conventional strategy for most late-industrialising countries. It was suggested, further, that even where export-oriented foreign industries are established in large numbers, they would generally have no decisive secondary effects in stimulating local industry through technology transfer or the development of skills or linkages. Thus a latecomer whose industrial growth depends on attracting much foreign industry would *continue* to be dependent on this process.

Most of this book has examined the experience of industry in Ireland in the light of the issues outlined above. The main findings are summarised below, followed by a presentation of the main conclusions.

Summary

Until the early nineteenth century Irish industry was expanding quite strongly by the standards of many countries at that time, indicating that local economic and social conditions were not particularly unfavourable for industrial development. But during the nineteenth century most industries in Ireland went into decline, except in the north east where industrialisation was comparable to major British industrial centres. The causes of this decline, and the contrasting industrialisation of the north east, can be traced to the fact that the earliest major centres of any particular mechanised industry gained increasing competitive advantages over relatively small centres or relatively late starters in mechanised industry. Most Irish industries, except for linen in the Belfast area, made a relatively late start in mechanisation and remained smaller in scale than competitors in Britain. So they mostly went into decline, indicating that difficulties for latecomers competing with somewhat more advanced economies developed quite early. As the size of successful industrial towns and firms grew rapidly, and as technological specialisation developed, increasingly formidable barriers to entry for newcomers would have been raised, simultaneous with the progressive elimination of previously existing small-scale industries.

The economic difference between the north east and the rest of Ireland underlay the political division of the island, since the economic and political withdrawal from the UK sought by most of the population would have been damaging to the interests of the industrial north east. The protectionist policy instituted in the new Irish Free State in the early 1930s did foster rapid industrial growth for about two decades but few new exports developed, so that chronic balance of payments crises eventually led to prolonged recession in the 1950s.

Against this background, it was widely accepted that new policy initiatives were called for in the 1950s and there was a high degree of consensus backing the re-introduction of an 'outward-looking' approach, without detailed selective state intervention in the market. After 1958, economic growth, especially industrial growth, showed a very marked improvement over the earlier experience of the 1950s. Exports grew rapidly as Irish manufactured exports' share of foreign markets increased significantly. Industrial employment increased almost continuously up to 1980, wage levels rose almost to equal UK levels, and industry diversified into a wider range of many technically advanced products. Consequently, Ireland is now widely regarded as an advanced industrial country and many people in Ireland itself would share this perception.

When one distinguishes the experience of indigenous and foreign firms, however, it is evident that indigenous industry contributed rather little to this apparent transformation. Since the removal of protection began in the mid-1960s, indigenous industry has continuously lost shares of the home market to competing imports while its exports have gained little compensating increase in shares of foreign markets. Indigenous manufacturing employment stopped growing after 1966 and fell sharply after 1980, and it is now probably lower than at any time since the 1940s. At the same time, unemployment and/or emigration have persisted throughout the period.

Basic processing sectors and sheltered non-traded sectors generally fared relatively well, however, while decline has been concentrated very disproportionately in internationally traded industries, particularly those in large-scale activities. There appears to have been little progress in developing indigenous industries in traded sectors with significant barriers to entry. Indeed the trend seems to have been more in the opposite direction, since there was a marked decline in large-scale activities newly opened to international trade. Similarly, examination of the largest indigenous manufacturing firms shows few examples engaged in internationally traded activities with barriers to entry for newcomers, and most of those which are engaged in such activities are exceptional cases which were established long ago and have not had to overcome such barriers as newcomers. While making little progress in 'upward' diversification, indigenous industry has also come under competitive pressure from low-wage NICs in some easily entered traded activities.

The inflow of new foreign export-oriented industries, therefore, has been mainly responsible for the apparent transformation of industry in Ireland. By 1980 foreign firms accounted for one-third of manufacturing employment and about 70% of manufactured exports, including nearly all exports of technically advanced products in sectors such as electronics and pharmaceuticals/fine chemicals. Although a small country with a population of just 3.5 million, the Republic of Ireland has become an important site for mobile transnational manufacturing industries, probably ranking in importance behind only about five or six LDCs or NICs as a base for export-oriented manufacturing TNCs. Most of the TNC subsidiaries in Ireland are fairly similar to those in the conventionally recognised LDCs or NICs in being primarily production units. Their operations often tend to be technically undemanding and require rather low inputs of locally produced materials and components, and thus are sufficiently 'foot-loose' or 'mobile' to choose locations outside advanced industrial areas. Ireland's attractions as a site, as compared with LDCs with much lower labour costs, seem to lie in a combination of geographical location, access to large markets, political 'reliability', an educated labour force, and other factors which reduce risks and information costs. And the attraction of Ireland as compared with European countries would lie mainly in tax and grant incentives and relatively low labour costs.

The nature of foreign firms in Ireland means that they have limited beneficial secondary effects for indigenous development such as transferring technology or developing local skills and linkages, though they do contribute to the balance of payments. They also appear to have had few undesirable effects on indigenous development. There is a tendency, however, for employment in these industries to decline some time after their establishment, leaving Ireland depending entirely on new, first-time foreign investors for net growth in manufacturing employment. But stronger competition for mobile foreign investment in Europe has emerged in the 1980s so that Ireland has been experiencing greater difficulty in attracting new foreign industries.

Chapter 8 looked briefly at a number of other late-industrialising countries which are also quite commonly referred to as examples of the success of the conventional strategy. It was concluded that three of the five most widely cited examples (Japan, South Korea and Taiwan) have progressed further than Ireland in developing indigenous industries in activities with substantial entry barriers, but have in fact departed significantly from the orthodox policies in doing so. Their policies were 'outward-looking' or 'export-oriented' only in the limited sense of emphasising the ultimate development of exports, but they did not in practice greatly favour free trade or indiscriminate freedom to foreign investment. Neither have they trusted in market forces to the same extent as Ireland, although they are certainly capitalist market economies. Rather, they have used selective and active state guidance and intervention to develop economies of scale, technology, marketing and external economies in important selected sectors where such action was required to overcome barriers to entry. The other two countries considered (Singapore and Hong Kong) do not appear to have had any more success than Ireland in developing indigenous industries in activities with important barriers to entry.

Principal Conclusions

The main conclusions which can be drawn from this book include some which are of general relevance, which will be discussed first, followed by other remaining points of particular relevance to the Republic of Ireland.

First, the findings of this study support the view that there are important difficulties impeding the industrial development of latecomers. These difficulties cannot generally be overcome by the conventionally recommended strategy of outward-looking policies without active and selective state intervention in the market. Important constraints on late development of indigenous industry arise from barriers to entry, which impede newcomers from developing many internationally traded industries. This conclusion arises from the fact that after more than two decades of implementing the conventional strategy, Irish indigenous industry remains very largely confined to sheltered non-traded sectors, basic processing industries and others which are relatively easily entered due to low entry barriers. At the same time there has been little sign of a trend of 'upward' diversification into other industries, and indeed the opposite trend has been more evident as Irish firms were squeezed out of some relatively large-scale activities which they had entered earlier with the aid of protection. And this lack of upward diversification compounded to some extent by competition from NICs in certain easily entered activities, has — as suggested in the 'alternative' view (see section 2.iii) —. resulted in low or negative indigenous manufacturing employment growth.

Also, unemployment and/or emigration have persisted throughout the period since the 1950s. This indicates that the constraints on late development of indigenous industry can be sufficiently serious to prevent full mobilisation of productive resources, even in a country where foreign industry plays an exceptionally large part. And the fact that Irish economic and social conditions have been quite favourable for development (see section 9.i) indicates that the constraints on latecomers present major obstacles even where favourable local conditions exist.

This general conclusion does not rest on observation of Ireland's experience alone. For a brief examination of other prominent examples of relatively successful latecomers relying on similar policies (Singapore and Hong Kong) indicates that they, too, have not overcome the suggested constraints on indigenous development. Rather their relatively rapid industrial growth has, like Ireland's, occurred due to exceptional circumstances and thus could not readily be repeated in many other countries. But Japan, South Korea and Taiwan have made significantly greater progress in indigenous industrial development and this can plausibly be attributed to the fact that their policies departed substantially from the conventional strategy, in ways which seem well designed to deal with the problems of overcoming entry barriers for latecomers. It may be concluded, therefore, that the practice of loosely labelling the policies of all these countries as 'outward-looking' or 'export oriented' is unhelpful, since it obscures the fact that there are very significant differences between them. It is probably the extent and nature of the state intervention practised by Japan, South Korea and Taiwan — the very element which the orthodox recommendation advises against — that has been crucial in accounting for their exceptional success in overcoming the constraints on latecomers.

The ultimately unsatisfactory experience of Ireland in the 1930s-1960s, and of many other latecomers, with a simple policy of protection — without further systematic intervention, such as Japan, South Korea and Taiwan used — indicates that protection alone is no longer sufficient to promote late development, though it may have been so in the last century when barriers to entry were less formidable. But Ireland's previous experience of industrial decline under an 'outward-looking' free market regime during the century before the 1930s also shows that the protectionist policy introduced then was not the original cause of the industrial stagnation which overtook the country in the 1950s. Rather protection was a temporarily useful, but ultimately unsatisfactory response to the long-standing problem of promoting late industrialisation.

The Republic of Ireland's rapid industrial growth under the conventional strategy in the 1960s and 1970s was due very largely to the fact that an exceptionally large proportion of mobile export-oriented foreign investment was attracted to the country. Since such investment occurs on only a limited scale worldwide, this was an *exceptional* experience which could not be readily repeated by many other latecomers and thus it offers no general support for recommending this type of strategy. Nevertheless, this strategy can evidently produce quite good results in some important respects for a small number of countries. But Ireland's experience with growth depending on foreign firms suggests that the growth achieved with this strategy can ultimately prove to be a temporary phenomenon — a phase which eventually passes. The earlier example of Puerto Rico establishes this conclusion more starkly. Consequently, it is necessary to be extremely cautious about applying the notion of a 'take-off into self-sustaining growth' (Rostow, 1960) to such cases.

Finally, it has been possible to observe, at various stages in Ireland's earlier history, the fact that the external influence of the dominant advanced country (Britain, in this case) played a significant part in forming or 'conditioning' the economy and society of Ireland, which is an important contention of the Dependency school. Even after independence was gained, the main political divisions in the new state, which persist to the present day, arose from issues of external relations with Britain.

To turn to some reflections which are relevant more specifically to the Republic of Ireland itself, it may be concluded that Ireland is not now an advanced industrial country in a sense comparable to most of the countries which are usually so described. Its living standards have indeed for long been closer to those of the developed countries than the LDCs but, over the long term, this has been a result quite largely of emigration and population decline which allowed the average incomes of the remaining population to be fairly high despite economic weakness. More recently, relatively high average incomes have also depended quite heavily on high agricultural prices under EEC policies, on foreign borrowing and on large-scale foreign investment in Ireland, while the strong indigenous industrial base that characterises most advanced industrial countries does not exist in Ireland.

This is important because it means that the country's present economic situation is particularly precarious, to a degree which is easily overlooked by those who see Ireland's experience since the 1950s in terms of a 'take-off' or industrial revolution comparable to the earlier experience of advanced industrial countries. At present, the future outlook for foreign investment, foreign borrowing and the EEC's agricultural policies are all somewhat uncertain, while the traditional outlet of emigration is less attractive than in the past due to high unemployment in Britain especially. Thus, the weakness of Irish indigenous industry is being increasingly felt as a fundamental problem requiring urgent remedies if unemployment is to be reduced from its present record level of over 17%.

As was argued in chapter 9, it will be particularly important for Ireland to develop more export industries, in view of the country's dependence on imports to sustain the economy. And it will be necessary to concentrate more on developing *indigenous* export industries, since foreign investment cannot be depended on to meet the country's needs. Control of relative labour costs is by no means the key to achieving such development, despite the emphasis often put on this factor. Rather, labour cost competitiveness may be regarded as, at most, a factor *facilitating* such development, the attainment of which will depend more importantly on the implementation of much more active selective state policies, designed to promote indigenous firms capable of overcoming barriers to entry.

In the last analysis, however, it cannot be certain whether even a latecomer using the most effective strategy can develop fully into an advanced industrial country in competition with the developed capitalist countries. The competitive advantages built up by the advanced countries over a long period are by now very great. For many LDCs, therefore, a less competitive and more co-operative world (or regional) economic system may be required before substantial industrial development is possible. But Ireland does seem *relatively* well placed to take up the challenge without waiting for such international change. This is because of such factors as its relatively strong administrative and educational structure, its access to major EC markets combined with the prospects for EC structural development assistance, and also its relatively small size. Its small size means that successful development of relatively few specialised industries would be sufficient. It also means that the impact of success on the advanced countries would be too small to provoke serious defensive action by them like the protectionism and/or diplomatic pressures which have followed from the rise of Japan and other NICs.

Notes

Chapter 2: The Problem of Late Industrialisation (pp. 8-31)

1. Little, Scitovsky and Scott (1970) and Balassa (1980) are good representatives of the conventional view, which is based on neo-classical economic theory. Brett (1987) gives a brief account of how it came to represent the prevailing orthodoxy since the 1960s.

2. Expressed in the terminology of the conventional neo-classical theory, to say that barriers to entry are widespread implies that 'imperfect competition' occurs very commonly, while 'perfect competition' is a special case and not really typical.

3. Some of this literature is discussed in Sutcliffe (1971, ch. 9).

4. In this connection, the example of the destruction of the Indian cotton industry by a flood of imports from Britain after the Napoleonic Wars is commonly mentioned. In chapter 3 we will see that Ireland had a similar experience at that time.

5. In a letter to Engels in 1867 (reprinted in Marx and Engels, 1971) Marx says that in the 1780s and 1790s Irish industry was flourishing, but that by the 1860s, under free trade with Britain, Ireland had been reduced to an agricultural district of England. He concludes that the regeneration of Irish industry required protection against Britain.

6. The common occurrence of market 'imperfections' associated with entry barriers in important industries has also been increasingly recognised recently in part of the mainstream economics literature on international trade, the so-called 'new international economics'; see, for example, Krugman, ed. (1986).

7. Kaldor (1972) remarks 'on an empirical level nobody doubts that in any economic activity which involves the processing or transformation of basic materials — in other words, in industry — increasing returns dominate the picture for the very reasons given by Adam Smith in the first chapter of the *Wealth of Nations*; reasons that are fundamental to the nature of technological processes and not to any particular technology'.

8. These figures are only approximate indications of order of magnitude, based on the assumption that a US industry typically produces enough to supply its own home market, and that market size for a typical industry in each country is proportionate to GDP.

9. A major example would be the car industry, in which the common pattern is for one or more very large firms to be surrounded in the same area by hundreds or even thousands of smaller ones supplying components for vehicles designed and assembled by the large company.

10. In an earlier era, there were the examples of the large textile and mechanical engineering centres which grew up early in the United Kingdom's industrial revolution when these technologies were newly developing. In the next chapter one of these centres, Belfast, is discussed, indicating how external economies were important at that time.

11. This arises from the definition of 'profit' as the expropriated product of labour, which arises *only* from the use of labour and therefore declines as a *rate* (in relation to capital employed) as the relative importance of labour as an input declines. This tendency has no exact counterpart in orthodox economics due to the difference of definition. But a similar tendency would follow from orthodox neo-classical theory — which sees profit as equal to the marginal product of capital — if it is assumed that the marginal efficiency of capital declines as the capital-labour ratio rises following sustained investment at a rate greater than the rate of growth of the labour force.

12. Yaffe (1972) stresses the importance of the (first-mentioned) tendency of the rate of profit to fall. Sweezy (1970) and Baran and Sweezy (1968) stress the (third-mentioned) 'realisation' crisis, leading to an underlying tendency to secular stagnation. Bienefeld and Innes (1976) simply outline all the possible tendencies, implying that *one way or another*, crises are inevitable.

13. Most foreign investment in manufacturing is still in developed countries. For example, in 1986, 81% of the assets abroad of US manufacturing companies was in the developed countries (US Department of Commerce, *Survey of Current Business*, August 1987).

14. Direct cost considerations may be offset to some extent by grants and tax concessions, but these are similar to cheap labour in so far as they imply paying out or foregoing part of the population's income.

15. Similarly, Singapore, Taiwan, South Korea and Hong Kong can have higher wages than other Asian countries while attracting much mobile foreign investment — because of political, locational or infrastructural attractions — but they could probably not expect to have wages rising very close to advanced country levels while still attracting large numbers of export-oriented foreign industries.

16. Cotton and woollen textiles, the first major mechanised industries which led Britain's industrial revolution and in which Britain — as the longest-established and most advanced producer — was highly dominant for a long period, are good examples of this process, since they are now technically mature and easily entered.

17. In fact, Irish industry had gained entry to some of the less easily entered sectors under an earlier protectionist policy, so that the period of outward-looking policies has seen some reversal of this process, with indigenous firms being squeezed out of larger-scale traded industries following the return of free trade.

Chapter 3: Irish Industry Before the Twentieth Century (pp. 32-52)

1. In fact, linen weaving had almost completely disappeared in the Belfast area by the 1800s (Monaghan, 1942; Green, 1949, p. 99).

2. The interests of cotton manufacturers increasingly lay in separation from Britain because the British cotton industry was growing increasingly dominant, whereas Britain had developed no such advantage in linen which was still not mechanised and which was, in any case, particularly strong in Ireland.

3. These figures may be somewhat unreliable. Also, many of the reported textile workers, being domestic spinners, would in fact have had little work by 1841 due to the mechanisation of spinning. It is clear, nevertheless, that large numbers were engaged in textiles and other industries at some earlier stage at least.

4. Machinery had been developed by 1790 for spinning *coarse* linen yarn, but this had been little used in Ireland; a few British centres had therefore captured the coarse linen trade but Irish fine linen was unaffected.

5. Another possible leading sector which might have stimulated some further industrialisation in Ireland was agricultural machinery (as in Denmark). But this possibility was closed off by the pattern of agriculture, which was relatively small in scale and increasingly dominated by grazing and therefore generated little demand for machinery.

6. Rosenberg (1976, ch. 1) shows that in the USA the skills and technology developed originally in firearms production made a decisive contribution to the subsequent development of other precision engineering industries. Since production of firearms in Britain was mainly concentrated in Birmingham and London, a similar pattern of development probably occurred there too.

7. The location of some major British industrial centres at the mining areas was probably due more to the early development there of engineering skills in the production of mining machinery, including steam engines, than to the advantages of proximity to coal and iron sources. Such an explanation is suggested by the rather similar pattern of engineering development which occurred in Belfast, starting with textile machinery and steam engines, in the absence of local coal and iron.

Chapter 4: Independence and Protection (pp. 53-71)

1. i.e. building, electricity, gas and other non-manufacturing 'industrial' activities, as well as manufacturing.

2. Essentially, Dominion status left the King of England as 'sovereign' of Ireland, with the limited functions of a constitutional monarch, while the more substantial powers of the UK parliament were transferred to the independent Dail.

3. The Labour Party derived much of its support from the remaining agricultural labourers, who were a declining group.

4. The difference between Fianna Fail's protectionism and Cumann na nGaedheal's favouring of freer trade could not be regarded as a major cause of the split over the Treaty and the consequent civil war. The Treaty did not rule out stiff protection and, in fact, Arthur Griffith himself, Sinn Fein's main advocate of protection, had led the delegation which signed it.

5. This calculation (and similar ones below) assumes that the output/employment ratio is the same for exports as for home sales; non-Food & Drink manufacturing employment is multiplied by the proportion of output of these industries going for export. If the output/employment ratio was higher for exports, which is the most likely bias, the export employment figure is even lower.

6. *The effective* tariff rates, on what were largely low value-added and assembly-type activities, would have been several times higher.

7. The absence of technologically demanding industries, even after 30 years of protection in the early 1960s, is indicated by the finding that industrial Research and Development was virtually non-existent at that time (*Science and Irish Economic Development*, 1966).

8. Admittedly, the measure which is most relevant in discussing balance of payments crises is the balance of payments itself, which tended to be less in deficit than the balance of trade due to invisible earnings such as tourism receipts, dividends on investments abroad, emigrants' remittances, etc. But net invisible earnings showed very little change from the late 1940s right through to the early 1960s (Meenan, 1970, p. 84), so that the changes in the trade deficit shown in tables 4.8 and 4.9 are a fair reflection of fluctuations in the balance of payments (for which we have not got figures in *constant* prices).

9. Kennedy and Dowling (1975, table 26) show that about 31% of the growth of such exports to the UK arose from increased market shares in 1953-58, the rest being attributable to growth of UK import demand, while the corresponding proportion for the influence of increased market shares in 1958-63 was even smaller. Thus unless the influence of other less important export markets was very different, two-thirds or more of this export growth would have resulted from holding constant shares of rapidly growing export markets.

10. According to the *Survey of Grant-aided Industry* (1967), firms setting up with New Industry grants (outside Shannon) from 1952 to March 1960 expected to be employing 7,800 people at full production. If they actually employed 50-60% of this number in 1960 (this is about the percentage which later experience suggests), they would have been employing 3,900 to 4,700 people. Assuming further that 22% of this employment was in *Irish-based* firms and that 75% of the foreign firms' employment was in manufacturing for export (these percentages are those for all New Grant-aided Industry in 1966), the foreign grant-aided firms, set up since 1952, would have employed about 2,300-2,700 people in export manufacturing in 1960 (outside Shannon).

11. *Direct* employment in export manufacturing is not the only important issue, of course, in the sense that improved exports (of anything) relaxes the foreign exchange constraint and enables employment to increase elsewhere too. The discussion here refers to employment figures as a measure partly because this illustrates fairly clearly the scale of activity referred to, and partly because it makes it possible to compare different components of the changes in the same terms.

12. Some particularly large latecomers, however, have managed to progress rather further with such policies, since in a very large market a fully competitive scale can more often be attained, and it may be worthwhile for foreign firms to establish (or license) more technologically advanced activities including more capital goods.

Chapter 5: Outward-looking Policies and Industrial Growth (pp. 72-96)

1. A more detailed account of these developments is contained in O'Malley (1980).

2. The one major exception was car assembly, in which the scale required for efficient operation of even one plant was greater than the size of the Irish market. This industry received special protective measures under the AIFTA agreement and the terms of EEC membership.

3. He was reviewing the First Programme and the Third Report of the Capital Investment Advisory Committee, as well as Economic Development. The arguments for freer trade, and indeed an assumption of its inevitability, were contained in these documents.

4. This was readily accepted by Britain, and it led to no change in such matters as free access to Britain and voting rights there for Irish emigrants, or trading relations with Britain.

5. As Chubb and Lynch (1969) point out in their introduction, it is significant that there is only one practising politician among the authors of the 25 documents they have edited which chart the changes in economic policy and administration in the 1950s and 1960s.

6. Evidence of the interconnected nature of Irish capitalist enterprises, with links between industry and services, especially the banks, is contained in Sinn Fein the Workers Party (1976).
7. Whitaker (1976a) has argued that the balance of payments constraint on demand expansion could not have been similarly overcome in the 1950s, pointing to the relatively small external reserves held by the Central Bank and to the limited scope for foreign borrowing before the appearance of the Eurodollar as a result of US trade deficits in the 1960s.
8. Garret FitzGerald was formerly a lecturer in economics in University College, Dublin and later became Minister for Foreign Affairs and Taoiseach, as the leader of Fine Gael. Noel Farley is a professor of economics in Bryn Mawr College, Pennsylvania. T.K. Whitaker was formerly secretary of the Department of Finance, Governor of the Central Bank of Ireland and later became a Senator.
9. Data on Irish wages are from tables in the back of the annual *Review and Outlook*. UK data are from the *Annual Abstract of Statistics*.
10. OECD, *Economic Survey of Ireland, 1987/88*.

Chapter 6: Irish Indigenous Industry (pp. 97-154)

1. Another difference from the preferred definition is the inclusion of foreign firms later taken over by Irish owners, but this appears to have occurred on only a minor scale. And in cases where the takeover by Irish owners occurred in the past few years they would still be classified as foreign in our data, as would be preferred.
2. It will be noted that the Total figures for 1973 differ slightly in tables 6.1 and 6.2 since IDA data are used in table 6.2, but in table 6.1 the *Trend* data are used for Totals (see appendix 1).
3. It might be argued that the stagnation of indigenous manufacturing employment over this lengthy period does not represent a particularly disappointing performance, since similar trends were in evidence in a number of advanced industrial countries. However there is an important difference in so far as these other countries were starting (in the early 1960s) from a much more advanced position in industrial development, such as Ireland had never reached, and were shifting resources increasingly into Services in line with a changing pattern of demand as high income levels are attained. Ireland, on the other hand, was simply failing to attain anything like a comparable level of indigenous industrial development (which would have entailed continuing growth of indigenous manufacturing employment long after it had slowed down in more advanced countries). The persistence of unemployment and/or emigration in Ireland indicates that there was a persistent failure to mobilise productive resources, not simply a proportionate shift of resources from employment in Industry to employment in Services as happened in more advanced economies.

4. The growth of New Foreign industry does not, of course, arise simply from expansion of a fairly constant group of companies, but was largely due to a continuous inflow of more new companies.

5. It can be estimated, from the sources used for table 6.3, that sales of New Foreign industry to the home market accounted for, at most, about 1% of all sales of manufactures to that market in 1966, 2% in 1973 and 3% in 1976; thus 'competing' imports take market shares almost exclusively from other industries.

6. The three series cover 1960-73, 1973-77 and 1977-79, and the inconsistency of definition between them is shown by the fact that the 1973 and 1977 figures differ somewhat in the two overlapping series for each of these years. They were joined together for figure 6.2 by taking the 1960-73 series unchanged, and then applying the proportionate increase in the share of competing imports in the home market found in the later series to the level reached by the end of the first series; e.g. by 1973, according to the first series, the share of competing imports stood at 23.6%; the 1973-77 series, however, gives a figure of 27.2%, rising to 30% by 1977, which is a proportionate increase of 30/27.2 or 1.103, which when multiplied by 23.6% gives 26.0%, the figure illustrated in the chart for 1977.

7. Home consumption equals gross output minus exports plus 'competing' Imports.

8. Food made up 53% of the exports of industries other than New Foreign firms in both 1966 and 1973 — see table 6.8.

9. The export-gross output ratio of *all* Drink & Tobacco stood at only 13% in 1960 declining to 12% in 1973. These figures could be only marginally affected by the inclusion of Foreign New industry which accounted for only 3% of the sector's employment by 1973.

10. This is similar to the concept of the 'effective tariff', which measures the level of protection in relation to value-added rather than final value.

11. 'Non-traded' should be understood to mean that relatively little international trade occurs, not taken literally as meaning no international trade in any circumstances.

12. See appendix 1 for derivation of these and similar figures for other sectors.

13. Car assembly, however, was exceptional in retaining a degree of protection until the 1980s, since firms were obliged to continue assembling if they wished to sell cars in the country; they could combine assembly with importing of cars, but could not import only. Nevertheless the industry began to run down, as firms sought ways round this obligation by guaranteeing employment in other activities. Car assembly in Ireland has now ceased.

14. It is possible that part of the explanation of more rapid employment decline in large plants is faster growth of labour productivity than in smaller ones, and thus not entirely due to a weaker performance as regards output. But the scale of the difference in employment

trends between large and small plants in the 'exposed' sectors makes it very unlikely that this is the main explanation of the trends. The fact that 37 out of 192 plants with over 100 employees in 1973 in the 'exposed' sectors had actually closed by 1980 suggests that there was a genuine decline here, particularly since there were hardly any closures among plants of this size in the 'sheltered' sectors, where only 5 out of 149 closed down.

15. Japan in the 1950s and 1960s is a good example of a country which spent heavily on domestic R & D, aimed at 'innovative imitation', while following a policy of importing advanced technology rather than attempting to develop fundamentally new technology itself.

    In the Irish context, the OECD (1974) and Cooper and Whelan (1973) argued that substantially more R & D would be required for Ireland to develop technologically advanced industries, even though they recommended relying heavily on imports of licensed technology.

16. It would not be valid, however, to make an exact comparison between the sectoral distribution of employment among the largest Irish firms and among all indigenous industry, because the large firms include some non-manufacturing activities. This does arise to a significant degree in the four large sectors mentioned, but is by no means confined to them. It is also an important consideration in Metals & Engineering, for example.

17. 'Irish Companies 1979', *The Irish Times*, 29/12/79.

18. 'Irish Companies 1978', *The Irish Times*, 1/1/79.

19. The figures given in appendix 2 for Guinness, and its no. 3 ranking, relate only to Guinness (Ireland), excluding operations of the Guinness Group in other countries. In total, Guinness would be the largest company to have originated in Ireland.

20. Relatively small scale can be overcome by special marketing advantages, such as 'tied' public houses, but generally returns to scale are important.

21. Thus most 'foreign' beers consumed in a country tend to be imported in only small quantities or, if larger quantities are involved, they are usually brewed locally under licence.

22. 'Guinness Stress on Cost-Cutting', *The Irish Times*, 15/7/81.

23. By far the most successful diversification in the Irish drinks industry, 'Bailey's' Irish cream liqueur — a blend of whiskey, cream and chocolate — was not developed by an Irish firm, but by the multinational subsidiary, Gilbeys, with the help of the parent company's R & D and marketing.

Chapter 7: Foreign Industries in Ireland (pp. 155-191)

1. US Department of Commerce, *Survey of Current Business*, June 1987.

2. Large concentrations of Japanese manufacturing investment in a few NICs such as Hong Kong and South Korea might, however,

cause them to rank higher than Ireland as sites for all TNC manufacturing.

3. Vernon (1966) had difficulty in thinking of more than a few examples of such export-oriented investments in the LDCs in the mid-1960s. Although such export industries have become much more common since then, Lall (1978) could still remark that 'the vast bulk of foreign manufacturing investment in LDCs has gone into protected import-substituting activities . . .', a remark which would probably be too strongly worded for the context of the late 1980s but no doubt it is still correct to say that export industries are in the minority among TNC operations in LDCs.

4. Helleiner mentions such products as textiles, sporting equipment, shoes and toys in this context, referring to Lary's (1968) list of such products found to be suitable for export from LDCs.

5. This foreign investment or participation in Irish manufacturing was subject to the Control of Manufactures Acts in force at that time, which required that majority ownership in new industrial projects should be in the hands of Irish citizens. For this reason foreign involvement took the form of licensing arrangements, managerial contracts, and minority participation in joint ventures. Thus although foreign participation in such ventures may frequently have been essential for their establishment, it would be rather difficult to assess the overall importance of foreign investment even if more complete data were available.

6. Thus the London Docklands Development Corporation used to feature in its advertisements the claims of many other local or regional development organisations in Britain that they are located within easy reach of London. These organisations all appear to see this as a factor worth stressing in attracting mobile investment — as does the London Docklands Development Corporation itself.

7. Among foreign firms in 1973, 24% of employment was in US firms, but their share rose to 45% by 1983. Japanese firms also began to invest in Ireland in the 1970s. In 1973, 55% of Irish exports went to the UK, and 21% to the rest of the EEC, but in 1980 the figures were respectively, 43% and 32%.

8. A much larger proportion of Irish projects would be in the Food sector, largely in activities which are naturally highly dispersed according to the catchment area for agricultural products. So in non-Food industries the highly decentralised location of foreign projects is probably even more marked in comparison with Irish projects.

9. Derived from O'Farrell (1984), table 12.

10. In these figures 'primary' exports include Food, Drink & Tobacco, and manufactured exports exclude them. All industries, Irish and foreign, are included. Import contents include direct and indirect imports, calculated using 1968 input-output relationships.

11. Reported by L. Connellan in Confederation of Irish Industry (1980b).

12. For example, the growth in sales of Baileys Irish Cream (produced by a multinational subsidiary) brought its cream supplier, Virginia Milk Products (another foreign subsidiary), into contentious competition with local firms for the year-round supply of the 26 million gallons of milk required in 1981. (*Sunday Tribune*, 22/11/81). Cadbury's have also been in dispute for supplies of milk.

13. Purchases of material inputs by non-food foreign firms are calculated using an estimate from IDA (1985) of materials purchases per employee by these firms, combined with the figure for employment of these firms from the IDA Annual Report 1983. Sales of indigenous industry are calculated using the sales per employee figure for indigenous industry in IDA (1985), combined with employment of indigenous industry from the IDA Annual Report 1983. Note that this probably overestimates somewhat the importance of foreign sector purchasing for indigenous industry, since some of the purchases included would be non-manufactured raw materials and some would be from other foreign firms in Ireland.

Chapter 8: The Experience of Other Latecomers with 'Outward-looking Policies' (pp. 192-214)

1. This was in some contrast to South Korea and Taiwan, which both have allotted a more important role to state enterprises. The difference is probably attributable to the initial weakness of Korean and Taiwanese private capitalists — unlike the large established private firms in Japan.

2. As an example of how these measures were used, the foreign exchange allocation for car imports stood at $13.7 million in 1953 but was reduced sharply to $0.6 million in 1954 when imports were thought to threaten domestic production; at the same time excise taxes on small and medium-size cars, in which Japanese producers were relatively strong, stood at 15-30% while a 50% rate was charged on large cars (Rosser, 1980).

3. See 'The Coming Assault on Communications Markets', *International Business Week*, 14/12/81, special issue on Japan.

4. For example, MITI had administrative rules requiring that the joint venture should be in a line in which the Japanese firm was experienced, that at least half the directors, the president and auditors must be Japanese, that the foreign firm should not have the deciding voice in certain specified key decisions, and that there must be limitations on the transfer of stock by Japanese firms (Rosser, 1980).

5. See, for example, 'The Business Intelligence Beehive', *International Business Week*, 14/12/81.

6. 'New Trade Winds: I Want Our People to Import More', *International Business Week*, 14/12/81.

7. As the *Financial Times* reports, 'South Korea may not quite deserve to be ranked as the most remarkable economic success story of the 1970s — that distinction probably should go to Taiwan . . . but South Korea certainly outclasses virtually every other country in the world. . .', Charles Smith, *Financial Times*, 2/4/79.

8. Charles Smith, *Financial Times* survey of South Korea, 2/4/79.

9. Indeed, if it were the case that foreign industry was largely responsible for industrial transformation in these countries, this would be difficult to reconcile with the argument that export-oriented foreign direct investment occurs on only a very limited scale worldwide. For South Korea, with a population of some 40 million, and Taiwan with about half of that number, could scarcely be described as small or insignificant cases.

10. Puerto Rico is another small economy which, like Ireland and Singapore, experienced rapid export-led industrial growth under the conventional policies, which was attributable very largely to foreign direct investment while indigenous firms were involved relatively little in manufacturing (see Villamil, 1979). But since this gave way to major economic problems in the 1970s (with unemployment rising to 23% by 1977), Puerto Rico is not often referred to now as an example of the success of this strategy — as it used to be in the 1950s and 1960s.

11. 'Singapore Builds Up Defence Industry in Economic Strategy', *Financial Times*, 30/11/83.

12. Owen, in Keith Hopkins (ed.), 1971, *Hong Kong: the Industrial Colony*, Oxford University Press.

Chapter 9: Constraints on Irish Industry and Future Prospects (pp. 215-257)

1. Telecommunications was the subject of a major investment programme in the early 1980s. The Confederation of Irish Industry (1980a) expressed itself broadly satisfied with the standards to be reached by the mid-1980s.

2. 'Reagan is Good for Ireland', *Business and Finance*, 15/1/81.

3. 'The Irish Worker is Just as Good as the German', *The Irish Times*, 28/9/83.

4. 'Ireland as a Manufacturing Base', *Allied Irish Banks Review*, No. 24, April 1981.

5. The establishment of this large number of new firms is consistent with stagnation in indigenous employment in the same period because the new firms have mostly remained small, while longer-established firms, which were in many cases quite large, tended to decline — see chapter 6.

6. It is interesting to speculate on the relative scale of these multinational operations. It seems probable that the companies mentioned employed over 20,000 people abroad by 1983, possibly over 30,000, as compared with a domestic indigenous

manufacturing work-force of 132,000. The proportion of employment abroad, at say, 15-23% or even more, would be higher than for some advanced industrial countries, mainly due to the large proportion of non-traded industries among Irish firms, which causes companies to go multinational as a mode of expansion.

7. Such views have been frequently expressed, in a short-term context, in the *Quarterly Bulletins* of the Central Bank of Ireland. Examples of a similar analysis in a longer-term context are National Economic and Social Council Report No. 26 (1976), the *Programme for National Development 1978-1981* (1979, ch. 8) and the *Report of the Committee on Costs and Competitiveness* (1981).

8. Of these outlets, investment abroad and increased consumption would be net absorbers of resources of the Irish economy, but takeovers or investment in property would not be net absorbers of resources, thus representing a transfer of the increased profits to others in the economy and not an explanation of the use to which they are finally put.

9. In Ireland, the level of labour costs does not arise directly as a determinant of agricultural output (which is the main material input for the industries referred to here), because the vast majority of the agricultural labour force are not employees, but owner-occupiers.

10. Consistent with the expectation that there would be little connection between profitability of foreign firms in Ireland and job-creating investment by them is the fact that they have generally been highly profitable according to the IDA, but their employment tends to decline a number of years after their establishment, rather than to increase over time, as seen in chapter 7.

11. It should be borne in mind, however, that investment abroad or in services might appear attractive to firms in this sector too. Examples of this were mentioned among large firms in section 6.iii, including Guinness, Carroll's and Waterford Glass.

12. The figures in table 9.2 are somewhat out of date. Data on manufacturing earnings (which are not quite the same as labour costs since they exclude social insurance costs) indicate that Irish labour costs probably came closer to UK levels by 1987 but remained slightly lower.

13. The price-elastic group includes, in addition, some activities with quite substantial entry barriers, particularly arising from scale and capital-intensity, such as many metals and chemicals.

14. This paper quotes evidence from Kaldor (1978), among other economists, as well as numerous 'business management' studies such as the European Management Forum (1980), who say 'the notion that competitiveness might be reduced to considerations of costs and productivity is a dangerous one', and the Boston Consulting Group's report to the French Commissariat du Plan: 'According to the BCG there are ten such mistaken preconceptions (about competitiveness) and the first consists in considering wages

and social costs as the primordial factor determining a firm's or an industry's capacity to compete successfully; there are many factors more important.'

15. This is in contrast to foreign projects which, McKeon says, are required to be independently viable, and to which grant payments are made only as incentives to locate in Ireland, not as subsidies to projects which would be non-viable without such assistance.

16. Cost-benefit analysis might show, of course, that *some* job creation should rationally be foregone if the costs to the economy for some projects are very great, but this is another matter.

17. These would include some of the oil-producing countries, as well as some others.

18. Ireland, for instance, does not seem capable of developing its tourist industry to the same degree as peripheral European countries in the Mediterranean area, such as Greece or Spain.

19. In a planned socialist economy, however, full employment can be arranged (by underemployment in some activities if necessary), but there may be no option of low or zero growth without political instability, if the population are aware of rising living standards elsewhere and aspire to match them.

20. Ultimately, however, import-substitution is not a substitute for export development. For if the goal of economic growth is achieved, it leads to expansion of imports of those products which have not been substituted by domestic production (and inevitably there will be many of these) and this can eventually raise the import bill above the level it stood at before import-substitution began.

21. Quoted by Eoin McVey, 'Still in the Vanguard of Job Creation', in supplement to *The Irish Times*, 30/12/81.

22. One factor militating against a very rapid development of these activities is that many of them would operate best in a context of close association with technically advanced industrial activities which are relatively lacking in Ireland. Also, as regards mobile foreign 'service industries', Ireland would seem to have little strong attraction for them as compared with major service centres in the same general region, such as the south east of England; in this it differs from places such as Singapore or Hong Kong which could reasonably be regarded as natural service centres for their region, with no major advanced centres nearby.

23. This post-war strategy of Japan was in some contrast to the views of orthodox economists who would have seen a different comparative advantage in a factor endowment consisting of 'a huge supply of underemployed labour, an extreme scarcity of capital and out-of-date technology. The obvious candidates for development were the labour-intensive industries: textiles, clothing, pottery, metal smallwares' (Allen, 1981).

24. The seventeen industries in the most extreme top right-hand cell are: motor vehicles; guided missiles and space vehicles; non-

cellulosic organic fibres; primary aluminium; electric lamps; cigarettes; turbines, turbine generator sets; household refrigerators, freezers; aircraft; tyres and inner tubes; aircraft engines and engine parts; photographic equipment and supplies; telephone and telegraph apparatus; malt beverages; sanitary paper products; environmental controls; aluminium sheet, plate and foil.

25. The 21 industries with concentration ratios of under 20 and average employment in top firms of under 1,000 are: typesetting; concrete blocks and bricks; wood pallets and skids; wood partitions and fixtures; screw machine products; metal plating and polishing; industrial patterns; fur goods; special product sawmills n.e.c.; bookbinding and related work; machinery except electrical n.e.c.; ready mixed concrete; special dies, tools and jigs; concrete products n.e.c.; signs and advertising displays; blouses; sheet metalwork; miscellaneous fabricated wire products; fabricated metal products n.e.c.; general industrial machinery n.e.c.; boat building and repairing. Note that those designated 'n.e.c.' are residual categories which may actually each contain quite a diverse range of industries. Some of these industries if properly defined, could be quite concentrated in themselves, but they would show up here as fragmented due to being grouped with other industries in one residual category.

26. O'Malley (1987) reports on a preliminary analysis of Metals & Engineering activities along the lines suggested here, with a view to identifying industries likely to be suitable as targets for development by Irish indigenous firms. Industries which appear to be worth detailed consideration include agricultural machinery (other than tractors and combine harvesters), process plants, mechanical handling equipment, precision toolmaking, medical instruments and equipment, measuring and checking instruments, special-purpose vehicles, small electrical appliances and specialised applications or systems in electronics.

27. By 1980, establishments accounting for 83% of manufacturing employment had received some form of IDA grant, and many of these companies were sheltered non-traded businesses being aided only to compete with one other.

Appendix 1

Data Sources for Chapter 6

TABLE 6.1

In table 6.1, the total employment figures are taken from the annual *Trend in Employment and Unemployment*, in which the figures are based on the Census of Population.

The employment figure for New and Small Foreign Industry for 1973 is from the Industrial Development Authority's annual Employment Survey which began in 1973. The results of this survey are not published in full, though the IDA quotes some of its results in reports, plans and press releases. I am very grateful to the IDA for making available to me the results of these surveys in some detail. For 1960 and 1966, New Foreign Industry employment is derived from the *Survey of Grant-aided Industry* (1967). The 1960 figure was obtained as explained in footnote 10 to chapter 4. The 1966 figure was obtained by distributing total actual grant-aided employment in the *Survey* (1967) between Irish and foreign firms in proportion to the employment projected in Irish and foreign firms at the time of grant approval, since an Irish/foreign breakdown of actual employment was not published. Any inaccuracy in the 1960 and 1966 figures would almost certainly be within a margin of 1,000 and therefore of little importance to the estimates for the 'Rest of Industry'.

The *Trend* series is used for all the totals, rather than the IDA's total when it is available from their own survey in 1973, in the interests of maintaining consistency over the whole period. And the *Trend* series was chosen, rather than the *Census of Industrial Production* which also covers the whole period, because the *Trend* series has a more similar definition to the IDA data, is closer to the IDA survey's totals in 1973-80, and therefore seems a better base from which to subtract a figure on foreign new industry taken from the IDA survey. The table below shows these three series, showing that the *Trend* and IDA data are fairly similar, while the CIP figures are smaller.

	1960	1966	1973	1979
Trend	172	198	222	239
IDA	—	—	215	236
CIP	151	175	205	228

The *Trend* and IDA series both cover all manufacturing, although the IDA series refers to January and the *Trend* to April of the year concerned, which would be the main factor accounting for the differences between them. The *CIP* series, however, excludes small enterprises with less than three workers, and is probably more precise in the matter of defining manufacturing workers within establishments that also engage in some service-type activities. These (and some omissions in its coverage, at least until 1979) are probably the main reasons for its smaller size.

As mentioned in the text, nationality is defined in the IDA data by nationality of ownership. 'New' industries are those which received the grants for new industrial projects under the grant scheme introduced for Designated (less-developed) Areas in 1952 and for other areas in 1956. 'Small' industries are those which received grants for new projects under the IDA's Small Industry programme which first started in 1967. (Only a very small minority of foreign grant-aided firms are 'Small'). These grant programmes would cover the vast majority of new foreign projects started since the 1950s. The *Survey of Grant-aided Industry* (1967) and McAleese (1971/72) estimated that only about 10% of new foreign projects failed to receive grants, and that these were well below average in size.

One slight problem with the figures as presented in table 6.1 arises from the fact that some old foreign plants established before 1952 have received grants for major expansions, and the practice in such cases is for the whole of a plant to be classified subsequently as new grant-aided. This means that some plants not included as New or Small Foreign in 1960 or 1966, but included instead in the 'Rest of Industry', would by 1966 or 1973 have been reclassified into New Foreign, thus artificially reducing employment in the 'Rest of Industry' in 1966 or 1973 below what it should be for purposes of comparison with earlier years. But the effect of this would not be very great since 'New' foreign firms established prior to 1952 employed only 5,900 people in 1973 of which only a fraction (probably under half) could be regarded as previously existing employment, prior to their major expansion; 3,000 or less is fairly small when compared with 186,000 employed in the 'Rest' in 1973. Also, these firms had falling employment in 1973-80 and possibly before 1973 too, so that had they, or part of them, been included in the 'Rest' there could still have been a decline in the 'Rest of Industry' in 1966-73. This problem of reclassification does not arise in the data after 1973 in table 6.2, since the classification of all firms for all these years was done with respect to their status at the end of the period (or at the time of closure if they had closed).

TABLE 6.2

This table is derived from the *IDA Employment Survey,* using their classifications, except that the Guinness brewery was reclassified as Irish rather than foreign.

TABLE 6.3

Gross output of All Industry is taken from the *Census of Industrial Production* (CIP). Gross output of New Foreign industry in 1985 is also taken from the CIP. Gross output of New Foreign industry in 1976 was derived by taking the gross output of all New Industry for 1976 from O'Loughlin, 1978 (table 6.11 grossed up by the population-sample ratios in table 6.1) and multiplying by the proportion of all New Industry sales accounted for by foreign rather than Irish firms (from O'Farrell and O'Loughlin, table 2.6). For 1973, gross output of New Foreign industry was derived by dividing the exports of these firms (McAleese, 1977, table 4.3) by their exports-gross output ratio (McAleese, 1977, table 4.2). Both the 1973 and 1976 estimates exclude foreign Small industries (which did not exist before 1967).

For 1966, gross output of New Foreign industry was estimated by taking gross output of all New industry (*Survey of Grant-aided Industry*, 1967, table 2.13) and multiplying by the proportion of New industry employment accounted for by foreign firms, as estimated for table 6.1. For 1960, New Foreign gross output was estimated by taking the New Foreign employment estimate from table 6.1, dividing it by total manufacturing employment and multiplying the resulting percentage by total gross output. These 1960 and 1966 estimates are a bit rough, therefore, but any error would have only a relatively small effect on the much larger estimates for the Rest of Industry derived by subtracting the New Foreign figure from the total. Industries at the Shannon estate are excluded from total gross output in 1960 and 1966 in the CIP; these are taken to be very largely New Foreign firms and they are excluded from our estimates of New Foreign gross output in those years, so as to avoid subtracting them from a total in which they are not included, when estimating gross output of industries other than New Foreign (i.e., The Rest). This means that the New Foreign estimates in 1960 and 1966 do not include Shannon, whereas the estimates for 1973, 1976 and 1985 do, producing some inconsistency. But the estimates for The Rest, which is our main interest here, do not suffer from such an inconsistency.

FIGURE 6.2

The data on 'Competing' Imports come from 3 different series. The 1960-73 series is that published regularly in the annual *Review and Outlook* for years up to 1973. The 1973-77 series was derived from the *Trade Statistics of Ireland* by summing up the imports of items regarded as 'competing', using a list kindly lent by Alan Matthews of Trinity College, Dublin, who used it to derive tables in Matthews (1980). The 1977-79 series is that supplied by the Department of Industry, Commerce and Tourism for Blackwell, Danaher and O'Malley's (1983) study of job losses in manufacturing. In this series, however, Competing Imports of Food were incomplete, so the Food figures were revised using the same method as for 1973-77.

TABLE 6.5

Total exports of manufactured goods are taken from the tables in the annual *Review and Outlook*, for 1960, 1966 and 1973. Where the coverage of these tables is slightly less than the *Census of Industrial Production* (as seen by the slightly lower level of gross output as compared with CIP gross output) exports are derived by multiplying the export/gross output ratio for each sector in the tables by the CIP gross output. For 1976, exports are derived by dividing the 1977 export figures supplied by the Department of Industry, Commerce and Tourism for Blackwell, Danaher and O'Malley's (1983) job loss study by the ratio of SITC 0 less 00 and 5-8 exports in 1977 to those in 1976.

Foreign New industry exports for 1973 are from McAleese (1977), table 4.3. For 1976, Foreign New industry exports are derived from O'Farrell and O'Loughlin (1980), by calculating the proportion of all New Industry exports accounted for by foreign firms in their sample survey (from their table 2.6) and multiplying this proportion by their figure for all New Industry exports (their table 2.4). For 1960 and 1966, Foreign New industry exports are derived by calculating 87.6% of the gross output estimates in table 6.3 (because McAleese, 1977, finds Foreign New industry exported 87.6% of output in 1973; O'Farrell and O'Loughlin, 1980, find 89.4% in 1976; the *Survey of Grant-aided Industry*, 1967, finds 85% for all New Industry, Foreign and Irish in 1966). The 1960 and 1966 estimates, therefore, are a bit rough, but unlikely to be so far in error as to misrepresent seriously the figures for the 'Rest of Industry' when subtracted from the total. Again, Shannon is excluded from both total exports and Foreign New industry exports in 1960 and 1966, but included in both in 1973 and 1976; this leads to some inconsistency in the time series for total and Foreign New industry but, as in the case of table 6.3, this does not produce any inconsistency in the series for the 'Rest of Industry' which is our main interest.

TABLE 6.6

Competing Imports and Home Consumption are derived in the same way as for figure 6.2.

TABLE 6.8

The 1960 export and gross output figures are for *all* industry outside the Shannon estate and therefore include a small number of Foreign New industries. The effect of this is probably to raise the overall export figure for 1960 by about £6 million, and the overall export-gross output ratio by about 1% above what it should be for industries other than New Foreign industry. The export-gross output ratios of certain sectors in 1960 are likely to be higher, therefore, than they should be if these New Foreign firms could be excluded — Metals & Engineering by perhaps 3 percentage points, Other/Drink & Tobacco by 2%, Textiles by 1% and Clothing & Footwear by 1%. For 1973, total exports by sector are derived as for table 6.5 and total gross output by sector is from the *Census of Industrial Production*; Shannon exports are included in the sectoral totals (because they are included in our Foreign New industry export figures which must be subtracted from the totals) by means of distributing Shannon exports for 1973 by sector according to the Department of Industry, Commerce and Tourism's figures for 1977 (Shannon exports are given as one figure in the *Trade Statistics*, not broken down by category). Foreign New industry exports for 1973 are from Dermot McAleese's survey (reported in McAleese, 1977), and I am grateful to him for allowing me access to some of his unpublished data.

EXPORT-GROSS OUTPUT RATIOS OF SUB-DIVISIONS OF THE TEN MAJOR SECTORS

These figures, in section 6.ii, are derived by using the *Census of Industrial Production* for gross output, while exports are derived from the *Trade Statistics of Ireland*, by summing up export items corresponding to the relevant production categories — using a list again provided by Alan Matthews and used in Matthews (1980). The export figures calculated in this way (for the ten major sectors) are close to the official *Review and Outlook* figures (which do not provide a more detailed breakdown than ten sectors) in 1973. The widest margin of difference among sectors mentioned in the text is only 8%, and mostly much less, for the export figure, so that when this is in turn expressed as an export-gross output ratio the margin of error is proportionately smaller — e.g., 4% for a ratio of 50% or 0.8% for a ratio of 10%, at the most. Since these figures are used only to illustrate whether an industry has a broadly high or low export-orientation, such a margin of error seems quite acceptable.

Appendix 2

The Largest Irish Firms

The table below lists 100 companies described as the top 100 Irish indigenous private-sector manufacturing companies. This list was drawn up from the *Irish Business*, January 1985, list of the top 500 companies of all types operating in Ireland. In this list, companies are ranked by sales during their last financial year prior to January 1985, from the Jefferson Smurfit Group's £686 million down to two companies on £3 million. From this list it was necessary to extract those companies definable as (a) 'indigenous' — meaning, as in the rest of chapter 6, majority Irish-owned or, more precisely, originally Irish-owned even if foreign-owned now (where this was known); (b) 'private sector', i.e., excluding state enterprises; and (c) 'manufacturing', meaning engaged in at least *some* manufacturing, since some companies combine manufacturing with other activities. The list would not be fully comprehensive but few very large companies would be left out.

As regards definitions, Irish ownership was generally established from the *IDA Employment Survey*. Most cases are fairly clear cut but there may still be a few misclassifications. There is no difficulty in distinguishing state from private enterprises. 'Manufacturing' companies are mostly clear from the description of their activities, but all were checked with the *IDA Employment Survey* (of manufacturing establishments). In cases where a firm's manufacturing is only part of its activities, it would be included only if the scale of its manufacturing seemed to be larger than that of the smallest companies included, judged on the basis of its manufacturing employment in the IDA Survey; again there may be a few misclassifications in this regard. Sales and employment figures for all firms listed below, however, are for the whole firm.

Some companies which appear large in terms of sales had very low employment, indicating very low manufacturing activity in terms of employment or value-added, mainly in the Food sector. (Unfortunately, value-added figures are not available for firms.) Since it seemed likely that it would give a distorted impression of the degree of concentration in Food if sales were used as the only criterion for inclusion in the list, a cut-off point of at least 100 employees was introduced.

Firms in the list have been classified by sector according to the nature of their *main* manufacturing activity, although some of them are involved in more than one sector; in two cases where companies could not be described as *predominantly* engaged in any one sector, they are described as 'multi-sectoral'.

Finally, the omission of one large Irish-owned company, Glen Dimplex, perhaps requires some explanation. Glen Dimplex is a manufacturer of small domestic electrical appliances, which had sales of £48 million in 1983-4 and would have been ranked no. 31 if included in the list. This company is now Irish owned but it consists mainly of overseas subsidiaries, and its Irish branch was originally foreign owned until it was taken over early in the company's development by the present Irish owners. Thus it does not really satisfy our particular definition of indigenous, meaning companies initially established in the Republic of Ireland by Irish owners. If nationality of present ownership were the sole criterion for inclusion, however, it would feature prominently in the list.

Table A2.1: The Top 100 Irish Indigenous Private-Sector Manufacturing Companies, 1983-84

	Company	Sales	Employ-ment	Main Activity	Main Manufacturing Sector
1.	Smurfit Group	£686m	12,119	Paper, Packaging & Print	Paper & Printing
2.	Cement Roadstone	£454m	7,322	Building Materials	Clay, Glass & Cement
3.	Guinness (Ireland)	£406m[1]	5,100	Brewing	Drink & Tobacco
4.	Purcell Exports	£313.4m	944	Meat Processing, Cattle Exports	Food
5.	Anglo Irish Meats	£253m	995	Beef Processing	Food
6.	Carroll Industries	£252.4m	1,325	Tobacco Manufacture	Drink & Tobacco
7.	Waterford Glass	£212.3m	6,717	Hand Made Crystal	Clay, Glass & Cement
8.	Avonmore Creameries	£210m	1,409	Milk Processing	Food
9.	Mitchelstown Co-op	£189.2m	2,000	Agricultural Co-operative	Food
10.	Irish Distillers	£185m	1,650	Distilling	Drink & Tobacco
11.	Waterford Co-op	£182m	1,200	Agricultural Co-operative	Food
12.	Kerry Co-op	£158.1m	1,350	Agricultural Co-operative	Food
13.	Cork Marts/IMP	£148m	750	Meat Processing	Food
14.	Ballyclough Co-op	£139.2m	1,037	Agricultural Co-operative	Food
15.	Golden Vale Co-op	£134.6m	984	Agricultural Co-operative	Food

	Company	Sales	Employment	Main Activity	Main Manufacturing Sector
16.	North Connaught Co-op	£90.8m	350	Agricultural Co-operative	Food
17.	Cantrell & Cochrane	£83.4m	1,280	Soft Drinks	Drink & Tobacco
18.	James Crean Holdings	£81.9m	700	Conglomerate, Soft Drinks	Drink & Tobacco
19.	Premier Hughes	£80m	1,521	Milk Processing, Distribution	Food
20.	Bailieboro Co-op	£80m	650	Agricultural Co-operative	Food
21.	O'Flaherty Holdings	£70m	615	Motor Assembly, Distribution	Metals & Engineering
22.	Halal Meat Packers	£69m	675	Meat Processing	Food
23.	Independent Newspapers	£65.2m	1,300	Printing/Publishing	Paper & Printing
24.	Killeshandra Co-op	£63m	192	Agricultural Co-operative	Food
25.	Odlum Mills	£58.6m	1,339	Flour Milling	Food
26.	Grassland Fertilisers	£55.8m	106	Fertiliser Manufacture, Distribution	Chemicals
27.	I.A.W.S.	£54m	230	Agricultural Inputs	Multi-sectoral
28.	Kildare Chilling Co.	£53m	230	Meat Processing	Food
29.	W. & R. Jacob	£51.7m	1,050	Biscuit Manufacture	Food

Table A2.1: The Top 100 Irish Indigenous Private-Sector Manufacturing Companies, 1983-84

	Company	Sales	Employ-ment	Main Activity	Main Manufacturing Sector
30.	Goulding Chemicals	£49.5m	195	Fertiliser Manufacture	Chemicals
31.	Youghal Carpets	£47.4m	1,725	Carpet Manufacture	Textiles
32.	Williams Group Tullamore	£45.2m	398	Drinks Manufacture	Drink & Tobacco
33.	Hanley Meats	£45m	490	Meat Processing	Food
34.	Clondalkin Group	£40.6m	921	Printing & Packaging	Paper & Printing
35.	Tunney Meat Packers	£39m	220	Meat Processing	Food
36.	Meadow Meats	£38m	140	Meat Processing	Food
37.	Drinagh Co-op	£37.2m	230	Agricultural Co-operative	Food
38.	John Daly Group	£36.3m	420	Soft Drinks	Drink & Tobacco
39.	Jones Group	£35.8m	600[2]	Shipping, Engineering	Metals & Engineering
40.	Nenagh Co-op	£34.8m	150	Agricultural Co-operative	Food
41.	McDonagh Group	£33m	250	Builders Providers	Wood & Furniture
42.	Lough Egish Co-op	£31.5m	200	Agricultural Co-operative	Food
43.	Tipperary Co-op	£30.7m	200	Agricultural Co-operative	Food
44.	Shannonside Co-op	£30.4m	140	Agricultural Co-operative	Food
45.	Irish Glass Bottle Co.	£28.9m	580	Glass Container Manufacture	Clay, Glass & Cement

	Company	Sales	Employ-ment	Main Activity	Main Manufacturing Sector
46.	Shannon Meats	£28m	278	Beef Processing	Food
47.	Kavanagh, Edward	£28m	100	Provender Milling	Food
48.	Savage Smyth & Co.	£26m	180	Soft Drinks	Drink & Tobacco
49.	Midwest Farmers' Co-op	£25.8m	110	Agricultural Co-operative	Food
50.	Gypsum Industries	£25.5m	500	Gypsum	Clay, Glass & Cement
51.	Monaghan Co-op	£25.3m	140	Agricultural Co-operative	Food
52.	Irish Ropes	£25m	566	Carpets, Ropes, Twine	Textiles
53.	M. J. Lyons Holdings	£25m	220	Meat Processing	Food
54.	Bacon Co. of Ireland	£24.7m	343	Pigmeat Processing	Food
55.	Irish Press	£23m	933	Printing & Publishing	Paper & Printing
56.	Sunbeam Wolsey	£22.7m	1,237	Knitwear	Textiles
57.	Kantoher Co-op	£22.6m	150	Agricultural Co-operative	Food
58.	Tayto	£22.5m	375	Snackfoods	Food
59.	Irish Leathers	£22m	400	Leather Tanners	Other Manufacturing
60.	Patton, David	£22m	169	Millers	Food
61.	Lisvaird Co-op	£21.8m	117	Agricultural Co-operative	Food
62.	Roscrea Bacon Factory	£21.8m	273	Pigmeat Processors	Food

Table A2.1: The Top 100 Irish Indigenous Private-Sector Manufacturing Companies, 1983-84

	Company	Sales	Employ-ment	Main Activity	Main Manufacturing Sector
63.	Minch, Norton & Co.	£21.5m	170	Malting	Drink & Tobacco
64.	Michael Byrne & Sons	£20m	280	Pigmeat Processors	Food
65.	TMG Group	£19.7m	465	Engineering	Metals & Engineering
66.	Carton Bros.	£19m	280	Poultry Processing	Food
67.	Mahon & McPhillips	£17.7m	530	Water Treatment Equipment/ Construction	Metals & Engineering
68.	Williams & Woods	£16.5m	245	Food Processing, Distribution	Food
69.	Spollen Concrete	£16m²	400	Concrete Products	Clay, Glass & Cement
70.	Monaghan Poultry Products	£15m	175	Poultry Processing	Food
71.	Irish Paper Products	£15m²	350	Paper Products	Paper & Printing
72.	Irish Times	£14.7m	510	Printers/Publishers	Paper & Printing
73.	Biocon Biochemicals	£14m	250	Enzyme Manufacture	Chemicals
74.	Woodfab Group	£14m	350	Sawmilling	Wood & Furniture
75.	Lunham Bros.	£14m	150	Bacon Curing	Food

	Company	Sales	Employment	Main Activity	Main Manufacturing Sector
76.	Moy Holdings	£13.8m	308	Insulation Materials, Construction	Clay, Glass & Cement
77.	S. & A.G. Davis	£13.4m	185	Flour/Animal Feed Milling	Food
78.	National Aluminium	£13m	500	Aluminium Windows/Doors	Metals & Engineering
79.	Doyle Group, D.B.	£12.5m^2	180	Meat Processing	Food
80.	Glen Abbey	£12.5m	722	Clothing Manufacture	Clothing & Footwear
81.	Maguire & Paterson	£10.2m	240	Match Manufacture	Other Manufacturing
82.	Lydonhouse Group	£9.3m	411	Bakers/Caterers	Food
83.	Thomas Crosbie & Co.	£9m^2	420	Printing/Publishing	Paper & Printing
84.	John Murphy & Sons	£8.7m	149	Meat Processing	Food
85.	Memory Computer	£8.2m	180	Computer Manufacturers	Metals & Engineering
86.	E. Burke & Sons	£8.1m	120	Pigmeat Processing	Food
87.	Milford (Donegal) Bakery	£7.6m	130	Baking & Milling	Food
88.	Campbell Seafoods	£7.6m	120	Fish Processing	Food
89.	Irish Co-operative Society	£7.4m	132	Box Manufacturers	Paper & Printing
90.	Lithographic Universal	£7m	150	Printing	Paper & Printing
91.	Dakota	£6.6m	204	Packing & Printing	Paper & Printing

Table A2.1: The Top 100 Irish Indigenous Private-Sector Manufacturing Companies, 1983-84

	Company	Sales	Employ-ment	Main Activity	Main Manufacturing Sector
92.	Hanlon Ireland	£6.2m	300	Ambulance Manufacture	Metals & Engineering
93.	Braids	£6.1m	264	Engineering & Textiles	Multi-sectoral
94.	Valley Ice Cream	£6m	150	Ice Cream Manufacture	Food
95.	RTD Group	£6m	226	Engineering	Metals & Engineering
96.	Killeen Corrugated Products	£5.7m	170	Corrugated Cases	Paper & Printing
97.	J. Murphy Structural Engineering	£5.7m	220	Structural Steel	Metals & Engineering
98.	Midland International	£5.6m	180	Bathroom Accessories	Other Manufacturing
99.	Western Pride	£5.5m	130	Bread & Confectionery	Food
100.	Lake Electronics	£5.5m	115	Telecommunications Equipment	Metals & Engineering

1. Sales (and ranking) refers to Guinness (*Ireland*) only.
2. Estimates.

Bibliography

Adams, F.G. and S. Ichimura, 1983. 'Industrial Policy in Japan', in F.G. Adams and L.R. Klein (eds.), *Industrial Policies for Growth and Competitiveness*, Lexington, Wharton Econometric Studies.

Allen, G.C., 1981. 'Industrial Policy and Innovation in Japan', in C. Carter (ed.), *Industrial Policy and Innovation*, London: Heinemann.

Baer, Werner, 1976. 'Technology, Employment and Development: Empirical Findings', *World Development*, Vol. 4, No. 2, pp. 121-130.

Bain, Joe, S., 1956. *Barriers to New Competition*, Cambridge (Mass.): Harvard University Press.

Balassa, Bela, 1980. *The Process of Industrial Development and Alternative Development Strategies*, World Bank Staff Working Paper No. 438, October.

Baran, Paul A. and Paul M. Sweezy, 1968. *Monopoly Capital*, Harmondsworth: Penguin.

Barratt Brown, Michael, 1974. *The Economics of Imperialism*, Harmondsworth: Penguin.

Bienefeld, Manfred and Duncan Innes, 1976. 'Capital Accumulation and South Africa', *Review of African Political Economy*, No. 7.

Blackwell, John, Gerard Danaher and Eoin O'Malley, 1983. *An Analysis of Job Losses in Irish Manufacturing Industry*, National Economic and Social Council report No. 67, Dublin: NESC.

Boltho, Andreas, 1985. 'Was Japan's Industrial Policy Successful?', *Cambridge Journal of Economics*, Vol. 9, No. 2, June.

Brett, E.A., 1987. 'States, Markets and Private Power in the Developing World: Problems and Possibilities', *IDS Bulletin*, Sussex, Vol. 18, No. 3, July.

British and Irish Communist Organisation, 1972. *The Economics of Partition*, Belfast: B & ICO.

Brock, Catherine, 1963/64. 'The CIO Industrial Survey', *Journal of the Statistical and Social Inquiry Society of Ireland*, Vol. 21, Part 2, pp. 176-188.

Brock, Catherine, 1965. *A Synthesis of Reports by Survey Teams on 22 Industries* — a report to the Committee on Industrial Organisation, Dublin: Stationery Office.

Brophy, Sean A., 1985. *The Strategic Management of Irish Enterprise 1934-1984*, Dublin: Smurfit Publications.

Buckley, Peter J., 1975. 'The Effects of Foreign Direct Investment on the Economy of the Irish Republic', Ph.D. Thesis, University of Lancaster.

Cardoso, F.H. and E. Faletto, 1979. *Dependency and Development in Latin America*, Berkeley: University of California Press.

Caves, Richard and Masu Uekusa, 1976. 'Industrial Organisation', in H. Patrick and H. Rosovsky (eds.), pp. 459-523.

Cheah Hock Beng, 1980. 'Export-Oriented Industrialisation and Dependent Development: the Experience of Singapore', *IDS Bulletin*, Sussex, Vol. 12, No. 1, December, pp. 35-41.

Chubb, Basil and Patrick Lynch (eds.), 1969. *Economic Development and Planning*, Dublin: Institute of Public Administration.

Coe, W.E., 1969. *The Engineering Industry of the North of Ireland*, Belfast: Institute of Irish Studies, Queen's University.

Cogan, J. and E. Onyenadum, 1981. 'Spin-Off Companies in the Irish Electronics Industry', *Journal of Irish Business and Administrative Research*, Vol. 3, No. 2, October, pp. 3-15.

Committee on Industrial Organisation, 1965. *Final Report*, Dublin: Stationery Office.

Confederation of Irish Industry, 1980a. *Industry 1980*, Business Series Paper No. 3, Dublin: CII.

Confederation of Irish Industry, 1980b. *Industry Report 1980*, Business Series Paper No. 4, Dublin: CII.

Connolly, James, 1973. *Labour in Irish History*, Dublin: New Books Publications. (First published 1910).

Cooper, C. and N. Whelan, 1973. *Science Technology and Industry in Ireland*, Report to the National Science Council, Dublin: Stationery Office.

Crotty, Raymond, 1966. *Irish Agricultural Production*, Cork: Cork University Press.

Crotty, Raymond, 1979. 'Capitalist Colonialism and Peripheralisation: the Irish Case', in D. Seers, B. Schaffer and M. Kiljunen (eds.), pp. 225-235.

Crotty, Raymond, 1986. *Ireland in Crisis: A Study in Capitalist Colonial Undevelopment*, Dingle: Brandon.

Cullen, L.M. (ed.), 1968. *The Formation of the Irish Economy*, Cork: Mercier Press.

Cullen, L.M., 1968a. 'The Irish Economy in the Eighteenth Century', in L.M. Cullen (ed.), pp. 9-21.

Cullen, L.M., 1968b. 'Irish Economic History: Fact and Myth', in L.M. Cullen (ed.), pp. 113-124.

Cullen, L.M., 1976. *An Economic History of Ireland Since 1660*, London: Batsford.

Cullen, L.M. and T.C. Smout (eds.), 1978. *Comparative Aspects of Scottish and Irish Economic and Social History 1600-1900*, Edinburgh: John Donald.

Cullen, L.M. and T.C. Smout, 1978. 'Economic Growth in Scotland and Ireland', in L.M. Cullen and T.C. Smout (eds.), pp. 3-18.

Dickson, David, 1978. 'Aspects of the Rise and Decline of the Irish Cotton Industry', in L.M. Cullen and T.C. Smout (eds.), pp. 100-115.

Dos Santos, Theotonio, 1973. 'The Crisis of Development Theory and the Problems of Dependence in Latin America', in H. Bernstein (ed.), *Underdevelopment and Development*, Harmondsworth: Penguin.

Dunning, John H., 1979. 'Explaining Changing Patterns of International Production: In Defence of the Eclectic Theory', *Oxford Bulletin of Economics and Statistics*, November.

Economic Development, 1958. Dublin: Stationery Office.

European Management Forum, 1980. *Report on the Competitiveness of European Industry*.

Farley, Noel J.J., 1973. 'Outward-Looking Policies and Industrialisation in a Small Economy: Some Notes on the Irish Case', *Economic Development and Cultural Change*, Vol. 21, No. 4, Part 1, July, pp. 610-628.

Federation of Irish Industries, 1968. *Challenge — Industry and Free Trade*, Dublin: FII.

FitzGerald, Garret, 1958. 'Grey, White and Blue: a Review of Three Recent Economic Publications', *Administration*, Vol. 6, No. 3. Reprinted in B. Chubb and P. Lynch (eds.), 1969.

FitzGerald, Garret, 1968. *Planning in Ireland*, Dublin and London: Institute of Public Administration, and Political and Economic Planning.

Fitzpatrick, Jim, 1981. *Industrialisation, Trade and Ireland's Development Cooperation Policy*, Advisory Council on Development Cooperation, Dublin.

Foley, Anthony, 1987. 'Indigenous Exports: Aspects of Firm and Sectoral Performance', Paper presented to Industrial Studies Association, Dublin.

Frank, Andre Gunder, 1969. *Capitalism and Underdevelopment in Latin America — Historical Studies of Chile and Brazil*, New York and London: Monthly Review Press.

Furtado, Celso, 1971. *Development and Underdevelopment*, Berkeley: University of California Press.

Garvin, Tom, 1974. 'Political Cleavages, Party Politics and Urbanisation in Ireland: the Case of the Periphery-Dominated Centre', *European Journal of Political Research*, 2, pp. 307-327.

Garvin, Tom, 1977. 'Nationalist Elites, Irish Voters and Irish Political Development: a Comparative Perspective', *Economic and Social Review*, Vol. 8, No. 3, April, pp. 161-186.

Gerschenkron, Alexander, 1962. *Economic Backwardness in Historical Perspective*, Cambridge (Mass.): Harvard UP.

Gill, Conrad, 1964. *The Rise of the Irish Linen Industry*, London: Oxford University Press.

Godfrey, Martin, 1980. 'Editorial: Is Dependency Dead?' *IDS Bulletin*, Sussex, Vol. 12, No. 1, December, pp. 1-4.

Goldstrom, J.M., 1968. 'The Industrialisation of the North East', in L.M. Cullen (ed.), pp. 101-112.

Green, E.R.R., 1949. *The Lagan Valley 1800-1850*, London: Faber and Faber.

Habakkuk, H.J., 1962. *American and British Technology in the Nineteenth Century*, Cambridge.

Helleiner, G.K., 1973. 'Manufactured Exports from the Less Developed Countries and Multinational Firms', *Economic Journal*, March, Vol. 83, No. 329, pp. 21-47.

Hirsch, Seev, 1976. 'An International Trade and Investment Theory of the Firm', *Oxford Economic Papers*, Vol. 28, July, pp. 258-270.

Hobsbawm, E.J., 1969. *Industry and Empire*, Pelican Economic History of Britain, Vol. 3, London: Pelican.

Hymer, Stephen, 1972. 'The Multinational Corporation and the Law of Uneven Development', in J. Bhagwati (ed.), *Economics and World Order — From the 1970s to the 1990s*, London: Macmillan, pp. 113-140.

Industrial Development Authority, 1978. *IDA Industrial Plan 1977-80*, Dublin: IDA.

Industrial Development Authority, 1979. *IDA Industrial Plan 1978-82*, Dublin: IDA.

Industrial Development Authority, 1985. *The Irish Economy Expenditures of the Irish Manufacturing Sector*, Dublin: IDA.

Industrial Policy, 1984. Dublin: Stationery Office.

Irish Congress of Trade Unions, 1984. *Confronting the Jobs Crisis*, Dublin: ICTU.

Jacoby, Neil, 1966. *US Aid to Taiwan*, New York and London: Praeger.

Johnston, Edith Mary, 1974. *Ireland in the Eighteenth Century*, Gill History of Ireland, Vol. 8, Dublin: Gill and Macmillan.

Kaldor, N., 1972. 'The Irrelevance of Equilibrium Economics', *Economic Journal*, December, Vol. 82, No. 328, pp. 1,237-1,255.

Kaldor, N. 1978, 'The Effect of Devaluations on Trade', in *Further Essays on Applied Economics,* London.

Kane, R.R., 1844. *The Industrial Resources of Ireland*, reprinted 1971, Shannon: Irish University Press.

Kennedy, Kieran A., 1971. *Productivity and Industrial Growth — The Irish Experience*, Oxford: Clarendon Press.

Kennedy, Kieran A., 1985. 'The Unemployment Crisis', John Busteed memorial lecture delivered at University College, Cork.

Kennedy, Kieran A. and Brendan R. Dowling, 1975. *Economic Growth in Ireland: the Experience Since 1947*, Dublin: Gill and Macmillan.

Kennedy, Kieran A. and Tom Healy, 1985. *Small-Scale Manufacturing in Ireland*, Dublin: The Economic and Social Research Institute.

Killeen, Michael J., 1975. Contribution to 'A Symposium on Increasing Employment in Ireland', *Journal of the Statistical and Social Inquiry Society of Ireland*, Vol. XXIII, pt. III, pp. 37-77.

Kindleberger, Charles P., 1980. 'Multinationals and the Small Open

Economy', *Journal of Irish Business and Administrative Research*, Vol. 2, No. 2, October, pp. 115-128.

Krause, Lawrence B. and Sueo Sekiguchi, 1976. 'Japan and the World Economy', in H. Patrick and H. Rosovsky (eds.), pp. 383-458.

Krugman, Paul R. (ed.), 1986. *Strategic Trade Policy and the New International Economics*, Cambridge (Mass.) and London: The MIT Press.

Lall, Sanjaya, 1978. 'Transnationals, Domestic Enterprises and Industrial Structure in Host LDCs: a Survey', *Oxford Economic Papers*, July, Vol. 30, No. 2, pp. 217-248.

Landes, David, 1965. 'Technological Change and Development in Western Europe 1750-1914', in H.J. Habakkuk and M. Postan (eds.), *Cambridge Economic History of Europe*, Vol. 6, Part 1, Cambridge.

Lary, Hal B., 1968. *Imports of Manufactures from Less Developed Countries*, National Bureau of Economic Research.

Lee, Joseph, 1968. 'Capital in the Irish Economy', in L.M. Cullen (ed.), pp. 53-63.

Lee, Joseph, 1969. 'Irish Agriculture: Review Article', *Agricultural History Review*, Vol. 17, Part 1, pp. 64-76.

Lee, Joseph, 1973. *The Modernisation of Irish Society 1848-1918*, Gill History of Ireland, Vol. 10, Dublin: Gill and Macmillan.

Lemass, Sean F., 1959. 'The Role of the State-Sponsored Bodies', *Administration*, Vol. 6, No. 4. Reprinted in Basil Chubb and Patrick Lynch (eds.), 1969.

Little, Ian, Tibor Scitovsky and Maurice Scott, 1970. *Industry and Trade in Some Developing Countries — A Comparative Study*, London, New York and Toronto: Oxford University Press (published for OECD).

Luedde-Neurath, Richard, 1980. 'Export-Orientation in South Korea: How Helpful is Dependency Thinking to its Analysis?', *IDS Bulletin*, Sussex, Vol. 12, No. 1, December, pp. 48-53.

Luedde-Neurath, Richard, 1984. 'State Intervention and Foreign Direct Investment in South Korea', *IDS Bulletin*, Sussex, Vol. 15, No. 2, April, pp. 18-25.

Lyons, F.S.L., 1976. *Ireland Since the Famine*, London: Fontana.

McAleese, Dermot, 1971a. 'Import Demand, Protection and the Effects of Trade Liberalisation on the Irish Economy', Ph.D. Thesis, Johns Hopkins University.

McAleese, Dermot, 1971b. *Effective Tariffs and the Structure of Industrial Protection in Ireland*, Paper No. 62, Dublin: Economic and Social Research Institute.

McAleese, Dermot, 1971/72. 'Capital Inflow and Direct Foreign Investment in Ireland 1952 to 1970', *Journal of the Statistical and Social Inquiry Society of Ireland*, Vol. XXII, Part IV, pp. 63-105.

McAleese, Dermot, 1977. *A Profile of Grant-Aided Industry in Ireland*, Dublin: Industrial Development Authority, Publication Series Paper 5.

302 *Industry and Economic Development*

McAleese, Dermot, 1978. 'Outward-Looking Policies, Manufactured Exports and Economic Growth: the Irish Experience', in M.J. Artis and A.R. Nobay (eds.), *Proceedings of the 1977 AUTE Conference*, London: Croom Helm, pp. 313-351.

McAleese, Dermot and Donagh McDonald, 1978. 'Employment Growth and the Development of Linkages in Foreign-Owned and Domestic Manufacturing Enterprises'', *Oxford Bulletin of Economics and Statistics*, November, Vol. 40, No. 4, pp. 321-339.

McKeon, John, 1980. 'Economic Appraisal of Industrial Projects in Ireland', *Journal of the Statistical and Social Inquiry Society of Ireland*.

Magaziner, Ira C. and Thomas M. Hout, 1980. *Japanese Industrial Policy*, London: Policy Studies Institute, Paper No. 585.

Maguire, Conor, 1979. *Research and Development in Ireland 1977*, Dublin: National Board for Science and Technology.

Mahfuzer Rahman, A.H.M., 1973. *Exports of Manufactures*, Rotterdam University Press.

Marx, Karl, 1977. *Capital*, Vols. I-III, London: Lawrence and Wishart.

Marx, Karl and Frederick Engels, 1971. *Ireland and the Irish Question*, Moscow: Progress Publishers.

Matthews, Alan, 1980. *EEC External Trade Policy: Its Relevance to Ireland*, Dublin: Irish Council of the European Movement.

Meenan, James, 1970. *The Irish Economy Since 1922*, Liverpool: Liverpool University Press.

Monaghan, John J., 1942. 'The Rise and Fall of the Belfast Cotton Industry', *Irish Historical Studies*, Vol. III, No. 9, pp. 1-17.

Myrdal, Gunnar, 1956. 'Development and Underdevelopment', National Bank of Egypt Fiftieth Anniversary Commemoration Lectures, Cairo.

National Economic and Social Council, 1976. *Prelude to Planning*, Paper No. 26, Dublin: Stationery Office.

National Economic and Social Council, 1981. *The Importance of Infrastructure to Industrial Development in Ireland*, by C.D. Foster, N. Segal, J. Dorgan, and S. Dewar, Paper 59, Dublin: Stationery Office.

National Economic and Social Council, 1982. *Policies for Industrial Development: Conclusions and Recommendations*, Paper No. 66, Dublin: NESC.

National Planning Board, 1984. *Proposals for Plan 1984-87*, Dublin: NPB.

Nayyar, Deepak, 1978. 'Transnational Corporations and Manufactured Exports from Poor Countries', *Economic Journal*, March, Vol. 88, No. 349, pp. 59-84.

Northcott, Jim, 1969/70. 'New Patterns of Development', contribution to a symposium on the Buchanan Report, *Journal of the Statistical and Social Inquiry Society of Ireland*, Vol. XXII, Part II, pp. 179-208.

Northern Ireland Economic Council, 1983. *The Duration of Industrial*

Development Assisted Employment, Report No. 40, Belfast: Northern Ireland Economic Development Office.

O'Brien, George, 1918. *The Economic History of Ireland in the Eighteenth Century*, Dublin and London: Maunsel.

O'Brien, George, 1921. *The Economic History of Ireland from the Union to the Famine*, Dublin and London: Maunsel.

O'Brien, Ronan, 1985. 'Technology and Industrial Development: The Irish Electronics Industry in an International Context', in J. Fitzpatrick and J. Kelly (eds.), *Perspectives on Irish Industry*, Dublin: Irish Management Institute.

OECD, 1974. *Reviews of National Science Policy — Ireland*, Paris: OECD.

OECD, 1978. *Policies for Stimulation of Industrial Innovation — Country Reports*, Vol. 11-2, Paris: OECD.

OECD, 1981. *The Notion of International Competitiveness: A Discussion Paper*, a report from the Directorate for Science, Technology and Industry, ref. DSTI/SPR/81.32, Paris: OECD.

OECD, 1985. *Economic Survey of Ireland 1984/85*, Paris: OECD.

O'Farrell, P.N., 1980. 'Multinational Enterprises and Regional Development: Irish Evidence', *Regional Studies*, Vol. 14, No. 2, pp. 141-150.

O'Farrell, P.N., 1984. 'Components of Manufacturing Employment Change in Ireland 1973-1981', *Urban Studies*, 21, pp. 155-176.

O'Farrell, P.N. and R. Crouchley, 1984. 'An Industrial and Spatial Analysis of New Firm Formation in Ireland', *Regional Studies*, Vol. 18, No. 3, pp. 221-236.

O'Farrell, P.N. and B. O'Loughlin, 1980. *An Analysis of New Industry Linkages in Ireland*, Dublin: Industrial Development Authority.

O'Leary, Jim, 1984. 'Some Implications of the Revisions to the Balance of Payments and the National Accounts', *The Irish Banking Review*, September.

O'Loughlin, Brian, 1978. 'The External Linkage Patterns of Grant-Aided Industry in Ireland', M.Sc. Thesis, UWIST.

O'Loughlin, Brian and P.N. O'Farrell, 1980. 'Foreign Direct Investment in Ireland: Empirical Evidence and Theoretical Implications', *Economic and Social Review*, April, Vol. 11, No. 3, pp. 155-185.

O'Malley, Eoin, 1980. *Industrial Policy and Development: A Survey of Literature from the Early 1960s to the Present*, National Economic and Social Council Report No. 56, Dublin: Stationery Office.

O'Malley, Eoin, 1981. 'The Decline of Irish Industry in the Nineteenth Century', *Economic and Social Review*, Vol. 13, No. 1, October, pp. 21-42.

O'Malley, Eoin, 1987. *The Irish Engineering Industry: Strategic Analysis and Policy Recommendations*, Dublin: The Economic and Social Research Institute.

O'Malley, E. and S. Scott, 1987. 'Determinants of Profit Outflows from Ireland', in J. Bradley, J. FitzGerald and R.A. Storey (eds.), *Medium-Term Review 1987-1992*, Dublin: The Economic and Social Research Institute.

O'Tuathaigh, Gearoid, 1972. *Ireland Before the Famine 1798-1848*, Gill History of Ireland, Vol. 9, Dublin: Gill and Macmillan.

Patrick, Hugh and Henry Rosovsky, 1976. 'Japan's Economic Performance: An Overview', in H. Patrick and H. Rosovsky (eds.), pp. 1-61.

Patrick, Hugh and Henry Rosovsky (eds.), 1976. *Asia's New Giant: How the Japanese Economy Works*, Washington D.C.: The Brookings Institution.

Peck, Merton and Shuji Tamura, 1976. 'Technology', in H. Patrick and H. Rosovsky (eds.), pp. 525-585.

Porter, Michael E., 1980. *Competitive Strategy — Techniques for Analysing Industries and Competitors*, London and New York: The Free Press.

Programme for Economic Expansion (first), 1958. Dublin: Stationery Office.

Programme for National Development 1978-1981, 1979. Dublin: Stationery Office.

Rosenberg, Nathan, 1976. *Perspectives on Technology*, Cambridge: Cambridge University Press.

Ross, Miceál, 1981. *Regional Industrial Policies in the Republic of Ireland: a Review of Economic Studies*, Glasgow: Centre for the Study of Public Policy, University of Strathclyde, Paper No. 85.

Rosser, Neil, 1980. 'Latecomer Advantage in the Eighties and the Lessons of Postwar Japanese Industrial Policy', M.A. Thesis, University of Sussex.

Rostow, W.W., 1960. *The Stages of Economic Growth*, London: C.U.P.

Ruane, Frances, 1976. 'Trade, Fiscal Policy and Industrialisation in the Small Open Economy: the Irish Experience', B.Phil. Thesis, Oxford.

Ruane, Frances, 1980. 'Optimal Labour Subsidies and Industrial Development in Ireland', *Economic and Social Review*, January, Vol. 11, No. 2, pp. 77-98.

Ryan, W.J.L., 1949. 'The Nature and Effects of Protective Policy in Ireland', Ph.D. Thesis, University of Dublin.

Schaffer, Bernard, 1979. 'Regional Development and Institutions of Favour: Aspects of the Irish Case', in D. Seers, B. Schaffer and M. Kiljunen (eds.)

Science and Irish Economic Development, Vols. I and II, 1966. Report of the Research and Technology Survey Team to the Minister for Industry and Commerce, Dublin: Stationery Office.

Seers, Dudley, 1980. 'Theoretical Aspects of Unequal Development at Different Spatial Levels', in D. Seers and C. Vaitsos (eds.), *Integration and Unequal Development: the Experience of the EEC*, London: Macmillan.

Seers, Dudley, Bernard Schaffer and Marja-Liisa Kiljunen (eds.), 1979. *Underdeveloped Europe: Studies in Core-Periphery Relations*, Hassocks: Harvester Press.

Sinn Fein the Workers Party (Research Section, Department of Economic Affairs), 1976. *The Banks*, Dublin: Repsol.

Sinn Fein the Workers Party (Research Section, Department of Economic Affairs), 1978. *The Irish Industrial Revolution*, Dublin: Repsol.

Stanton, Richard, 1979. 'Foreign Investment and Host-Country Politics: the Irish Case', in D. Seers, B. Schaffer and M. Kiljunen (eds.).

Stewart, J.C., 1976. 'Foreign Direct Investment and Emergence of a Dual Economy', *Economic and Social Review*, Vol. 7, No. 2, January, pp. 173-197.

Sunkel, O., 1973. 'Transnational Capitalism and National Disintegration in Latin America', *Social and Economic Studies*, March.

Survey of Grant-Aided Industry, 1967. Survey Team's report to the Industrial Development Authority, Dublin: Stationery Office.

Sutcliffe, R.B., 1971. *Industry and Underdevelopment*, London: Addison-Wesley.

Sweeney, John, 1973. 'Foreign Companies in Ireland', *Studies*, Autumn/Winter.

Sweezy, Paul M., 1970. *The Theory of Capitalist Development*, New York and London: Monthly Review Press (first published 1942).

Teeling, John, 1975. 'The Evolution of Offshore Investment', D.B.A. Thesis, Harvard University.

Telesis Consultancy Group, 1982. *A Review of Industrial Policy*, National Economic and Social Council Report No. 64, Dublin: NESC.

Third Programme: Economic and Social Development 1969-72, 1969. Dublin: Stationery Office.

Thomas, Clive Y., 1974. *Dependence and Transformation*, New York and London: Monthly Review Press.

Vaughan, R.N., 1978. 'Profits, Finance and Growth', in B.R. Dowling and J. Durkan (eds.), *Irish Economic Policy: a Review of Major Issues*, Dublin: Economic and Social Research Institute.

Vernon, Raymond, 1966. 'International Investment and International Trade in the Product Cycle', *Quarterly Journal of Economics*, May, Vol. LXXX, No. 2, pp. 190-207.

Vernon, Raymond, 1970. 'Future of the Multinational Enterprise', in Charles P. Kindleberger (ed.), *The International Corporation*, Cambridge (Mass.) and London: MIT Press, pp. 373-400.

Villamil, J.J. (ed.), 1979. *Transnational Capitalism and National Development*, Hassocks: Harvester.

Villamil, Jose J., 1979. 'Puerto Rico 1948-1976: The Limits of Dependent Growth', in J.J. Villamil (ed.), pp. 241-260.

Wade, Robert, 1984. 'Dirigisme Taiwan-style', *IDS Bulletin*, Sussex, Vol. 15, No. 2, April, pp. 65-70.

Wall, Maureen, 1968. 'Catholics in Economic Life', in L.M. Cullen (ed.), pp. 37-51.

Whitaker, T.K., 1953. 'The Finance Attitude', *Administration*, Vol. 2, No. 3. Reprinted in Basil Chubb and Patrick Lynch (eds.), 1969.

Whitaker, T.K., 1973. 'From Protection to Free Trade — the Irish Experience', *Administration*, Winter, Vol. 21, No. 4, pp. 405-423.

Whitaker, T.K., 1976a. 'The Irish Economy Since the Treaty', *Central Bank of Ireland Annual Report*.

Whitaker, T.K., 1976b. 'Economic and Social Planning — Planning Irish Development', in *Economic and Social Planning*, Papers of the Irish Congress of Trade Unions Summer Course.

Yaffe, David, 1972. 'The Marxian Theory of Crisis, Capital and the State', *Conference of Socialist Economist's Bulletin*, Winter.

Yamamura, Kozo, 1986. 'Caveat Emptor: The Industrial Policy of Japan', in Paul R. Krugman (ed.), pp. 169-209.